Running On Emptiness

Running On Emptiness

THE PATHOLOGY
OF CIVILIZATION

John Zerzan

Running on Emptiness ©2002 John Zerzan

ISBN: 0-922915-75-X

Feral House
P.O. Box 13067
Los Angeles, CA 90013

www.feralhouse.com
info@feralhouse.com

Design by Linda Hayashi

10 9 8 7 6 5 4 3 2 1

CONTENTS

INTRODUCTION
by Theresa Kintz

This collection of essays from civilization's most cogent living critic demands consideration. Consideration of the indisputable fact that no matter where you're from ten thousand years ago your ancestors were stone-age anarchists. Consideration of the significance of how for 99 percent of human history people walked gently on the earth, lived free in harmony with wild nature and each other accomplishing everything they needed to accomplish in their daily lives using a stone, bone, wood tool technology. It demands we consider why all artifacts have politics and how when we use tools they use us back. It requires we consider how human nature was originally one and part of a whole and now we lament that we are lost and alienated from one another.

It is in this context that we are then forced to consider the following questions: What are the origins of this estrangement? Why do we ignore the nature of our own bodies and minds? Who decided we needed mechanization, electricity, nuclear power, automobiles or computer technology? Has one single man-made item been a necessary improvement on the earth? Why do we put the survival of all species on the planet in peril for our exclusive comfort and gratification? How did we come to dedicate our lives to maintaining this mad tangle of supply and demand that we call civilization? And finally, what will it take for us to give up on the artificiality of our grim modern lives and cleave instead to what is natural?

For two decades, author John Zerzan's research has focused intently on these issues. As one of only a handful of scholars to do so seriously, Zerzan is the most important writing from a definitively anarchist point of view. His work has contributed to the development of a perspective that seeks to merge anarchist socio-political analysis with radical deep-green environmental thought, engendering a revolutionary green anarchist outlook with a dual focus on social and environmental issues and the interplay between the two. Inspired equally by anti-authoritarian and radical green viewpoints this dynamic and thought-provoking analytical framework has come to be referred to as anarcho-primitivism (AP). Some essential elements of the analysis are:

- Society as we know it now in the industrialized world is pathological and the civilizing impulses of certain dominant groups and individuals are effectively to blame.
- Trends in communication towards acts of symbolic representation have obstructed human being's ability to directly experience one another socially, and alienated us from the rest of the natural world.
- Humanity basically took a wrong turn with the advent of animal domestication and sedentary agriculture, which laid the foundation for the exploitation of the earth, facilitated the growth of hierarchical social structures and subsequently the ideological control of the many by the few.
- All technology besides the stone-age techniques of hunter-gatherers is inherently detrimental to social relations and set the stage for the ecological catastrophe now being brought on by the technoindustrial system.

While AP aspires to inform and enlighten with regards to the anthropological and archaeological knowledge it imparts, the primary purpose is to articulate non-negotiable social discontent and exhort and incite revolutionary social change. Illustrating how contemporary society is the product of thousands of years of social struggles and complex technological changes demonstrates that the current state of affairs we find ourselves in is neither inevitable nor desirable in light of what is known about cultural processes. Anarcho-primitivist thought and action is intentionally provocative. Zerzan is not arguing for "going back," rather he is arguing for going forward, towards a future primitive. Green anarchists who will shun identification with all "isms" (perceived as categorical constructions imposed by the civilization they struggle against) are unified by the recognition that it is important not only to understand the genesis of the totality in theory, but also to decide for oneself how to effectively resist in practice and do so. And there is no place where theory has been put into practice more successfully than in the Oregon community John Zerzan has been a part of since 1981.

It was in 1999 that Eugene moved onto the frontlines of the green anarchist movement in a big way after mainstream media noticed the community's vocal support of the rioting Black Bloc during the anti-World Trade Organization protests in Seattle. The "Eugene Anarchists" quickly received widespread notoriety with Eugene subsequently dubbed "the anarchist capital of America." An appearance on the TV news magazine *60 Minutes* followed by interviews with major magazines meant the intense media attention went on unabated for months.

Those of us who had been around for a while couldn't remember a time when the words anarchy and anarchist were bandied about more in popular culture. The fact it was mostly in association with the truly radical anarchism of the anarcho-primitivists inevitably caused a backlash from within the more conventional anarchist community. The AP perspective, despite being the most vibrant and active, remains a contested point of view, as traditional anarchists continue to press on with an anti-authoritarian agenda designed to appeal to a disaffected proletariat, focusing on distribution of wealth and class dimensions of contemporary society rather than the fundamental structures that engender it. Within these circles the AP perspective is perceived as too extreme, the critique of technology too radical and the prescriptions for social change impossible to ever actualize. Still, anarcho-primitivists have persisted in confronting the old guard in the pages of radical periodicals like *Green Anarchist* (UK), *Green Anarchy* (US), *Black Clad Messenger, Disorderly Conduct, Live Wild or Die* and the Coalition Against Civilization newsletter *Species Traitor*. Their use of thought-provoking, impudent and absurdly humorous agit-prop to communicate specific elements of their profound critique is a self-conscious affirmation of their commitment to blatant incitement. Nothing is sacred and that is the point.

Eugene was also the home of the *Earth First! Journal* from 1991 to 2000. It was a time that saw this once vital radical periodical slide into a pattern of liberal-oriented, uninspired hand-wringing as Zerzan often pointed out in its letters pages. But in large part due to the Journal's presence a unique intersection of some very special people occurred there in the mid-nineties. It was the successful Warner Creek forest defense campaign that first drew the scores of young people who would leave their homes in cities to take up precarious existence hundreds of feet off the ground in tree villages. In 1998 a new occupation with a

more chaotic and anarchic bent was initiated at Fall Creek outside
Eugene. The Red Cloud Thunder treesitters spent their days and nights
in constant vigil, sometimes going for months without ever touching
the ground, using their bodies to protect the centuries-old stands of
ancient forest destined for lumber mills in the Pacific Northwest.

Once these forest defenders had excommunicated themselves from
civilization and taken up residence in communal social groups in the
woodlands they came to identify completely with this landscape. It was
reflected in their daily interactions with one another and with the
forest. The stories and poetry they wrote in defense of the wild were
poignant and affective. Their desire to reject modern industrial society
was utterly authentic, heartfelt and spiritual. They were deliberately re-
wilding themselves through acts of confrontation and defiance, and
fundamentally changing their lives.

The activists in the trees were intimately familiar with the various
elements of environmentalist discourse and many had gone through a
progression from "shallow ecology"— a commitment to recycling, supporting local conservation projects, becoming vegetarians, to a "deep
ecology"— rejecting reformist approaches, losing faith in legal means of
protection, and finally questioning the foundations of industrial society
in general. Some, disenfranchised and disenchanted bourgeoisie, had
majored in environmental studies where they learned the essentials of
biology, chemistry, physics, etc., but found the scientistic ecological
analysis profoundly lacking from political and spiritual perspectives.
Some were working-class urban runaways searching for a way out of the
cage of civilization, looking for a community of resistance where they
could share skills and fight the good fight for the wild. What they all
had in common by the time they went to live in trees was a feeling of
profound affinity with wild nature and a desire to immerse themselves
in natural systems, to come to a degree of understanding that would
never be achieved in crowded industrial urban environments or by
reading books and attending lectures. What they desired was a sense of
place, a feeling of connection to all living things. For the Fall Creek
forest defenders taking direct action in defense of the wild was not
about abstract political arguments or scientific rationale, it was about
truly doing away with the nature/culture dualism, rejecting civilization
and defining one's self as a member of the community of all beings.

At the same time activists who remained in urban areas were thoroughly rejecting the lifestyle it dictates. Their resistance took the form of declaring liberated zones within the confines of the cities. In addition to Zerzan's Whiteaker neighborhood in Eugene that provided essential ground support for the trees, there was also the Minnehaha Free State in Minneapolis, Minnesota. Minnehaha was particularly significant with respect to the unique alliance local Earth First! activists established with indigenous Native Americans there. The joint occupation began at a prehistoric archaeological site due to be destroyed by a highway re-route when a group of Earth First!ers and members of the Mendota tribe began squatting in evacuated houses just before demolition. The Minnehaha Free State was an intentional community where an atmosphere of mutual aid and fellowship flourished. Supported by many in the surrounding local community, the coalition of activists confronted the state and held up the road project for several months until the governor sent in the National Guard to remove the protesters in what would be the largest police action in Minnesota history.

This is just a brief description of the social context in which the essays in *Running on Emptiness* were written in the years between 1995 and 2001. Most premiered in the pages of those radical periodicals that Zerzan regularly contributes to. This current compilation continues the work began in previous volumes, *Future Primitive* and *Elements of Refusal*, by looking into possible ways out of this dismal ascent into violence, oppression, hatred, environmental exploitation and human misery that is civilization. As I write this introduction in the autumn of 2001 the world is apparently gearing up for WWIII. Running on emptiness, indeed. Interestingly, heads of states are referring to what is going on as a "clash of civilizations"—how true, for a change. The regimes currently challenging the West's supremacy are authoritarian entities no less civilized than capitalist America. The only differences between the combatants are down to access to resources, position in global power structures and technological sophistication. It's been going on like this for thousands of years. Even a cursory overview of history shows that as long as civilizations have existed they've made war on each other—always have, always will. As usual there will be no real revolutionary potential as both sides promote ideologies based on control, repression and fear.

Current analysis of the situation barely scratch the surface, leaving
the underlying causes for this persistent pattern of confrontation unexamined. America and its allies with their ahistorical blinders on arro-
gantly view Western civilization as invincible. Rest assured, so did the
Egyptian Pharaohs, the Roman Emperors and the Ottoman Caliphs . . .
but where are they now? Did the Mayan peasants or leaders envision
their city-states someday covered by jungle (perhaps the peasants actually
did, is that why it happened)? What do we really expect someplace like
Manhattan or London will look like in 500, 5,000, 50,000 years? The
truth is that as long as skyscrapers, military industrial complexes, investment bankers and jet airplanes exist the possibility exists they'll collide. It
was inevitable that one day the World Trade Center and the Pentagon,
as physical manifestations of imperialist America's economic power and
military might would someday lie in ruins. It has just happened sooner
rather than later. In light of recent events it seems more important than
ever to reflect on what is at the foundation of this clash of civilizations
and John Zerzan's work provides an important starting point.

Our general understanding of ways of life in the past has been radically altered from the once dominant Hobbesian view of pre-civilized life
as nasty, brutish and short, when civilization was thought to be a necessary condition for making us better humans. Rethinking the characteristics of the categories of primitive vs. modern is one of the main themes
of the opening essays which address, in various terms, the failures of
symbolic thought. As Zerzan argues, when we removed ourselves from
the direct experience of the sensual world through reification, time and
language we became less stimulated by our senses. As we immerse ourselves in the world of objectification and abstraction, we see the triumph
of the symbols for reality over the reality of experience itself.

The false consciousness of symbolic representation and its consequences are evidenced in the domination of nature, division of labor,
co-ordination of action, standardization of technique, institution of
social and ritual rules and finally, industrial behavior. It is this constel-
lation of cultural practices that precipitated, as Zerzan writes, "the fall
from simplicity and fullness of life directly experienced" resulting in
the alienated society in which we now live. By seeking to understand
the process by which this came about, Zerzan continues his anarcho-
primitivist project of demystifying this alienation, speaking in terms of

watershed events, moments where decisions were made, cultures chose
paths, resistance to the civilizing impulses was overcome and the next
stage of the domestication of humans and of nature was attained. It is
an accumulation that buries each stage under the rubble of ideology
and legitimization so that one sees only the surface with eyes conditioned by alienated existence.

It is undeniable that modern socio-political organization, material
culture and resource distribution has become so complicated that
scholars in any field of study would be hard pressed to make sense of
the root causes or potential effects. But should this preclude us from
trying? In the part of North America where Zerzan lives small groups
of egalitarian, stone-age hunter-gatherers were getting along just fine
until confronted by the first Europeans less than 200 years ago. Now
wage slaves there pay taxes, drive to work in cars and return to electri-
fied homes at night to check email on computers and watch satellite
TV reports on cloning. How did this happen?

Working as an archaeologist for the last decade, I've observed first-
hand how 14,000 years of continuous Native American occupation left
the scant legacy of ephemeral hearth features, delicate spear points and
broken pieces of pottery prehistoric archaeologists study. But what lies
on the land now, after only a few hundred years since colonization and
industrialization? . . . superfund sites, nuclear warheads, factory farms,
denuded forests, poisoned rivers and dying industrial towns with
already crumbling inner-cities. Archaeologists recognize how all this
alteration of matter our society engages in now is unprecedented in
terms of the scope of the distribution and essential durability of the
composite materials modern technology is capable of creating. One
thing archaeology demonstrates beyond a reasonable doubt is that
there is no such thing as "away" when one speaks about throwing
things like arrowheads, broken dishes, glass, spent nuclear fuel, asphalt,
refrigerators, autos, computers, diapers away. What is going to be the
fate of all these concrete, plastic, metal, toxic, complicated, real, material, empirical objects our modern material culture produces? It
appears that most people operate under the mistaken impression that
these things our culture is so busy making are going to be functioning
"forever," or at least a modified version of them will be. Archaeologists
know that's not likely to be true and we confront the enormity of this

realization every day. The simple truth is that every generation of humans to come is going to have to deal with the complex social and environmental impacts of our modern civilization.

Zerzan should really be commended for his efforts toward taking the data and theory being produced by archaeologists and trying to make it relevant to us in the real world. It is possible to construct some very cogent arguments against civilization using worldwide archaeological research as evidence, as Zerzan demonstrates. Archaeologists themselves could become very effective social critics of rampant technological change, hierarchical class systems and unsustainable industrial development if they chose to interpret the evidence they study in such a light. By focusing on certain issues addressed in archaeological theory like the effects of over-exploitation of resources surrounding human habitations, the outcomes of increasing social stratification, the consequences of proliferating complexity in material culture and resource distribution, the potential for conflicts as a result of scarcity, etc., one can come to some very different conclusions about the wisdom of the pro-technology, pro-industrial agenda the dominant forces in Western culture have deemed progressive and in the global society's best interest.

Unfortunately my academic colleagues are reluctant to engage in the kind of political debate Zerzan is trying to start, yet I know that none in the field could deny that all of the so-called achievements of man are only monuments to overwhelming pride and hubris, as he so plainly argues. Everybody, not just the archaeologists, knows people managed to live perfectly fine for thousands of years without electricity or automobiles—what better evidence than that can you have that it is possible? It is our involvement in society that creates the false perception of such needs. Here the Green Anarchist tendencies expressed in the AP analysis emerge as the remnants of a bygone consciousness with the potential to re-awaken the immediacy of life and the affinity with wild nature that humanity experienced in pre-civilization.

Zerzan has written in great detail about how technology now props up the totalizing system of capital that has emptied the meaning from everyday life. While Zerzan has much in common with other contemporary critics of technology such as Ellul, Marcuse and Adorno, he is unwilling to let this domination of the machine over our daily lives go unchallenged. The fact that he had enough guts to be the lone voice of dissent in front of an audience of technology cheerleaders at Stanford University is telling of how he views his work. Insisting technology is neutral, like many anarchists do, allows one to avoid demonstrating it is positive or negative. The armed-to-the-teeth U.S. Right says, "guns don't kill people, people kill people" but obviously if guns didn't exist no one would be killed by guns. Guns are not neutral; they are weapons of death when they are used at all. Neither is technology neutral; one can cite a multitude of ways our commitment to keeping the technoindustrial system in running order exerts insidious control over our daily lives. Technology assists the state in its repression of dissent, decreases human freedom and happiness, destroys the natural world and turns all of us into biomechanical appendages of the megamachine.

The dual commodification of labor and of time, as Zerzan points out, is relentless and he calls for a negative reconsideration of time from its initial role as a socially learned symbolic abstraction through to the notion of linear time and progress to the subordination of the working class where time is money. Time's reckoning alienates us from the present and from experiencing the rich wholeness of unmediated existence, separating humans from the ebb and flow of being by mathematizing our very being with its all consuming measuring presence and insistence on perfect and universal ordering.

In the middle section of essays Zerzan addresses postmodernism. His critique of radical relativist tendencies is much needed and compelling. He begins with an explanation of why he hates *Star Trek* and finishes with a swat at post-modern intellectual ostriches "confident to only contemplate what appears within their limited field of vision, ignoring the past and present in favor of the always tentative and mostly uncritical examination of the parochial and the particular and rejoicing in its own depthlessness." The essay on how PBS "programming" (the very word!) leads us all toward a more manageable society does much to undermine its public-interest pretense by highlighting how well the content suits those who maintain the system of class and capital. Picking up on the popular media's christening of the youth of the '90s as the generation "that couldn't care less" JZ comments on how our age of nihilism, post-modernism's essential accomplice, is evidence of the widespread social pathology of civilization.

While post-modernism has indeed become very adept at deconstruction Zerzan is correct to argue it fails miserably as a philosophical
discourse when, overwhelmed by the complexity of history and society,
it proclaims "Why bother with truth if nothing can be done about
reality anyway." His scathing critique of nihilist post-modernism would
send shudders down the spines of leftist academics if they had any. And
speaking of leftist academics, Zerzan asks in one essay, "Who is Noam
Chomsky?" Well, not an anarchist anyway . . . a left-leaning professor
with little time for questioning authority, technology or anything as
radical as that, perhaps? And "Who is Hakim Bey?" A hip PM cynic
evidently happy with the totality of oppression and its physical manifestation technology, perhaps? Zerzan slices through Bey's thick anti-prim-
itivist rhetoric to reveal a thinly veiled racket in Bey's Temporary
Autonomous Zone spiel. Several of the essays address what lengths the
ruling order will go to deny reality, e.g. a modern psychiatry that
ignores the very real strains and stresses of life in the technoindustrial
prison. In preferring to treat the individual as in need of re-program-
ming to better meet the requirements of the system that oppresses
rather than encouraging efforts toward liberation the profession
attempts to narcotize the populace into accepting their lot in life. It is a
tactic that reduces human suffering to an aberration with biological or
genetic roots and is a horrific example of the pathology of civilization.

This collection also contains a series of short, sharp essays offering
fresh perspectives on current events, e.g. the meaning of Waco and
Jonestown and the reactionary response of leftists to the gauntlet
thrown down in front of civilization by FC. The profound anti-civilization argument put forth in the anarchist essay *Industrial Society and
Its Future* (the so-called Unabomber Manifesto) brought to mind atti-
tudes held by many involved early on in the Earth First! movement
who, like FC, realized it was industrial society itself that posed the
most significant threat to Mother Earth and human freedom. It was
disappointing to see how quickly vocal minorities within the radical
green and the anarchist milieus sought to distance themselves from
FC's campaign against the exploiters. Not Zerzan, though, and his
support of Kaczynski has never wavered.

Those who know him personally know John always talks with
people about his ideas, not to them. In "Enemy of the State," inter-

viewer Derrick Jensen notes that Zerzan both defies the stereotype of the bomb-throwing anarchist and shrinks from the role of guru by refusing to play the wise old anarchist handing down pearls of wisdom. Their in-depth discussion offers clarification of some of the more general and persistent misunderstandings surrounding the anti-authoritarian, anti-civilization critique. Along with the autobiographical sketch, "So How Did You Become an Anarchist?" (a previously unpublished, welcome addition to this collection), these two pieces shed considerable light on the author's past and present. In writing about himself a perhaps overly modest Zerzan leaves much out, but does present a brief overview of his Catholic family roots, forays into the educational system, intellectual catalysts, social experiences with labor unions, the Situationists and various radical publications, his gradual embrace of anarchism, his relationship with Kaczynski and life in the anarchist community of Eugene.

Zerzan's use of an academic (yet accessible) writing style and copious citations from primary research material means he is sometimes accused of asking a lot of the reader, as if presenting something as complex as an analysis of all of human history would ever be easy. No, he is not writing the "The History of Civilization for Dummies"—because he does not view his audience in those terms. But you don't have to have a Ph.D. in archaeology to understand the points Zerzan is making. Prehistory is all around us, it is there for everyone to observe and contemplate. Don't believe me? Please get up now and go gaze out of the nearest window for a moment. Imagine the same landscape there before you 10,000 years ago and just think about what the lives of the people living there would have been like. Turn off the radio and television, unplug the computer and the telephone, look past the concrete, tune out the noise of the traffic and visualize what it must have been like living in an ecologically sustainable, socially harmonious world. The question of how we got from the stone age to the space age should be of interest to all human inhabitants of planet earth. Zerzan argues that in understanding the primitive past we take the first step toward rejecting the pathological present and actualizing a future primitive. It is a radical idea that certainly deserves our consideration.

Running On Emptiness: The Failure Of Symbolic Thought

To what degree can it be said that we are really living? As the substance of culture seems to shrivel and offer less balm to troubled lives, we are led to look more deeply at our barren times. And to the place of culture itself in all this.

An anguished Ted Sloan asks (1996), "What is the problem with modernity? Why do modern societies have such a hard time producing adults capable of intimacy, work, enjoyment, and ethical living? Why is it that signs of damaged life are so prevalent?" According to David Morris (1994), "Chronic pain and depression, often linked and occasionally even regarded as a single disorder, constitute an immense crisis at the center of postmodern life." We have cyberspace and virtual reality, instant computerized communication in the global village; and yet have we ever felt so impoverished and isolated?

Just as Freud predicted that the fullness of civilization would mean universal neurotic unhappiness, anti-civilization currents are growing in response to the psychic immiseration that envelops us. Thus symbolic life, essence of civilization, now comes under fire.

It may still be said that this most familiar, if artificial, element is the least understood, but felt necessity drives critique, and many of us feel driven to get to the bottom of a steadily worsening mode of existence. Out of a sense of being trapped and limited by symbols comes the thesis that the extent to which thought and emotion are tied to symbolism is the measure by which absence fills the inner world and destroys the outer world.

We seem to have experienced a fall into representation, whose depths and consequences are only now being fully plumbed. In a fundamental sort of falsification, symbols at first mediated reality and then replaced it. At present we live within symbols to a greater degree than we do within our bodily selves or directly with each other.

The more involved this internal representational system is, the more distanced we are from the reality around us. Other connections, other cognitive perspectives are inhibited, to say the least, as symbolic communication and its myriad representational devices have accomplished an alienation from and betrayal of reality.

This coming between and concomitant distortion and distancing is ideological in a primary and original sense; every subsequent ideology is an echo of this one. Debord depicted contemporary society as exerting a ban on living in favor of its representation: images now in the saddle, riding life. But this is anything but a new problem. There is an imperialism or expansionism of culture from the beginning. And how much does it conquer? Philosophy today says that it is language that thinks and talks. But how much has this always been the case?

Symbolizing is linear, successive, substitutive; it cannot be open to its whole object simultaneously. Its instrumental reason is just that: manipulative and seeking dominance. Its approach is "let a stand for b" instead of "let a be a." Language has its basis in the effort to conceptualize and equalize the unequal, thus bypassing the essence and diversity of a varied, variable richness.

Symbolism is an extensive and profound empire, which reflects and makes coherent a world view, and is itself a world view based upon withdrawal from immediate and intelligible human meaning.

James Shreeve, at the end of his *Neanderthal Enigma* (1995), provides a beautiful illustration of an alternative to symbolic being. Meditating upon what an earlier, non-symbolic consciousness might have been like, he calls forth important distinctions and possibilities:

" . . . where the modern's gods might inhabit the land, the buffalo, or the blade of grass, the Neandertal's spirit was the animal or the grass blade, the thing and its soul perceived as a single vital force, with no need to distinguish them with separate names. Similarly, the absence of artistic expression does not preclude the apprehension of what is artful about the world. Neandertals did not paint their caves with the images of animals. But perhaps they had no need to distill life into representations, because its essences were already revealed to their senses. The sight of a running herd was enough to inspire a surging sense of beauty. They had no drums or bone flutes, but they could listen to the booming rhythms of the wind, the earth, and each other's heartbeats, and be transported."

Rather than celebrate the cognitive communion with the world that Shreeve suggests we once enjoyed, much less embark on the project of seeking to recover it, the use of symbols is of course widely considered the hallmark of human cognition. Goethe said, "Everything is a symbol," as industrial capitalism, milestone of mediation and alienation, took off. At about the same time Kant decided that the key to philosophy lies in the answer to the question, "What is the ground of the relation of that in us which we call 'representation' to the object?" Unfortunately, he divined for modern thought an ahistorical and fundamentally inadequate answer, namely that we are simply not constituted so as to be able to understand reality directly. Two centuries later (1981), Emmanuel Levinas came much closer to the mark with "Philosophy, in its very diachrony, is the consciousness of the breakup of consciousness."

Eli Sagan (1985) spoke for countless others in declaring that the need to symbolize and live in a symbolic world is, like aggression, a human need so basic that "it can be denied only at the cost of severe psychic disorder." The need for symbols—and violence—did not always obtain, however. Rather, they have their origins in the thwarting and fragmenting of an earlier wholeness, in the process of domestication from which civilization issued. Apparently driven forward by a gradually quickening growth in the division of labor that began to take hold in the Upper Paleolithic, culture emerged as time, language, art, number, and then agriculture.

The word culture derives from the Latin *cultura*, referring to cultivation of the soil; that is, to the domestication of plants and animals—and of ourselves in the bargain. A restless spirit of innovation and anxiety has largely been with us ever since, as continually changing symbolic modes seek to fix what cannot be redressed without rejecting the symbolic and its estranged world.

Following Durkheim, Leslie White (1949) wrote, "Human behavior is symbolic behavior; symbolic behavior is human behavior. The symbol is the universe of humanity." It is past time to see such pronouncements as ideology, serving to shore up the elemental falsification underneath a virtually all-encompassing false consciousness. But if a fully developed symbolic world is not, in Northrop Frye's bald claim (1981), in sum "the charter of our freedom," anthropologist Clifford Geertz (1965) comes closer to the truth in saying that we are generally dependent on "the guidance provided by systems of significant symbols." Closer yet is Cohen (1974), who observed that "symbols are essential for the development and maintenance of social order." The ensemble of symbols represents the social order and the individual's place in it, a formulation that always leaves the genesis of this arrangement unquestioned. How did our behavior come to be aligned by symbolization?

Culture arose and flourished via domination of nature, its growth a measure of that progressive mastery that unfolded with ever greater division of labor. Malinowski (1962) understood symbolism as the soul of civilization, chiefly in the form of language as a means of coordinating action or of standardizing technique, and providing rules for social, ritual, and industrial behavior.

It is our fall from a simplicity and fullness of life directly experienced, from the sensuous moment of knowing, which leaves a gap that the symbolic can never bridge. This is what is always being covered over by layers of cultural consolations, civilized detouring that never recovers lost wholeness. In a very deep sense, only what is repressed is symbolized, because only what is repressed needs to be symbolized. The magnitude of symbolization testifies to how much has been repressed; buried, but possibly still recoverable.

Imperceptibly for a long while, most likely, division of labor very slowly advanced and eventually began to erode the autonomy of the individual and a face-to-face mode of social existence. The virus destined to become full-blown as civilization began in this way: a tentative thesis supported by all that victimizes us now. From initial alienation to advanced civilization, the course is marked by more and more reification, dependence, bureaucratization, spiritual desolation, and barren technicization.

Little wonder that the question of the origin of symbolic thought, the very air of civilization, arises with some force. Why culture should exist in the first place appears, increasingly, a more apt way to put it. Especially given the enormous antiquity of human intelligence now established, chiefly from Thomas Wynn's persuasive demonstration (1989) of what it took to fashion the stone tools of about a million years ago. There was a very evident gap between established human capability and the initiation of symbolic culture, with many thousands of generations intervening between the two.

Culture is a fairly recent affair. The oldest cave art, for example, is in the neighborhood of 30,000 years old, and agriculture only got underway about 10,000 years ago. The missing element during the vast interval between the time when I.Q. was available to enable symbolizing, and its realization, was a shift in our relationship to nature. It seems plausible to see in this interval, on some level that we will perhaps never fathom, a refusal to strive for mastery of nature. It may be that only when this striving for mastery was introduced, probably non-consciously, via a very gradual division of labor, did the symbolizing of experiences begin to take hold.

But, it is so often argued, the violence of primitives—human sacrifice, cannibalism, head-hunting, slavery, etc.—can only be tamed by symbolic culture/civilization. The simple answer to this stereotype of the primitive is that organized violence was not ended by culture, but in fact commenced with it. William J. Perry (1927) studied various New World peoples and noted a striking contrast between an agricultural group and a non-domesticated group. He found the latter "greatly inferior in culture, but lacking [the former's] hideous customs." While virtually every society that adopted a domesticated relationship to nature, all over the globe, became subject to violent practices, the non-agricultural knew no organized violence. Anthropologists have long focused on the Northwest Coast Indians as a rare exception to this rule of thumb. Although essentially a fishing people, at a certain point they took slaves and established a very hierarchical society. Even here, however, domestication was present, in the form of tame dogs and tobacco as a minor crop.

We succumb to objectification and let a web of culture control us and tell us how to live, as if this were a natural development. It is anything but that, and we should be clear about what culture/civilization has in fact given us, and what it has taken away.

The philosopher Richard Rorty (1979) described culture as the assemblage of claims to knowledge. In the realm of symbolic being the senses are depreciated, because of their systematic separation and atrophy under civilization. The sensual is not considered a legitimate source of claims to truth.

We humans once allowed a full and appreciative reception to the total sensory input, what is called in German *umwelt*, or the world around us. Heinz Werner (1940, 1963) argued that originally a single sense obtained, before divisions in society ruptured sensory unity. Surviving non-agricultural peoples often exhibit, in the interplay and interpenetration of the senses, a very much greater sensory awareness and involvement than do domesticated individuals (E. Carpenter 1980). Striking examples abound, such as the Bushmen, who can see four moons of Jupiter with the unaided eye and can hear a single-engine light plane seventy miles away (Farb 1978).

Symbolic culture inhibits human communication by blocking and otherwise suppressing channels of sensory awareness. An increasingly technological existence compels us to tune out most of what we could experience. The William Blake declaration comes to mind:

> If the doors of perception were cleansed, everything would appear to man as it is, infinite. For man has closed himself up, 'till he sees all things through narrow chinks of his cavern.

Laurens van der Post (1958) described telepathic communication among the Kung in Africa, prompting Richard Coan (1987) to characterize such modes as "representing an alternative, rather than a prelude to the kind of civilization in which we live."

In 1623 William Drummond wrote, "What sweet contentments doth the soul enjoy by the senses. They are the gates and windows of its knowledge, the organs of its delight." In fact, the "I," if not the "soul," doesn't exist in the absence of bodily sensations; there are no non-sensory conscious states.

But it is all too evident how our senses have been domesticated in a symbolic cultural atmosphere: tamed, separated, arranged in a revealing hierarchy. Vision, under the sign of modern linear perspective, reigns because it is the least proximal, most distancing of the senses. It has been the means by which the individual has been transformed into a spectator, the world into a spectacle, and the body an object or specimen. The primacy of the visual is no accident, for an undue elevation of sight not only situates the viewer outside what he or she sees, but enables the principle of control or domination at base. Sound or hearing as the acme of the senses would be much less adequate to domestication because it surrounds and penetrates the speaker as well as the listener.

Other sensual faculties are discounted far more. Smell, which loses its importance only when suppressed by culture, was once a vital means of connection with the world. The literature on cognition almost completely ignores the sense of smell, just as its role is now so circumscribed among humans. It is, after all, of little use for purposes of domination; considering how smell can so directly trigger even very distant memories, perhaps it is even a kind of anti-domination faculty. Lewis Thomas (1983) remarked that "The act of smelling something, anything, is remarkably like the act of thinking itself." And if it isn't it very likely used to be and should be again.

Tactile experiences or practices are another sensual area we have been expected to relinquish in favor of compensatory symbolic substitutes. The sense of touch has indeed been diminished in a synthetic, work-occupied, long-distance existence. There is little time for or emphasis on tactile stimulation or communication, even though such deprival causes clearly negative outcomes. Nuances of sensitivity and tenderness become lost, and it is well known that infants and children who are seldom touched, carried and caressed are slow to develop and are often emotionally stunted.

Touching by definition involves feeling; to be "touched" is to feel emotionally moved, a reminder of the earlier potency of the tactile sense, as in the expression "keep in touch." The lessening of this category of sensuousness, among the rest, has had momentous consequences. Its renewal, in a re-sensitized, reunited world, will bring a likewise momentous improvement in living. As Tommy cried out, in

The Who's rock opera of the same name, "See me, feel me, touch me, heal me. . . ."

As with animals and plants, the land, the rivers, and human emotions, the senses come to be isolated and subdued. Aristotle's notion of a "proper" plan of the universe dictated that "each sense has its proper sphere." Freud, Marcuse and others saw that civilization demands the sublimation or repression of the pleasures of the proximity senses so that the individual can be thus converted to an instrument of labor. Social control, via the network of the symbolic, very deliberately disempowers the body. An alienated counter-world, driven on to greater estrangement by ever-greater division of labor, humbles one's own somatic sensations and fundamentally distracts from the basic rhythms of one's life.

The definitive mind-body split, ascribed to Descartes' 17th century formulations, is the very hallmark of modern society. What has been referred to as the great "Cartesian anxiety" over the specter of intellectual and moral chaos, was resolved in favor of suppression of the sensual and passionate dimension of human existence. Again we see the domesticating urge underlying culture, the fear of not being in control, now indicting the senses with a vengeance. Henceforth science and technology have a theoretic license to proceed without limits, sensual knowledge having been effectively eradicated in terms of claims to truth or understanding.

Seeing what this bargain has wrought, a deep-seated reaction is dawning against the vast symbolic enterprise that weighs us down and invades every part of us. "If we do not 'come to our senses' soon," as David Howes (1991) judged, "we will have permanently forfeited the chance of constructing any meaningful alternatives to the pseudo-existence which passes for life in our current 'Civilization of the Image.'" The task of critique may be, most centrally, to help us see what it will take to reach a place in which we are truly present to each other and to the world.

The first separation seems to have been the sense of time which brings a loss of being present to ourselves. The growth of this sense is all but indistinguishable from that of alienation itself. If, as Lévi-Strauss put it, "the characteristic feature of the savage mind is its timelessness," living in the here and now becomes lost through the mediation of cultural interventions. Presentness is deferred by the

symbolic, and this refusal of the contingent instant is the birth of
time. We fall under the spell of what Eliade called the "terror of
history" as representations effectively oppose the pull of immediate
perceptual experience.

Mircea Eliade's *Myth of the Eternal Return* (1954) stresses the fear
that all primitive societies have had of history, the passing of time. On
the other hand, voices of civilization have tried to celebrate our immersion in this most basic cultural construct. Leroi-Gourhan (1964), for
instance, saw in time orientation "perhaps the human act par excel-
lence." Our perceptions have become so time-governed and time satu-
rated that it is hard to imagine time's general absence: for the same
reasons it is so difficult to see, at this point, a non-alienated, non-symbolic, undivided social existence.

History, according to Peterson and Goodall (1993), is marked by
an amnesia about where we came from. Their stimulating *Visions of
Caliban* also pointed out that our great forgetting may well have begun
with language, the originating device of the symbolic world. Comparative linguist Mary LeCron Foster (1978, 1980) believes that language
is perhaps less than 50,000 years old and arose with the first impulses
toward art, ritual and social differentiation. Verbal symbolizing is the
principal means of establishing, defining, and maintaining the cultural
world and of structuring our very thinking.

As Hegel said somewhere, to question language is to question
being. It is very important, however, to resist such overstatements and
see the distinction, for one thing, between the cultural importance of
language and its inherent limitations. To hold that we and the world
are but linguistic creations is just another way of saying how pervasive
and controlling is symbolic culture. But Hegel's claim goes much too
far, and George Herbert Mead's assertion (1934) that to have a mind
one must have a language is similarly hyperbolic and false.

Language transforms meaning and communication but is not synonymous with them. Thought, as Vendler (1967) understood, is essentially independent of language. Studies of patients and others lacking all
aspects of speech and language demonstrate that the intellect remains
powerful even in the absence of those elements (Lecours and Joanette
1980; Donald 1991). The claim that language greatly facilitates
thought is likewise questionable, inasmuch as formal experiments with

children and adults have not demonstrated it (G. Cohen 1977). Language is clearly not a necessary condition for thinking (see Kertesz 1988, Jansons 1988).

Verbal communication is part of the movement away from a face-to-face social reality, making feasible physical separateness. The word always stands between people who wish to connect with each other, facilitating the diminution of what need not be spoken to be said. That we have declined from a non-linguistic state begins to appear a sane point of view. This intuition may lie behind George W. Morgan's 1968 judgment that "Nothing, indeed, is more subject to depreciation and suspicion in our disenchanted world than the word."

Communication outside civilization involved all the senses, a condition linked to the key gatherer-hunter traits of openness and sharing. Literacy ushered us into the society of divided and reduced senses, and we take this sensory deprivation for granted as if it were a natural state, just as we take literacy for granted.

Culture and technology exist because of language. Many have seen speech, in turn, as a means of coordinating labor, that is, as an essential part of the technique of production. Language is critical for the formation of the rules of work and exchange accompanying division of labor, with the specializations and standardizations of nascent economy paralleling those of language. Now guided by symbolization, a new kind of thinking takes over, which realizes itself in culture and technology. The interdependence of language and technology is at least as obvious as that of language and culture, and results in an accelerating mastery over the natural world intrinsically similar to the control introduced over the once autonomous and sensuous individual.

Noam Chomsky, chief language theorist, commits a grave and reactionary error by portraying language as a "natural" aspect of "essential human nature," innate and independent of culture (1966, 1992). His Cartesian perspective sees the mind as an abstract machine which is simply destined to turn out strings of symbols and manipulate them. Concepts like origins or alienation have no place in this barren techno-schema. Lieberman (1975) provides a concise and fundamental correction: "Human language could have evolved only in relation to the total human condition."

The original sense of the word define is, from Latin, to limit or bring to an end. Language seems often to close an experience, not to help ourselves be open to experience. When we dream, what happens is not expressed in words, just as those in love communicate most deeply without verbal symbolizing. What has been advanced by language that has really advanced the human spirit? In 1976, von Glasersfeld wondered "whether, at some future time, it will still seem so obvious that language has enhanced the survival of life on this planet."

Numerical symbolism is also of fundamental importance to the development of a cultural world. In many primitive societies it was and is considered unlucky to count living creatures, an anti-reification attitude related to the common primitive notion that to name another is to gain power over that person. Counting, like naming, is part of the domestication process. Division of labor lends itself to the quantifiable, as opposed to what is whole in itself, unique, not fragmented. Number is also necessary for the abstraction inherent in the exchange of commodities and is prerequisite to the take-off of science and technology. The urge to measure involves a deformed kind of knowledge that seeks control of its object, not understanding.

The sentiment that "the only way we truly apprehend things is through art" is a commonplace opinion, one which underlines our dependence on symbols and representation. "The fact that originally all art was 'sacred'" (Eliade, 1985), that is, belonging to a separate sphere, testifies to its original status or function.

Art is among the earliest forms of ideological and ritual expressiveness, developed along with religious observances designed to hold together a communal life that was beginning to fragment. It was a key means of facilitating social integration and economic differentiation (Dickson, 1990), probably by encoding information to register membership, status, and position (Lumsden and Wilson 1983). Prior to this time, somewhere during the Upper Paleolithic, devices for social cohesion were unnecessary; division of labor, separate roles, and territoriality seem to have been largely non-existent. As tensions and anxieties started to emerge in social life, art and the rest of culture arose with them in answer to their disturbing presence.

Art, like religion, arose from the original sense of disquiet, no doubt subtly but powerfully disturbing in its newness and its encroaching gradualness. In 1900 Hirn wrote of an early dissatisfac-

tion that motivated the artistic search for a "fuller and deeper expression" as "compensation for new deficiencies of life." Cultural solutions,
however, do not address the deeper dislocations that cultural "solutions" are themselves part of. Conversely, as commentators as diverse as
Henry Miller and Theodor Adorno have concluded, there would be no
need of art in a disalienated world. What art has ineffectively striven to
capture and express would once again be a reality, the false antidote of
culture forgotten.

Art is a language and so, evidently, is ritual, among the earliest cultural and symbolic institutions. Julia Kristeva (1989) commented on
"the close relation of grammar to ritual," and Frits Staal's studies of
Vedic ritual (1982, 1986, 1988) demonstrated to him that syntax can
completely explain the form and meaning of ritual. As Chris Knight
(1996) noted, speech and ritual are "interdependent aspects of one and
the same symbolic domain."

Essential for the breakthrough of the cultural in human affairs,
ritual is not only a means of aligning or prescribing emotions; it is also
a formalization that is intimately linked with hierarchies and formal
rule over individuals. All known tribal societies and early civilizations
had hierarchical organizations built on or bound up with a ritual structure and matching conceptual system.

Examples of the link between ritual and inequality, developing
even prior to agriculture, are widespread (Gans 1985, Conkey 1984).
Rites serve a safety valve function for the discharge of tensions generated by emerging divisions in society and work to create and maintain
social cohesion. Earlier on there was no need of devices to unify what
was, in a non-division of labor context, still whole and unstratified.

It has often been said that the function of the symbol is to disclose
structures of the real that are inaccessible to empirical observation.
More to the point, in terms of the processes of culture and civilization,
however, is Abner Cohen's contention (1981, 1993) that symbolism
and ritual disguise, mystify and sanctify irksome duties and roles and
thus make them seem desirable. Or, as David Parkin (1992) put it, the
compulsory nature of ritual blunts the natural autonomy of individuals
by placing them at the service of authority.

Ostensibly opposed to estrangement, the counter-world of public
rites is arrayed against the current of historical direction. But, again,

this is a delusion, since ritual facilitates the establishment of the cultural order, bedrock of alienated theory and practice. Ritual authority structures play an important part in the organization of production (division of labor) and actively further the coming of domestication. Symbolic categories are set up to control the wild and alien; thus the domination of women proceeds, a development brought to full realization with agriculture, when women become essentially beasts of burden and/or sexual objects. Part of this fundamental shift is movement toward territorialism and warfare; Johnson and Earle (1987) discussed the correspondence between this movement and the increased importance of ceremonialism.

According to James Shreeve (1995), "In the ethnographic record, wherever you get inequality, it is justified by invoking the sacred." Relatedly, all symbolism, says Eliade (1985), was originally religious symbolism. Social inequality seems to be accompanied by subjugation in the non-human sphere. M. Reinach (quoted in Radin, 1927) said, "thanks to magic, man takes the offensive against the objective world." Cassirer (1955) phrased it this way: "Nature yields nothing without ceremonies."

Out of ritual action arose the shaman, who was not only the first specialist because of his or her role in this area, but the first cultural practitioner in general. The earliest art was accomplished by shamans, as they assumed ideological leadership and designed the content of rituals.

This original specialist became the regulator of group emotions, and as the shaman's potency increased, there was a corresponding decrease in the psychic vitality of the rest of the group (Lommel, 1967). Centralized authority, and most likely religion too, grew out of the elevated position of the shaman. The specter of social complexity was incarnated in this individual who wielded symbolic power. Every head man and chief developed from the primacy of this figure in the lives of others in the group.

Religion, like art, contributed to a common symbolic grammar needed by the new social order and its fissures and anxieties. The word is based on the Latin *religare*, to tie or bind, and a Greek verbal stem denoting attentiveness to ritual, faithfulness to rules. Social integration, required for the first time, is evident as impetus to religion.

It is the answer to insecurities and tensions, promising resolution and transcendence by means of the symbolic. Religion finds no basis for its existence prior to the wrong turn taken toward culture and the civilized (domesticated). The American philosopher George Santayana summed it up well with, "Another world to live in is what we mean by religion."

Since Darwin's *Descent of Man* (1871) we have understood that human evolution greatly accelerated culturally at a time of insignificant physiological change. Thus symbolic being did not depend on waiting for the right gifts to evolve. We can now see, with Clive Gamble (1994), that intention in human action did not arrive with domestication/agriculture/civilization.

The native denizens of Africa's Kalahari Desert, as studied by Laurens van der Post (1976), lived in "a state of complete trust, dependence and interdependence with nature," which was "far kinder to them than any civilization ever was." Egalitarianism and sharing were the hallmark qualities of hunter-gatherer life (G. Isaac 1976, Ingold 1987, 1988, Erdal and Whiten 1992, etc.), which is more accurately called gatherer-hunter life, or the foraging mode. In fact, the great bulk of this diet consisted of plant material, and there is no conclusive evidence for hunting at all prior to the Upper Paleolithic (Binford 1984, 1985).

An instructive look at contemporary primitive societies is Colin Turnbull's work (1961, 1965) on pygmies of the Ituri forest and their Bantu neighbors. The pygmies are foragers, living with no religion or culture. They are seen as immoral and ignorant by the agriculturalist Bantu, but enjoy much greater individualism and freedom. To the annoyance of the Bantu, the pygmies irreverently mock the solemn rites of the latter and their sense of sin. Rejecting territorialism, much less private holdings, they "move freely in an uncharted, unsystematized, unbounded social world," according to Mary Douglas (1973).

The vast era prior to the coming of symbolic being is an enormously prominent reality and a question mark to some. Commenting on this "period spanning more than a million years," Tim Ingold (1993) called it "one of the most profound enigmas known to archaeological science." But the longevity of this stable, non-cultural epoch has a simple explanation: as F. Goodman (1988) surmised, "It was such a harmonious existence, and such a successful adaptation, that it did not materially alter for many thousands of years."

Culture triumphed at last with domestication. The scope of life became narrower, more specialized, forcibly divorced from its previous grace and spontaneous liberty. The assault of a symbolic orientation upon the natural also had immediate outward results. Early rock drawings, found 125 miles from the nearest recorded trickle of water in the Sahara, show people swimming. Elephants were still somewhat common in some coastal Mediterranean zones in 500 BC, wrote Herodotus. Historian Clive Ponting (1992) has shown that every civilization has diminished the health of its environment.

And cultivation definitely did not provide a higher-quality or more reliable food base (M.N. Cohen 1989, Walker and Shipman 1996), though it did introduce diseases of all kinds, almost completely unknown outside civilization (Burkett 1978, Freund 1982), and sexual inequality (M. Ehrenberg 1989, A. Getty 1996). Frank Waters' *Book of the Hopi* (1963) gives us a stunning picture of unchecked division of labor and the poverty of the symbolic: "More and more they traded for things they didn't need, and the more goods they got, the more they wanted. This was very serious. For they did not realize they were drawing away, step by step, from the good life given them."

A pertinent chapter from *The Time Before History* (1996) by Colin Tudge bears a title that speaks volumes, "The End of Eden: Farming." Much of an underlying epistemological distinction is revealed in this contrast by Ingold (1993): "In short, whereas for farmers and herdsmen the tool is an instrument of control, for hunters and gatherers it would better be regarded as an instrument of revelation." And Horkheimer (1972) bears quoting, in terms of the psychic cost of domestication/domination of nature: "the destruction of the inner life is the penalty man has to pay for having no respect for any life other than his own." Violence directed outward is at the same time inflicted spiritually, and the outside world becomes transformed, debased, as surely as the perceptual field was subjected to fundamental redefinition. Nature certainly did not ordain civilization; quite the contrary.

Today it is fashionable, if not mandatory, to maintain that culture always was and always will be. Even though it is demonstrably the case that there was an extremely long non-symbolic human era, perhaps one hundred times as long as that of civilization, and that culture has gained only at the expense of nature, one has it from all sides that the symbolic—like alienation—is eternal. Thus questions of origins and destinations are meaningless. Nothing can be traced further than the semiotic in which everything is trapped.

But the limits of the dominant rationality and the costs of civilization are too starkly visible for us to accept this kind of cop-out. Since the ascendance of the symbolic humans have been trying, through participation in culture, to recover an authenticity we once lived. The constant urge or quest for the transcendent testifies that the hegemony of absence is a cultural constant. As Thomas McFarland (1987) found, "culture primarily witnesses the absence of meaning, not its presence."

Massive, unfulfilling consumption, within the dictates of production and social control, reigns as the chief everyday consolation for this absence of meaning, and culture is certainly itself a prime consumer choice. At base, it is division of labor that ordains our false and disabling symbolic totality. "The increase in specialization . . ." wrote Peter Lomas (1996), "undermines our confidence in our ordinary capacity to live."

We are caught in the cultural logic of objectification and the objectifying logic of culture, such that those who counsel new ritual and other representational forms as the route to a re-enchanted existence miss the point completely. More of what has failed for so long can hardly be the answer. Lévi-Strauss (1978) referred to "a kind of wisdom [that primitive peoples] practiced spontaneously and the rejection of which, by the modern world, is the real madness."

Either the non-symbolizing health that once obtained, in all its dimensions, or madness and death. Culture has led us to betray our own aboriginal spirit and wholeness, into an ever-worsening realm of synthetic, isolating, impoverished estrangement. Which is not to say that there are no more everyday pleasures, without which we would lose our humanness. But as our plight deepens, we glimpse how much must be erased for our redemption.

1997

TIME AND ITS DISCONTENTS

The dimension of time seems to be attracting great notice, to judge
from the number of recent movies that focus on it, such as *Back to the
Future, Terminator, Peggy Sue Got Married*, etc. Stephen Hawking's *A
Brief History of Time* (1988) was a best-seller and became, even more
surprisingly, a popular film. Remarkable, in addition to the number of
books that deal with time, are the larger number which don't, really,
but which feature the word in their titles nonetheless, such as Virginia
Spate's *The Color of Time: Claude Monet* (1992). Such references have
to do, albeit indirectly, with the sudden, panicky awareness of time,
the frightening sense of our being tied to it. Time is increasingly a key
manifestation of the estrangement and humiliation that characterize
modern existence. It illuminates the entire, deformed landscape and
will do so ever more harshly until this landscape and all the forces that
shape it are changed beyond recognizing.

This contribution to the subject has little to do with time's fascination for film-makers or TV producers, or with the current academic
interest in geologic conceptions of time, the history of clock technology and the sociology of time, or with personal observations and counsels on its use. Neither aspects nor excesses of time deserve as much
attention as time's inner meaning and logic. For despite the fact that
time's perplexing character has become, in John Michon's estimation,

"almost an intellectual obsession" (1988), society is plainly incapable of dealing with it.

With time we confront a philosophical enigma, a psychological mystery, and a puzzle of logic. Not surprisingly, considering the massive reification involved, some have doubted its existence since humanity began distinguishing "time itself" from visible and tangible changes in the world. As Michael Ende (1984) put it: "There is in the world a great and yet ordinary secret. All of us are part of it, everyone is aware of it, but very few ever think of it. Most of us just accept it and never wonder over it. This secret is time."

Just what is "time"? Spengler declared that no one should be allowed to ask. The physicist Richard Feynman (1988) answered, "Don't even ask me. It's just too hard to think about." Empirically as much as in theory, the laboratory is powerless to reveal the flow of time, since no instrument exists that can register its passage. But why do we have such a strong sense that time does pass, ineluctably and in one particular direction, if it really doesn't? Why does this "illusion" have such a hold over us? We might just as well ask why alienation has such a hold over us. The passage of time is intimately familiar, the concept of time mockingly elusive; why should this appear bizarre, in a world whose survival depends on the mystification of its most basic categories?

We have gone along with the substantiation of time so that it seems a fact of nature, a power existing in its own right. The growth of a sense of time—the acceptance of time —is a process of adaptation to an ever more reified world. It is a constructed dimension, the most elemental aspect of culture. Time's inexorable nature provides the ultimate model of domination.

The further we go in time the worse it gets. We inhabit an age of the disintegration of experience, according to Adorno. The pressure of time, like that of its essential progenitor, division of labor, fragments and disperses all before it. Uniformity, equivalence, separation are byproducts of time's harsh force. The intrinsic beauty and meaning of that fragment of the world that is not-yet-culture moves steadily toward annihilation under a single cultures-wide clock. Paul Ricoeur's assertion that "we are not capable of producing a concept of time that is at once cosmological, biological, historical and individual," fails to notice how they are converging.

Concerning this "fiction" that upholds and accompanies all the forms of imprisonment, "the world is filled with propaganda alleging its existence," as Bernard Aaronson (1972) put it so well. "All awareness," wrote the poet Denise Levertov (1974), "is an awareness of time," showing just how deeply alienated we are in time. We have become regimented under its empire, as time and alienation continue to deepen their intrusion, their debasement of everyday life. "Does this mean," as David Carr (1986) asks, "that the 'struggle' of existence is to overcome time itself?" It may be that exactly this is the last enemy to be overcome.

In coming to grips with this ubiquitous yet phantom adversary, it is somewhat easier to say what time is not. It is not synonymous, for fairly obvious reasons, with change. Nor is it sequence, or order of succession. Pavlov's dog, for instance, must have learned that the sound of the bell was followed by feeding; how else could it have been conditioned to salivate at that sound? But dogs do not possess time consciousness, so before and after cannot be said to constitute time.

Somewhat related are inadequate attempts to account for our all but inescapable sense of time. The neurologist Gooddy (1988), rather along the lines of Kant, describes it as one of our "subconscious assumptions about the world." Some have described it, no more helpfully, as a product of the imagination, and the philosopher J.J.C. Smart (1980) decided that it is a feeling that "arises out of metaphysical confusion." McTaggart (1934), F.H. Bradley (1930), and Dummett (1978) have been among 20th century thinkers who have decided against the existence of time because of its logically contradictory features, but it seems fairly plain that the presence of time has far deeper causes than mere mental confusion.

There is nothing even remotely similar to time. It is as unnatural and yet as universal as alienation. Chacalos (1989) points out that the present is a notion just as puzzling and intractable as time itself. What is the present? We know that it is always now; one is confined to it, in an important sense, and can experience no other "part" of time. We speak confidently of other parts, however, which we call "past" and "future." But whereas things that exist in space elsewhere than here continue to exist, things that don't exist now, as Sklar (1992) observes, don't really exist at all.

Time necessarily flows; without its passage there would be no sense of time. Whatever flows, though, flows with respect to time. Time therefore flows with respect to itself, which is meaningless owing to the fact that nothing can flow with respect to itself. No vocabulary is available for the abstract explication of time apart from a vocabulary in which time is already presupposed. What is necessary is to put all the givens into question. Metaphysics, with a narrowness that division of labor has imposed from its inception, is too narrow for such a task.

What causes time to flow, what is it that moves it toward the future? Whatever it is, it must be beyond our time, deeper and more powerful. It must depend as Conly (1975) had it, "upon elemental forces which are continually in operation."

William Spanos (1987) has noted that certain Latin words for culture not only signify agriculture or domestication, but are translations from Greek terms for the spatial image of time. We are, at base, "time-binders," in Alfred Korzybski's lexicon (1948); the species, due to this characteristic, creates a symbolic class of life, an artificial world. Time-binding reveals itself in an "enormous increase in the control over nature." Time becomes real because it has consequences, and this efficacy has never been more painfully apparent.

Life, in its barest outline, is said to be a journey through time; that it is a journey through alienation is the most public of secrets. "No clock strikes for the happy one," says a German proverb. Passing time, once meaningless, is now the inescapable beat, restricting and coercing us, mirroring blind authority itself. Guyau (1890) determined the flow of time to be "the distinction between what one needs and what one has," and therefore "the incipience of regret." Carpe diem, the maxim counsels, but civilization forces us always to mortgage the present to the future.

Time aims continually toward greater strictness of regularity and universality. Capital's technological world charts its progress by this, could not exist in its absence. "The importance of time," wrote Bertrand Russell (1929), lies "rather in relation to our desires than in relation to truth." There is a longing that is as palpable as time has become. The denial of desire can be gauged no more definitively than via the vast construct we call time.

Time, like technology, is never neutral; it is, as Castoriadis (1991)

rightly judged, "always endowed with meaning." Everything that commentators like Ellul (1964) have said about technology, in fact, applies
to time, and more deeply. Both conditions are pervasive, omnipresent,
basic, and in general as taken for granted as alienation itself. Time, like
technology, is not only a determining fact but also the enveloping
element in which divided society develops. Similarly, it demands that
its subjects be painstaking, "realistic," serious, and above all, devoted to
work. It is autonomous in its overall aspect, like technology; it goes on
forever of its own accord.

But like division of labor, which stands behind and sets in motion
time and technology, it is, after all, a socially learned phenomenon.
Humans, and the rest of the world, are synchronized to time and its
technical embodiment, rather than the reverse. Central to this dimension—as it is to alienation per se—is the feeling of being a helpless
spectator. Every rebel, it follows, also rebels against time and its relent-
lessness. Redemption must involve, in a very fundamental sense,
redemption from time.

"Time is the accident of accidents," according to Epicurus. Upon
closer examination, however, its genesis appears less mysterious. It has
occurred to many, in fact, that notions such as "the past," "the
present," and "the future" are more linguistic than actual or physical.
The neo-Freudian theorist Lacan, for example, decided that the time
experience is essentially an effect of language. A person with no language would likely have no sense of the passage of time. R.A. Wilson
(1980), moving much closer to the point, suggested that language was
initiated by the need to express symbolic time. Gosseth (1972) argued
that the system of tenses found in Indo-European languages developed
along with consciousness of a universal or abstract time. Time and language are coterminous, decided Derrida (1982): "to be in the one is to
be in the other." Time is a symbolic construct immediately prior, relatively speaking, to all the others and which requires language for its
actualization.

Paul Valéry (1962) referred to the fall of the species into time as sig-
nalling alienation from nature; "by a sort of abuse, man creates time," he
wrote. In the timeless epoch before this fall, which constituted the overwhelming majority of our existence as humans, life, as has often been
said, had a rhythm but not a progression. It was the state when the soul

could "gather in the whole of its being," in Rousseau's words, in the absence of temporal strictures, "where time is nothing to the soul." Activities themselves, usually of a leisurely character, were the points of reference before time and civilization; nature provided the necessary signals, quite independent of "time." Humanity must have been conscious of memories and purposes long before any explicit distinctions were drawn among past, present, and future (Fraser, 1990). Furthermore, as the linguist Whorf (1956) estimated, "preliterate ['primitive'] communities, far from being subrational, may show the human mind functioning on a higher and more complex plane of rationality than among civilized men."

The largely hidden key to the symbolic world is time; indeed it is at the origin of human symbolic activity. Time thus occasions the first alienation, the route away from aboriginal richness and wholeness. "Out of the simultaneity of experience, the event of Language," says Charles Simic (1971) "is an emergence into linear time." Researchers such as Zohar (1982) consider faculties of telepathy and precognition to have been sacrificed for the sake of evolution into symbolic life. If this sounds far-fetched, the sober positivist Freud (1932) viewed telepathy as quite possibly "the original archaic means through which individuals understand one another." If the perception and apperception of time relate to the very essence of cultural life (Gurevich 1976), the advent of this time sense and its concomitant culture represent an impoverishment, even a disfigurement, by time.

The consequences of this intrusion of time, via language, indicate that the latter is no more innocent, neutral, or assumption-free than the former. Time is not only, as Kant said, at the foundation of all our representations, but, by this fact, also at the foundation of our adaptation to a qualitatively reduced, symbolic world. Our experience in this world is under an all-pervasive pressure to be representation, to be almost unconsciously degraded into symbols and measurements. "Time," wrote the German mystic Meister Eckhart, "is what keeps the light from reaching us."

Time awareness is what empowers us to deal with our environment symbolically; there is no time apart from this estrangement. It is by means of progressive symbolization that time becomes naturalized, becomes a given, is removed from the sphere of conscious cultural production. "Time becomes human in the measure to which it becomes actualized in narrative," is another way of putting it (Ricoeur 1984). The symbolic accretions in this process constitute a steady throttling of instinctive desire; repression develops the sense of time unfolding. Immediacy gives way, replaced by the mediations that make history possible—language in the forefront.

One begins to see past such banalities as "time is an incomprehensible quality of the given world" (Sebba 1991). Number, art, religion make their appearances in this "given" world, disembodied phenomena of reified life. These emerging rites, in turn, Gurevitch (1964) surmises, lead to "the production of new symbolic contents, thus encouraging time leaping forward." Symbols, including time, of course, now have lives of their own, in this cumulative, interacting progression. David Braine's *The Reality of Time and the Existence of God* (1988) is illustrative. It argues that it is precisely time's reality which proves the existence of God; civilization's perfect logic.

All ritual is an attempt, through symbolism, to return to the timeless state. Ritual is a gesture of abstraction from that state, however, a false step that only leads further away. The "timelessness" of number is part of this trajectory, and contributes much to time as a fixed concept. In fact, Blumenberg (1983) seems largely correct in assaying that "time is not measured as something that has been present all along; instead it is produced, for the first time, by measurement." To express time we must, in some way, quantify it; number is therefore essential. Even where time has already appeared, a slowly more divided social existence works toward its progressive reification only by means of number. The sense of passing time is not keen among tribal peoples, for example, who do not mark it with calendars or clocks.

Time: an original meaning of the word in ancient Greek is division. Number, when added to time, makes the dividing or separating that much more potent. The non-civilized often have considered it "unlucky" to count living creatures, and generally resist adopting the practice (e.g. Dobrizhoffer 1822). The intuition for number was far from spontaneous and inevitable, but "already in early civilizations," Schimmel (1992) reports, "one feels that numbers are a reality having as it were a magnetic power field around them." It is not surprising that among ancient cultures with the strongest emerging senses of time—Egyptian, Babylonian, Mayan—we see numbers associated with ritual figures and deities; indeed the Mayans and Babylonians both had number gods (Barrow 1992).

Much later the clock, with its face of numbers, encouraged society to abstract and quantify the experience of time still further. Every clock reading is a measurement that joins the clock watcher to the "flow of time." And we absently delude ourselves that we know what time is because we know what time it is. If we did away with clocks, Shallis (1982) reminds us, objective time would also disappear. More fundamentally, if we did away with specialization and technology, alienation would be banished.

The mathematizing of nature was the basis for the birth of modern rationalism and science in the West. This had stemmed from demands for number and measurement in connection with similar teachings about time, in the service of mercantile capitalism. The continuity of number and time as a geometrical locus were fundamental to the Scientific Revolution, which projected Galileo's dictum to measure all that is measurable and make measurable that which is not. Mathematically divisible time is necessary for the conquest of nature, and for even the rudiments of modern technology.

From this point on, number-based symbolic time became crushingly real, an abstract construction "removed from and even contrary to every internal and external human experience" (Syzamosi 1986). Under its pressure, money and language, merchandise and information have become steadily less distinguishable, and division of labor more extreme.

To symbolize is to express time consciousness, for the symbol embodies the structure of time (Darby 1982). Clearer still is Meerloo's formulation: "To understand a symbol and its development is to grasp human history in a nutshell." The contrast is the life of the non-civilized, lived in a capacious present that cannot be reduced to the single moment of the mathematical present. As the continual now gave way to increasing reliance upon systems of significant symbols (language, number, art, ritual, myth) dislodged from the now, the further abstraction, history, began to develop. Historical time is no more inherent in reality, no less an imposition on it, than the earlier, less choate forms of time.

In a slowly more synthetic context, astronomical observation is invested with new meanings. Once pursued for its own sake, it comes to provide the vehicle for scheduling rituals and coordinating the activities of complex society. With the help of the stars, the year and its divisions exist as instruments of organizational authority (Leach 1954). The formation of a calendar is basic to the formation of a civilization. The calendar was the first symbolic artifact that regulated social behavior by keeping track of time. And what is involved is not the control of time but its opposite: enclosure by time in a world of very real alienation. One recalls that our word comes from the Latin *calends*, the first day of the month, when business accounts had to be settled.

"No time is entirely present," said the Stoic Chrysippus, and meanwhile the concept of time was being further advanced by the underlying Judeo-Christian tenet of a linear, irreversible path between creation and salvation. This essentially historical view of time is the very core of Christianity; all the basic notions of measurable, one-way time can be found in St. Augustine's (fifth-century) writings. With the spread of the new religion the strict regulation of time, on a practical plane, was needed to help maintain the discipline of monastic life. Bells summoning the monks to prayer eight times daily were heard far beyond the confines of the cloister, and thus a measure of time regulation was imposed on society at large. The population continued to exhibit "*une vaste indifférence au temps*" throughout the feudal era, according to Marc Bloch (1940), but it is no accident that the first public clocks adorned cathedrals in the West. Worth noting in this regard is the fact that the calling of precise prayer times became the chief externalization of medieval Islamic belief.

The invention of the mechanical clock was one of the most important turning points in the history of science and technology; indeed of all human art and culture (Synge 1959). The improvement in accuracy presented authority with enhanced opportunities for oppression. An early devotee of elaborate mechanical clocks, for example, was Duke Gian Galeazzo Visconti, described in 1381 as "a sedate but crafty ruler with a great love of order and precision" (Fraser 1988). As Weizenbaum (1976) wrote, the clock began to create "literally a new reality . . . that was and remains an impoverished version of the old one."

A qualitative change was introduced. Even when nothing was happening, time did not cease to flow. Events, from this era on, are put into this homogeneous, objectively measured, moving envelope—and this unilinear progression incited resistance. The most extreme were the chiliast, or millenarian, movements, which appeared in various parts of Europe from the 14th into the 17th centuries. These generally took the form of peasant risings which aimed at recreating the primal egalitarian state of nature and were explicitly opposed to historical time. These utopian explosions were quelled, but remnants of earlier time concepts persisted as a "lower" stratum of folk consciousness in many areas.

During the Renaissance, domination by time reached a new level as public clocks now tolled all twenty-four hours of the day and added new hands to mark the passing seconds. A keen sense of time's all-consuming presence is the great discovery of the age, and nothing portrays this more graphically than the figure of Father Time. Renaissance art fused the Greek god Kronos with the Roman god Saturn to form the familiar grim deity representing the power of Time, armed with a fatal scythe signifying his association with agriculture/domestication. The Dance of Death and other medieval *memento mori* artifacts preceded Father Time, but the subject is now time rather than death.

The seventeenth century was the first in which people thought of themselves as inhabiting a particular century. One now needed to take one's bearings within time. Francis Bacon's *The Masculine Birth of Time* (1603) and *A Discourse Concerning a New Planet* (1605) embraced the deepening dimension and revealed how a heightened sense of time could serve the new scientific spirit. "To choose time is to save time," he wrote, and "Truth is the daughter of time." Descartes followed, introducing the idea of time as limitless. He was one of the first advocates of the modern idea of progress, closely related to that of unbounded linear time, and characteristically expressing itself in his famous invitation that we become "masters and possessors of nature."

Newton's clockwork universe was the crowning achievement of the Scientific Revolution in the seventeenth century, and was grounded in his conception of "Absolute, true and mathematical time, of itself and from its own nature, flowing equably without relation to anything eternal." Time is now the grand ruler, answering to no one, influenced by nothing, completely independent of the environment: the model of unassailable authority and perfect guarantor of unchanging alienation.

Classical Newtonian physics in fact remains, despite changes in science, the dominant, everyday conception of time.

The appearance of independent, abstract time found its parallel in the emergence of a growing, formally free working class forced to sell its labor power as an abstract commodity on the market. Prior to the coming of the factory system but already subject to time's disciplinary power, this labor force was the inverse of the monarch Time: free and independent in name only. In Foucault's judgment (1973), the West had become a "carceral society" from this point on. Perhaps more directly to the point is the Balkan proverb, "A clock is a lock."

In 1749 Rousseau threw away his watch, a symbolic rejection of modern science and civilization. Somewhat more in the dominant spirit of the age, however, were the gifts of 51 watches to Marie Antoinette upon her engagement. The word is certainly appropriate, as people had to "watch" the time more and more; watches would soon become one of the first consumer durables of the industrial era.

William Blake and Goethe both attacked Newton, the symbol of the new time and science, for his distancing of life from the sensual, his reduction of the natural to the measurable. Capitalist ideologue Adam Smith, on the other hand, echoed and extended Newton, by calling for greater rationalization and routinization. Smith, like Newton, labored under the spell of an increasingly powerful and remorseless time in promoting further division of labor as objective and absolute progress.

The Puritans had proclaimed waste of time the first and in principle the deadliest of sins (Weber 1921); this became, about a century later, Ben Franklin's "Time is money." The factory system was initiated by clockmakers and the clock was the symbol and fountainhead of the order, discipline and repression required to create an industrial proletariat.

Hegel's grand system in the early 19th century heralded the "push into time" that is History's momentum; time is our "destiny and necessity," he declared. Postone (1993) noted that the "progress" of abstract time is closely tied to the "progress" of capitalism as a way of life. Waves of industrialism drowned the resistance of the Luddites; appraising this general period, Lyotard (1988) decided that "the illness of time was now incurable."

An increasingly complex class society requires an ever larger array of time signals. Fights against time, as Thompson (1967) and Hohn (1984) have pointed out, gave way to struggles over time; resistance to being yoked to time and its inherent demands was defeated in general, replaced, typically, by disputes over the fair determination of time schedules or the length of the work day. [In an address to the First International (July 28, 1868), Karl Marx advocated, by the way, age nine as the time to begin work.]

The clock descended from the cathedral, to court and courthouse, next to the bank and railway station, and finally to the wrist and pocket of each decent citizen. Time had to become more "democratic" in order to truly colonize subjectivity. The subjection of outer nature, as Adorno and others have understood, is successful only in the measure of the conquest of inner nature. The unleashing of the forces of production, to put it another way, depended on time's victory in its long-waged war on freer consciousness. Industrialism brought with it a more complete commodification of time, time in its most predatory form yet. It was this that Giddens (1981) saw as "the key to the deepest transformations of day-to-day social life that are brought about by the emergence of capitalism."

"Time marches on," as the saying goes, in a world increasingly dependent on time and a time increasingly unified. A single giant clock hangs over the world and dominates. It pervades all; in its court there is no appeal. The standardization of world time marks a victory for the efficient/machine society, a universalism that undoes particularity as surely as computers lead to homogenization of thought.

Paul Virilio (1986) has gone so far as to foresee that "the loss of material space leads to the government of nothing but time." A further provocative notion posits a reversal of the birth of history out of maturing time. Virilio (1991), in fact, finds us already living within a system of technological temporality where history has been eclipsed. ". . . the primary question becomes less one of relations to *history* than one of relations to *time*."

Such theoretical flights aside, however, there is ample evidence and testimony as to time's central role in society. In "Time—The Next Source of Competitive Advantage" (July-August, 1988 *Harvard Business Review*), George Stark, Jr. discusses it as pivotal in the positioning

of capital: "As a strategic weapon, time is the equivalent of money, productivity, quality, even innovation." Time management is certainly not
confined to the corporations; Levine's 1985 study of publicly accessible
clocks in six countries demonstrated that their accuracy was an exact
gauge of the relative industrialization of national life. Paul Adler's
January-February, 1993 *Harvard Business Review* offering, "Time-and-
Motion Regained," nakedly champions the neo-Taylorist standardization
and regimentation of work: behind the well-publicized "workplace
democracy" window dressing in some factories remains the "time-and-
motion discipline and formal bureaucratic structures essential for efficiency and quality in routine operations."

It is clear that the advent of writing facilitated the fixation of time
concepts and the beginning of history. But as the anthropologist
Goody (1986) points out, "oral cultures are often only too prepared to
accept these innovations." They have already been conditioned, after
all, by language itself. McLuhan (1962) discussed how the coming of
the printed book, and mass literacy, reinforced the logic of linear time.

Life was steadily forced to adapt. "For now hath time made me his
numbering clock," wrote Shakespeare in *Richard II*. "Time," like
"rich," was one of the favorite words of the Bard, a time-haunted
figure. A hundred years later, Defoe's Robinson Crusoe reflected how
little escape from time seemed possible. Marooned on a desert island,
Crusoe is deeply concerned with the passage of time; keeping close
track of his affairs, even in such a setting, meant above all keeping
track of the time, especially as long as his pen and ink lasted.

Northrop Frye (1950) saw the "alliance of time and Western man"
as the defining characteristic of the novel. Ian Watt's *The Rise of the
Novel* (1957) likewise focused on the new concern with time that stimulated the novel's emergence in the eighteenth century. As Jonathan
Swift told it in *Gulliver's Travels* (1726), his protagonist never did anything without looking at his watch. "He called it his oracle, and said it
pointed out the time for every action of his life." The Lilliputians concluded that the watch was Gulliver's god. Sterne's *Tristram Shandy*
(1760), on the eve of the Industrial Revolution, begins with the
mother of Tristram interrupting his father at the moment of their
monthly coitus: "'Pray, my dear,' quoth my mother, 'have you not
forgot to wind up the clock?'"

In the nineteenth century Poe satirized the authority of clocks, linking them to bourgeois superficiality and obsession with order. Time is the real subject of Flaubert's novels, according to Hauser (1956), as Walter Pater (1901) sought in literature the "wholly concrete moment" which would "absorb past and future in an intense consciousness of the present," similar to Joyce's celebration of "epiphanies." In *Marius the Epicurean* (1909), Pater depicts Marius suddenly realizing "the possibility of a real world beyond time." Meanwhile Swinburne looked for a respite beyond "time-stricken lands" and Baudelaire declared his fear and hatred of chronological time, the devouring foe.

The disorientation of an age wracked by time and subject to the acceleration of history has led modern writers to deal with time from new and extreme points of view. Proust delineated interrelationships among events that transcended conventional temporal order and thus violated Newtonian conceptions of causation. His thirteen-volume *À la Recherche du Temps Perdu* (1925), usually rendered in English as *Remembrance of Things Past*, is more literally and accurately translated as *Searching for Lost Time*. In it he judges that "a minute freed from the order of time has recreated in us . . . the individual freed from the order of time," and recognizes "the only environment in which one could live and enjoy the essence of things, that is to say, entirely outside time."

Philosophy in the twentieth century has been largely preoccupied with time. Consider the misguided attempts to locate authentic time by thinkers as different as Bergson and Heidegger, or the latter's virtual deification of time. A.A. Mendilow's *Time and the Novel* (1952) reveals how the same intense interest has dominated the novels of the century, in particular those of Joyce, Woolf, Conrad, James, Gide, Mann, and of course, Proust. Other studies, such as Church's *Time and Reality* (1962), have expanded this list of novelists to include, among others, Kafka, Sartre, Faulkner, and Vonnegut.

And of course time-struck literature cannot be confined to the novel. T.S. Eliot's poetry often expressed a yearning to escape time-bound, time-ridden conventionality. "Burnt Norton" (1941) is a good example, with these lines:

Time past and time future

Allow but a little consciousness.
To be conscious is not to be in time.

Samuel Beckett, early in his career (1931), wrote pointedly of "the poisonous ingenuity of Time in the science of affliction." The play *Waiting for Godot* (1955) is an obvious candidate in this regard, and so is his Murphy (1957), in which time becomes reversible in the mind of the main character. When the clock may go either way, our sense of time, and time itself, vanishes.

Turning to what is commonly called psychology, we again come upon one of the most fundamental questions: Is there really a phenomenon of time that exists apart from any individual, or does it reside only in one's perceptions of it? Husserl, for example, failed to show why consciousness in the modern world seems to inevitably constitute itself in time. We know that experiences, like events of every other kind, are neither past, present nor future in themselves.

Whereas there was little sociological interest in time until the 1970s, the number of studies of time in the literature of psychology has increased rapidly since 1930 (Lauer 1988). Time is perhaps hardest of all to define "psychologically." What is time? What is the experience of time? What is alienation? What is the experience of alienation? If the latter subject were not so neglected the obvious interrelationship would be made clear.

Davies (1977) termed time's passage "a psychological phenomenon of mysterious origin" and concluded (1983), "the secret of mind will only be solved when we understand the secret of time." Given the artificial separation of the individual from society, which defines their field, it is inevitable that such psychologists and psychoanalysts as Eissler (1955), Loewald (1962), Namnum (1972), and Morris (1983) have encountered "great difficulties" in studying time!

At least a few partial insights have been achieved, however. Hartcollis (1983), for instance, noted that time is not only an abstraction but a feeling, while Korzybski (1948) had already taken this further with his observation that "'time' is a feeling, produced by conditions of this world. . . ." In all our lives we are "waiting for Godot," according to Arlow (1986), who believed that our experience of time arises out of unfulfilled emotional needs. Similarly, Reichenbach (1956) had termed anti-time philosophies, like religion, "documents of emotional dissatisfaction." In Freudian terms, Bergler and Roheim (1946) saw the passage of time as symbolizing separation periods originating in early infancy. "The calendar is an ultimate materialization of separation anxiety." If informed by a critical interest in the social and historical context, the implications of these undeveloped points could become serious contributions. Confined to psychology, however, they remain limited and even misleading.

In the world of alienation no adult can contrive or decree the freedom from time that the child habitually enjoys—and must be made to lose. Time training, the essence of schooling, is vitally important to society. This training, as Fraser (1989) very cogently puts it, "bears in almost paradigmatic form the features of a civilizing process." A patient of Joost Meerlo (1970) "expressed it sarcastically: 'Time is civilization,' by which she meant that scheduling and meticulousness were the great weapons used by adults to force the youngsters into submission and servility." Piaget's studies (1946, 1952) could detect no innate sense of time. Rather, the abstract notion of "time" is of considerable difficulty to the young. It is not something they learn automatically; there is no spontaneous orientation toward time (Hermelin and O'Connor 1971, Voyat 1977).

Time and *tidy* are related etymologically, and our Newtonian idea of time represents perfect and universal ordering. The cumulative weight of this ever more pervasive pressure shows up in the increasing number of patients with time anxiety symptoms (Lawson 1990). Dooley (1941) referred to "the observed fact that people who are obsessive in character, whatever their type of neurosis, are those who make most extensive use of the sense of time. . . ." Pettit's "Anality and Time" (1969) argued convincingly for the close connection between the two, as Meerloo (1966), citing the character and achievements of Mussolini and Eichmann, found "a definite connection between time compulsion and fascistic aggression."

Capek (1961) called time "a huge and chronic hallucination of the human mind"; there are few experiences indeed that can be said to be timeless. Orgasm, LSD, a life "flashing before one's eyes" in a moment of extreme danger . . . these are some of the rare, evanescent situations intense enough to escape from time's insistence.

Timelessness is the ideal of pleasure, wrote Marcuse (1955). The passage of time, on the other hand, fosters the forgetting of what was and what can be. It is the enemy of eros and deep ally of the order of repression. The mental processes of the unconscious are in fact timeless, decided Freud (1920): ". . . time does not change them in any way and the idea of time cannot be applied to them." Thus desire is already outside of time. As Freud said in 1932: "There is nothing in the Id that corresponds to the notion of time; there is no recognition of the passage of time."

Marie Bonaparte (1940) argued that time becomes ever more plastic and obedient to the pleasure principle insofar as we loosen the bonds of full ego control. Dreams are a form of thinking among noncivilized peoples (Kracke 1987); this faculty must have once been much more accessible to us. The Surrealists believed that reality could be much more fully understood if we could make the connection to our instinctive, subconscious experiences; Breton (1924), for example, proclaimed the radical goal of a resolution of dream and conscious reality.

When we dream the sense of time is virtually nonexistent, replaced by a sensation of presentness. It should come as no surprise that dreams, which ignore the rules of time, would attract the notice of those searching for liberatory clues, or that the unconscious, with its "storms of impulse," frightens those with a stake in the neurosis we call civilization. Norman O. Brown (1959) saw the sense of time or history as a function of repression; if repression were abolished, he reasoned, we would be released from time. Similarly, Coleridge (1801) recognized in the man of "methodical industry" the origin and creator of time.

In his *Critique of Cynical Reason* (1987), Peter Sloterdijk called for the "radical recognition of the Id without reservation," a narcissistic self-affirmation that would laugh in the face of morose society. Narcissism has of course traditionally been cast as wicked, the "heresy of self-love." In reality that meant it was reserved for the ruling classes, while all others (workers, women, slaves) had to practice submission and self-effacement (Fine 1980). The narcissist symptoms are feelings of emptiness, unreality, alienation, life as no more than a succession of moments, accompanied by a longing for powerful autonomy and self-esteem (Alford 1988, Grunberger 1979). Given the appropriateness of these "symptoms" and desires it is little wonder that narcissism can be seen as a potentially emancipatory force (Zweig 1980). Its demand for total satisfaction is obviously a subversive individualism, at a minimum.

The narcissist "hates time, denies time" (letter to author, Alford 1993) and this, as always, provokes a severe reaction from the defenders of time and authority. Psychiatrist E. Mark Stern (1977), for instance: "Since time begins beyond one's control one must correspond to its demands. . . . Courage is the antithesis of narcissism." This condition, which certainly may include negative aspects, contains the germ of a different reality principle, aiming at the non-time of perfection wherein being and becoming are one and including, implicitly, a halt to time.

> I'm not a scientist but I do know that all things begin and end in eternity.
>
> —*The Man Who Fell to Earth*, Walter Tevis

Science, for our purposes, does not comment on time and estrangement with anywhere near the directness of, say, psychology. But science can be re-construed to shed light on the topic at hand, because of the many parallels between scientific theory and human affairs.

"Time," decided N.A. Kozyrev (1971), "is the most important and the most mysterious phenomenon of Nature. Its notion is beyond the grasp of imagination." Some scientists, in fact, have felt (e.g. Dingle 1966) that "all the real problems associated with the notion of time are independent of physics." Science, and physics in particular, may indeed not have the last word; it is another source of commentary, however, though itself alienated and generally indirect.

Is "physical time" the same as the time of which we are conscious; if not, how does it differ? In physics, time seems to be an undefined basic dimension, as much a taken-for-granted given as it is outside the realm of science. This is one way to remind ourselves that, as with every other kind of thinking, scientific ideas are meaningless outside their cultural context. They are symptoms of and symbol for the ways of living that give rise to them. According to Nietzsche, all writing is inherently metaphorical, even though science is rarely looked at this way. Science has developed by drawing an increasingly sharp separation between inner and outer worlds, between dream and "reality". This has been accomplished by the mathematization of nature, which has largely meant that the scientist proceeds by a method that debars him or her from the larger context, including the origins and significance of his/her projects. Nonetheless, as H.P. Robinson (1964) stated, "the cosmologies which humanity has set up at various times and in various localities inevitably reflect the physical and intellectual environment, including above all the interests and culture of each society."

Subjective time, as P.C.W. Davies pointed out (1981), "possesses apparent qualities that are absent from the 'outside' world and which are fundamental to our conception of reality"—principally the "passing" of time. Our sense of separation from the world owes largely to this discrepancy. We exist in time (and alienation), but time is not found in the physical world. The time variable, though useful to science, is a theoretical construct. "The laws of science," Stephen Hawking (1988) explained, "do not distinguish between past and future." Einstein had gone further than this some thirty years earlier; in one of his last letters, he wrote that "People like us, who believe in physics, know that the distinction between past, present and future is only a stubborn, persistent illusion." But science partakes of society in other ways concerning time, and very deeply. The more "rational" it becomes, the more variations in time are suppressed. Theoretical physics geometrizes time by conceiving it as a straight line, for example. Science does not stand apart from the cultural history of time.

As implied above, however, physics does not contain the idea of a present instant of time that passes (Park 1972). Furthermore, the fundamental laws are not only completely reversible as to the 'arrow of time'—as Hawking noted—but "irreversible phenomena appear as the result of the particular nature of our human cognition," according to Watanabe (1953). Once again we find human experience playing a decisive role, even in this most "objective" realm. Zee (1992) put it this way: "Time is that one concept in physics we can't talk about without dragging in, at some level, consciousness."

Even in seemingly straightforward areas ambiguities exist where time is concerned. While the complexity of the most complex species may increase, for example, not all species become more complex, prompting J.M. Smith (1972) to conclude that it is "difficult to say whether evolution as a whole has a direction."

In terms of the cosmos, it is argued, "time's arrow" is automatically indicated by the fact that the galaxies are receding away from each other. But there seems to be virtual unanimity that as far as the basics of physics are concerned, the "flow" of time is irrelevant and makes no sense; fundamental physical laws are completely neutral with regard to the direction of time (Mehlberg 1961, 1971, Landsberg 1982, Squires 1986, Watanabe 1953, 1956, Swinburne 1986, Morris 1983, Mallove 1987, D'Espagnat 1989, etc.). Modern physics even provides scenarios in which time ceases to exist and, in reverse, comes into existence. So why is our world asymmetric in time? Why can't it go backward as well as forward? This is a paradox, inasmuch as the individual molecular dynamics are all reversible. The main point, to which I will return later, is that time's arrow reveals itself as complexity develops, in striking parallel with the social world.

The flow of time manifests itself in the context of future and past, and they in turn depend on a referent known as the now. With Einstein and relativity, it is clear that there is no universal present: we cannot say it is "now" throughout the universe. There is no fixed interval at all that is independent of the system to which it refers, just as alienation is dependent on its context.

Time is thus robbed of the autonomy and objectivity it enjoyed in the Newtonian world. It is definitely more individually delineated, in Einstein's revelations, than the absolute and universal monarch it had been. Time is relative to specific conditions and varies according to such factors as speed and gravitation. But if time has become more "decentralized," it has also colonized subjectivity more than ever before. As time and alienation have become the rule throughout the world, there is little solace in knowing that they are dependent on varying circumstances. The relief comes in acting on this understanding; it is the invariance of alienation that causes the Newtonian model of independently flowing time to hold sway within us, long after its theoretical foundations were eliminated by relativity.

Quantum theory, dealing with the smallest parts of the universe, is known as the fundamental theory of matter. The core of quantum theory follows other fundamental physical theories, like relativity, in making no distinction in the direction of time (Coveney and Highfield 1991). A basic premise is indeterminism, in which the movement of particles at this level is a matter of probabilities. Along with such elements as positrons, which can be regarded as electrons moving backward in time, and tachyons, faster-than-light particles that generate effects and contexts reversing the temporal order (Gribbin 1979, Lindley 1993), quantum physics has raised fundamental questions about time and causality. In the quantum microworld common acausal relationships have been discovered that transcend time and put into question the very notion of the ordering of events in time. There can be "connections and correlations between very distant events in the absence of any intermediary force or signal" and which occur instantaneously (Zohar 1982, Aspect 1982). That phenomena in which action taken now affects the course of events that have already happened is an inescapable phenomenon of quantum, or particle physics.

Gleick (1992) summed up the situation as follows: "With simultaneity gone, sequentiality was foundering, causality was under pressure, and scientists generally felt themselves free to consider temporal possibilities that would have seemed far-fetched a generation before." At least one approach in quantum physics has attempted to remove the notion of time altogether (J.G. Taylor 1972); D. Park (1972), for instance, said, "I prefer the atemporal representation to the temporal one."

The bewildering situation in science finds its match in the extremity of the social world. Alienation, like time, produces ever greater oddities and pressures: the most fundamental questions finally, almost necessarily, emerge in both cases.

St. Augustine's fifth century complaint was that he didn't understand what the measurement of time really consisted of. Einstein, admitting the inadequacy of his comment, often defined time as "what a clock measures." Quantum physics, for its part, posits the inseparability of measurer and what is measured. Via a process physicists don't claim to understand fully, the act of observation or measurement not only reveals a particle's condition but actually determines it (Pagels 1983). This has prompted the question, "Is everything—including time—built from nothingness by acts of observer-participancy?" Again a striking parallel, for alienation, at every level and from its origin, requires exactly such participation, virtually as a matter of definition.

Time's arrow—irrevocable, one-direction-only time—is the monster that has proven itself more terrifying than any physical projectile. Directionless time is not time at all, and Cambel (1993) identifies time directionality as "a primary characteristic of complex systems." The time-reversible behavior of atomic particles is "generally commuted into behavior of the system that is irreversible," concluded Schlegel (1961). If not rooted in the micro world, where does time come from? Where does our time-bound world come from? It is here that we encounter a provocative analogy. The small scale world described by physics, with its mysterious change into the macro world of complex systems, is analogous to the "primitive" social world and the origins of division of labor, leading to complex, class-divided society with its apparently irreversible "progress".

A generally held tenet of physical theory is that the arrow of time is dependent on the Second Law of Thermodynamics (e.g. Reichenbach 1956), which asserts that all systems tend toward ever greater disorder or entropy. The past is thus more orderly than the future. Some proponents of the Second Law (e.g. Boltzmann 1866) have found in entropic increase the very meaning of the past-future distinction.

This general principle of irreversibility was developed in the middle decades of the 19th century, beginning with Carnot in 1824, when industrial capitalism itself reached its apparent non-reversible point. If evolution was the century's optimistic application of irreversible time, the Second Law of Thermodynamics was its pessimistic one. In its original terms, it pictured a universe as an enormous heat engine running down, where work became increasingly subject to inefficiency and disorder. But nature, as Toda (1978) noticed, is not an engine, does not work, and is not concerned with "order" or "disorder". The cultural aspect of this theory—namely, capital's fear for its future—is hard to miss.

One hundred and fifty years later, theoretical physicists realize that the Second Law and its supposed explanation of the arrow of time cannot be considered a solved problem (Néeman 1982). Many supporters of reversible time in nature consider the Second Law too superficial, a secondary law not a primary one (e.g. Haken 1988, Penrose

1989). Others find the very concept of entropy ill-defined and problematic, and, related to the charge of superficiality, it is argued that the
phenomena described by the Second Law can be ascribed to particular
initial conditions and do not represent the workings of a general principle (Davies 1981, Barrow 1991). Furthermore, not every pair of
events that bear the "afterward" relation the one to the other bear an
entropic difference. The science of complexity (with a wider scope
than chaos theory) has discovered that not all systems tend toward disorder (Lewin 1992), also contrary to the Second Law. Moreover, isolated systems, in which no exchanges with the environment are
allowed, display the Second Law's irreversible trend; even the universe
may not be such a closed system. In fact, we don't know whether the
total entropy of the universe is increasing, decreasing, or remaining
stationary.

Despite such aporias and objections, a movement toward an "irreversible physics" based on the Second Law is underway, with quite
interesting implications. 1977 Nobel Laureate Ilya Prigogine seems to
be the most tireless and public advocate of the view that there is an
innate unidirectional time at all levels of existence. Whereas the fundamentals of every major scientific theory, as noted, are neutral with
respect to time, Prigogine gives time a primary emphasis in the universe. Irreversibility is for him and his like-minded fellow believers an
over-arching primal axiom. In supposedly nonpartisan science, the
question of time has clearly become a political matter.

Prigogine (1985), in a symposium sponsored by Honda and promoting such projects as Artificial Intelligence: "Questions such as the
origin of life, the origin of the universe, or the origin of matter, can no
longer be discussed without recourse to irreversibility." It is no coinci-
dence that non-scientist Alvin Toffler, America's leading cheerleader for
a high-tech world, provided an enthusiastic forward for one of the basic
texts of the pro-time campaign, Prigogine and Stenger's *Order Out of
Chaos* (1984). Prigogine disciple Ervin Laszlo, in a bid to legitimate and
extend the dogma of universally irreversible time, asks whether the laws
of nature are applicable to the human world. He soon answers, in
effect, his own disingenuous question (1985): "The general irreversibility of technological innovation overrides the indeterminacy of individual points of bifurcation and drives the processes of history in the

observed direction from primitive tribes to modern techno-industrial states." How "scientific"! This transposition from the "laws of nature" to the social world could hardly be improved on as a description of time, division of labor, and the mega-machine crushing the autonomy or "reversibility" of human decision. Leggett (1987) expressed this perfectly: "So it would seem that the arrow of time which appears in the apparently impersonal subject of thermodynamics is intimately related to what we, as human agents, can or cannot do."

It is deliverance from "chaos" which Prigogine and others promise the ruling system, using the model of irreversible time. Capital has always reigned in fear of entropy or disorder. Resistance, especially resistance to work, is the real entropy, which time, history, and progress constantly seek to banish. Prigogine and Stenger (1984) wrote: "Irreversibility is either true on all levels or none." All or nothing, always the ultimate stakes of the game.

Since civilization subjugated humanity we have had to live with the melancholy idea that our highest aspirations are perhaps impossible in a world of steadily mounting time. The more that pleasure and understanding are deferred, moved out of reach—and this is the essence of civilization—the more palpable is the dimension of time. Nostalgia for the past, fascination with the idea of time travel, and the heated quest for increased longevity are some of the symptoms of time sickness, and there seems to be no ready cure. "What does not elapse in time is the lapse of time itself," as Merleau-Ponty (1962) realized.

In addition to the general antipathy at large, however, it is possible to point out some recent specifics of opposition. The Society for the Retardation of Time was established in 1990 and has a few hundred members in four European countries. Less whimsical than it may sound, its members are committed to reversing the contemporary acceleration of time in everyday life, toward the aim of being allowed to live more satisfying lives. Michael Theunissen's *Negative Theology of Time* appeared in 1991, aimed explicitly at what it sees as the ultimate human enemy. This work has engendered a very lively debate in philosophical circles (Penta 1993), due to its demand for a negative reconsideration of time.

"Time is the one single movement appropriate to itself in all its parts," wrote Merleau-Ponty (1962). Here we see the fullness of alienation in the separated world of capital. Time is thought of by us before its parts; it thus reveals the totality. The crisis of time is the crisis of the whole. Its triumph, apparently well established, was in fact never complete as long as anyone could question the first premises of its being.

Above Lake Silviplana, Nietzsche found the inspiration for *Thus Spake Zarathustra*. "Six thousand feet above men and time . . ." he wrote in his journal. But time cannot be transcended by means of a lofty contempt for humanity, because overcoming the alienation that it generates is not a solitary project. In this sense I prefer Rexroth's (1968) formulation: "the only Absolute is the Community of Love with which Time ends."

Can we put an end to time? Its movement can be seen as the master and measure of a social existence that has become increasingly empty and technicized. Averse to all that is spontaneous and immediate, time more and more clearly reveals its bond with alienation. The scope of our project of renewal must include the entire length of this joint domination. Divided life will be replaced by the possibility of living completely and wholly—timelessly—only when we erase the primary causes of that division.

1994

AGAINST TECHNOLOGY

A humanities symposium called "Discourse @ Networks
200" was held at Stanford University over the course of
several months in 1997. The following talk on April 23
represents the only dissent to the prevailing high-tech
orientation/appreciation.

John Zerzan: Thanks for coming. I'll be your Luddite this afternoon.
The token Luddite, so that it falls on me to uphold this unpopular or
controversial banner. The emphasis will be on breadth more than
depth, and in rather reified terms, owing to time considerations. But I
hope it won't disable whatever cogency there might be to these somewhat general remarks.

It seems to me we're in a barren, impoverished, technicized place
and that these characteristics are interrelated. Technology claims that it
extends the senses; but this extension, it seems, ends up blunting and
atrophying the senses, instead of what this promise claims. Technology
today is offering solutions to everything in every sphere. You can
hardly think of one for which it doesn't come up with the answer. But
it would like us to forget that in virtually every case, it has created the
problem in the first place that it comes round to say that it will transcend. Just a little more technology. That's what it always says. And I
think we begin to see the results ever more clearly today.

The computer cornucopia, as everything becomes wired into the computer throughout society, offers variety, the riches of complete access, and yet, as Frederick Jameson said, we live in a society that is the most standardized in history.

Let's look at it as a "means and ends" proposition, as in means and ends must be equally valid. Technology claims to be neutral, merely a tool, its value or meaning completely dependent on how it is used. In this way it hides its ends by cloaking its means. If there is no way to understand what it is in terms of an essence, inner logic, historical embeddedness or other dimension, then what we call technology escapes judgment. We generally recognize the ethical precept that you can't achieve valid or good ends with deficient or invalid means, but how do we gauge that unless we look at the means? If it's something we're not supposed to think about in terms of its essential being, its foundations, it's impossible. I mean, you can repeat any kind of cliché. This is the kind of thing that one hopes is not a cliché because the means and ends thesis is a moral value that I think does have validity.

A number of people or cases could be brought up to further illuminate this. For example, Marx early on was concerned with what technology is, what production and the means of production are, and determined, as many, many people have, that it's at base division of labor. And hence it is a vital question how stunting or how negative division of labor is. But Marx went on from that banality, which doesn't get very much examined, as we know, to very different questions, such as which class owns and controls the technology and means of production, and how does the dispossessed class, the proletariat, seize that technology from the bourgeoisie. This was quite a different emphasis from examining and evaluating technology, and represents an abandonment of his earlier interest.

Of course, by that point, Marx certainly felt that technology is a positive good. Today the people who say that it's merely a tool, a neutral thing, that it's purely a matter of instrumental use of technology, really believe that technology is a positive thing. But they want to be a little more canny about it, so again, my point is that if you say it's neutral, then you avoid testing the truth claim that it's positive. In other words, if you say it's negative or positive, you have to look at what it is. You have to get into it. But if you say it's neutral, that has worked pretty well at precluding this examination.

Next, I want to provide a quote that keeps coming back to me, a very pregnant quote from a brilliant mathematician—and it's not Ted Kaczynski. It's the British mathematician, Alan Turing, and some of you, I'm sure, know that he established many of the theoretical foundations for the computer in the 1930s and '40s. Also, it would be worth mentioning that he took his own life in the '50s because of a prosecution stemming from the fact that he was gay, somewhat like the action against Oscar Wilde about 50 years earlier. Anyway, I mention that—and I don't want to belittle the tragic fact that he was gay and this was his end because of it—but he took his life by painting an apple with cyanide and biting into it, and it makes me think of the forbidden fruit of the tree of knowledge and whether he was saying something about that, as we know what happened with that. We have work, agriculture, misery and technology out of that. And I also wonder, in passing, about Apple computers. Why would they use an apple? It's kind of a mystery to me. [laughter]

But anyway, after this digression, the quote that I was trying to get to here. In the middle of an article for the journal *Mind* in 1950, he said, "I believe that at the end of the century, the use of words in general educated opinion will have altered so much that one will be able to speak of machines thinking without expecting to be contradicted." Now, what I think is of a lot of interest here is that he doesn't say that by the end of the century we'll have computing machines (they were still called computing machines at that time) that have advanced so far that people won't have any trouble understanding, now, that machines think. He says, ". . . the use of words in general educated opinion will have altered so much."

Now, I'm giving a reading of this which is probably different from what he had in mind, but when you think about it, this has to do with this question of the interrelationship of society and technology. I think he was quite right; again, not because artificial intelligence—it wasn't called that back then, of course—had advanced so far. Actually, it hasn't made very good on its ambitious claims, as I understand it. But some people now entertain that notion very seriously. In fact, there's even a small but considerable literature on whether machines feel and at what point machines live. And that isn't because Artificial Intelligence has gone very far, it seems to me. In the early '80s, there was an awful lot of talk about "just around the corner," and I'm not an expert on AI, but I don't think it has gone very far. It plays a pretty good game of chess, I guess, but I don't think it's anywhere near these other achievements, or levels.

I think what explains the change in perception about computers is the deformation caused by the massive amount of alienation that has happened in the past 50 years or so. That's why some, and I hope not many, hold to this point about computers living.

In terms of what they are capable of, it seems to me, when you have the distance narrowing between humans and machines in the sense that if we are becoming more machine-like, it's easier to see the machine as more human-like. I don't want to be overly dramatic about it, but I think people more and more wonder, is this living or are we just going through the motions? What's happening? Is everything being leached out of life? Is the whole texture and values and everything kind of draining away? Well, that would take many other lectures, but it's not so much the actual advance of the technology. If machines can be human, humans can be machines. The truly scary point is the narrowing of the distance between the two.

Another quotation to similarly mark this descent, if you will, is a short one from a computer communications expert, J.C.R. Licklider. In 1968 he said, "In the future, we'll be able to communicate more effectively through a machine than face-to-face." If that isn't estrangement, I don't know what is. At the same time, one striking aspect in terms of cultural development is that the concept of alienation is disappearing, has almost disappeared. If you look at the indices of books in the last, say, 20 years, it isn't there any more. It has become so banal, I guess, what's the point of talking about it?

I was reading a recent review on another subject by the political theorist, Anthony Giddens, I think it's Sir Anthony Giddens, actually. He found it remarkable that "capitalism has disappeared as an object of study, just when it has removed any alternative to itself." One might think, what else is there to study in the absence of any other system? But no one talks about it. It's just a given. It's another commonplace that is apparently just accepted and not scrutinized.

And, of course, capital is increasingly technologized. A kind of
obvious point. The people who think that it's about surfing the Net
and exchanging e-mail with your cousin in Idaho or something, obviously neglect the fact that the movement of capital is the computer's
basic function. The computer is there for faster transactions, the faster
movement of commodities and so on. That shouldn't even have to be
pointed out.

So anyway, back to the theme of how the whole field or ground-
work moves and our perception of technology and the values we attach
to it change, usually pretty imperceptibly. Freud said that the fullness
of civilization will mean universal neurosis. And that sounds kind of
too sanguine, when you think about it. I'm very disturbed by what I
see.

I live in Oregon, where the rate of suicide among 15- to 19-year
olds has increased 600% since 1961. I find it hard to see this as other
than youth getting to the threshold of adulthood and society and
looking out, and what do they see? They see this bereft place. I'm not
saying they consciously go through that sort of formulation, but some
kind of assessment takes place, and some just opt out.

A study of several of the most developed countries is showing that
the rate of serious depression doubles about every ten years. So I guess
that means if there aren't enough people on anti-depressants right now,
just to get through the day, we'll all be taking them before long. You
can just extrapolate from this chilling fact. If you look for a reason
why that won't keep going, what would that be without a pretty total
change?

And many other things. The turn away from literacy. That's a
pretty basic thing that is somewhat baffling, but it isn't baffling if you
think that people are viscerally turning away from what doesn't have
meaning anymore. The outbursts of multiple homicides. That used to
be unheard of, even in this violent country, just a few decades ago.
Now it's spreading to all the other countries. You can hardly pick up
the paper without seeing some horrendous thing in McDonald's or at a
school or someplace in Scotland or New Zealand, as well as L.A. or
wherever in the U.S.

Rancho Santa Fe. You probably remember this quote from the
news. It's from a woman who was part of the Heaven's Gate group

there. "Maybe I'm crazy, but I don't care. I've been here 31 years, and there's nothing here for me." I think that speaks for quite a lot of people who are surveying the emptiness, not just cult members.

So we're seeing the crisis of inner nature, the prospect of complete dehumanization, linking up with the crisis of outer nature, which is obviously ecological catastrophe. And I won't bore you with the latter; everybody here knows all its features, the accelerating extinction of species, etc. etc. Up in Oregon, for example, the natural, original forest is virtually one hundred percent gone; the salmon are on the verge of extinction. Everybody knows this. And it's so greatly urged along by the movement of technology and all that is involved there.

Marvin Minsky—I think this was in the early '80s—said that the brain is a three-pound computer made of meat. He's one of the leading AI people. And we have all the rest. We have Virtual Reality. People will be flocking to that, just to try to get away from an objective social existence that is not too much to look at or deal with. The cloning of humans, obviously, is just a matter of probably months away. Fresh horrors all the time.

Education. Get the kids linked up when they're five or so to the computer. They call it "knowledge production." And that's the best thing you could say about it.

I want to read one quote here from Hans Moravec from Carnegie-Mellon, who is a contributor to the periodical *Extropy*. He says, "The final frontier will be urbanized ultimately into an arena where every bit of activity is a meaningful computation. The inhabited portion of the universe will be transformed into a cyberspace. We might then be tempted to replace some of our innermost mental processes with more cyberspace-appropriate programs purchased from artificial intelligence and so, bit by bit, transform ourselves into something much like it. Ultimately, our thinking procedures could be totally liberated from any traces of our original body, indeed of any body." I don't think that requires any comment.

But, of course, there have been contrary voices. There have been analysis by people who been pretty worried about the whole development. One of the best is Horkheimer and Adorno's *Dialectic of Enlightenment*, written in the '40s. If technology is not neutral, they argue very forcefully, reason isn't a neutral thing either, when you think about it. They raise a critique of what they call "instrumental reason," that reason, under the sign of civilization and technology, is fundamentally biased toward distancing and control. I'm not going to try to sum up the whole thing in a few words, but one of the memorable parts of this was their look at Odysseus from the *Odyssey*, from Homer, one of the basic texts of European civilization, where Odysseus is trying to sail past the sirens. Horkheimer and Adorno demonstrate that this depicts at a very early point the tension between the sensuous, Eros, pre-history, pre-technology, and the project of going past that and doing something else. Odysseus has his oarsmen tie him to the mast, and stuff their own ears with wax, so he won't be tempted by pleasure and he can get through to the repressive, non-sensuous life of civilization and technology.

Of course, there are many other markers of estrangement. Descartes, 350 years ago: "We have to become the masters and possessors of nature." But what I think is also worth pointing out in a critique like Horkheimer and Adorno's and many others, is that they feel that they have to add the idea that, well, after all, if nature isn't subdued, that if society doesn't subdue nature, society always will be subjected to nature and, in effect, there probably won't be any society. So they always put that caveat, that qualification, which is to their credit for honesty; but it puts a brake on the implications of their critique. It makes it less a black-and-white thing, obviously, because, well, we can't really get away from domination of nature, and that's what the whole thing is based on, our very existence. We can criticize the technological life, but where would we be without it?

But something that I think has very, very enormous implications has happened in the last 20 or 30 years, and I don't think it has yet got out very much. There has been a wholesale revision in scholarly ideas of what life outside of civilization really was. One of the basic ideological foundations for civilization, for religion, the state, police, armies, everything else, is that you've got a pretty bloodthirsty, awful, subhuman condition before civilization. It has to be tamed and tutored and so on. It's Hobbes. It's that famous idea that the pre-civilized life was nasty, brutish and short, and so to rescue or enable humanity away from fear and superstition, from this horrible condition into the light of civilization, you have to do that. You have to have what Freud called the "forcible renunciation of instinctual freedom." You just have to. That's the price.

Anyway, that turns out to be completely wrong. Certainly, there are disagreements about some of the parts of the new paradigm, some of the details, and I think most of the literature doesn't draw out its radical implications. But since about the early '70s, we have a starkly different picture of what life was like in the two million or so years before civilization, a period that ended about 10,000 years ago, almost no time at all.

Prehistory is now characterized more by intelligence, egalitarianism and sharing, leisure time, a great degree of sexual equality, robusticity and health, with no evidence at all of organized violence. I mean, that's just staggering. It's virtually a wholesale revision. We're still living, of course, with the cartoonish images, the caveman pulling the woman into the cave, Neanderthal meaning somebody who is a complete brute and subhuman, and so on. But the real picture has been wholly revised.

I won't take time here to go into the evidence and the arguments, but I want to mention just a couple of them. For example, how do we know about sharing? That sounds like some kind of '60s assertion, right? But it's simple things like examining the evidence around hearths, around fire sites, probably in impermanent settlements. If you found around one fire you've got all the goodies there, well, that looks like the chief and everybody else has little or nothing. But if everybody has about exactly the same amount of stuff, it argues for a condition of equality. Thomas Wynn has helped us see prehistoric intelligence in a different light. He drew on Piaget quite a bit in terms of what is congealed and/or concealed in even a simple stone tool, and he kind of deconstructed it to bring out, I think, about eight different stages and steps and aspects to what it takes to actually take something like that and make a tool out of it. And he concluded—and this hasn't been refuted that I see anywhere in the literature—that at least a million years ago, Homo had an intelligence equal to that of the adult human today. So one would have said, well, okay, even if it was kind of rosy prior to culture, our distant ancestors were just so dim they couldn't figure out how to establish agriculture, hierarchy and all the other wonderful things. But if that's not true, then you start looking at the whole picture quite differently.

One other thing: the book *Stone Age Economics* by Marshall
Sahlins came out in 1972, and a lot of his argument is based on existing hunter-gatherer peoples, on just simply seeing how much they
worked. Which was very, very little. By the way, he was the chairman
of the anthropology department at the University of Michigan, so
we're not talking about some crank, or a marginal figure. If you look at
the literature in anthropology and archaeology, you see quite amazing
corrections to what we had thought. It makes you start to think, I
guess perhaps civilization wasn't such a good idea. The question that
was always asked was why did it take humanity so long to figure out
agriculture? I mean, they just thought of it yesterday, relatively, less
than 10,000 years ago.

Now the question is, why did they ever take up agriculture?
Which is really the question of why did they ever take up civilization?
Why did they ever start our division-of-labor-based technology? If we
once had a technology, if you want to call it that, based on pretty
much zero division of labor, for me that has pretty amazing implications and makes me think that somehow it's possible to get back there
in some way or another. We might be able to reconnect to a higher
condition, one that sounds to me like a state of nearness to reality, of
wholeness.

I'm getting pretty close to the end here. I want to mention Heidegger. Heidegger, of course, is thought of by many as one of the
deepest or most original thinkers of the century. He felt that technology is the end of philosophy, and that's based on his view that as technology encompasses more and more of society, everything becomes
grist for it and grist for production, even thinking. It loses its separateness, its quality of being apart from that. His point is worth mentioning just in passing.

And now I get to one of my favorite topics, postmodernism,
which I think is exactly what Heidegger would have had in mind if
he had stuck around long enough to see it. I think that here we have
a rather complete abdication of reason with postmodernism in so
many ways, and it's so pervasive, and so many people don't seem to
know what it is. Though we are completely immersed in it, few even
now seem to have a grasp of it. Perhaps this, in its way, is similar to
the other banalities I referred to earlier. Namely, that which has over-

powered what is alien to it is simply accepted and rarely analyzed.

So I started having to do some homework, and I've done some writing on it since, and one of the fundamental things—and sorry, for people who already know this—comes from Lyotard in the '70s, in a book called *The Postmodern Condition*. He held that postmodernism is fundamentally "antipathy to meta-narratives," meaning it's a refusal of totality, of the overview, of the arrogant idea that we can have a grasp of the whole. It's based on the idea that the totality is totalitarian. To try to think that you can get some sense of the whole thing, that's no good. And I think a lot of it, by the way, is a reaction against Marxism, which held sway for so long in France among the intelligentsia; I think there was an overreaction because of that.

So you have an anti-totality outlook and an anti-coherence outlook, even, because that too is suspect and even thought to be a nasty thing. After all, and here's the one thing in which he probably concurred with Horkheimer and Adorno, what has Enlightenment thinking brought us? What has modernist, overview, totality-oriented thinking got us? Well, you know, Auschwitz, Hiroshima, neutron bombs. You don't have to defend those things, though, to get a sense that maybe postmodernism is throwing everything away and has no defenses against, for one thing, an onrushing technology.

Similarly, postmodernists are against the idea of origins. They feel that the idea of origins is a false one (these are all big generalizations; there are probably some with slightly different emphases). We are in culture. We have always been in culture. We always will be in culture. So we can't see outside of culture. So something like nature versus culture is just a false notion. Thus they deny that, too, and further inhibit understanding the present. You can't go back to any origins or beginning points of causation or development. Relatedly, history is a fairly arbitrary fiction; one version is about as good as another.

There's also emphasis on the fragmentary, pluralism, diversity, the random. But I ask you, where is the random? Where is the diversity? Where is it? To me, the world is getting so stark and monolithic in terms of the general movement of things and what the meaning of this movement is. To play around with this emphasis on margins and surfaces, this attitude that you can't get below the surface, to me is ethical and intellectual cowardice. "Truth and meaning?" Well, that's just nonsense. That's passé. Always put terms like those in quotes. You see pretty much everything in quotes when you look at postmodern writing. So it's a lot of irony, of course. Irony verging on cynicism is the thing you can now see everywhere in popular culture. In terms of postmodernism, that's close to the whole thing. Everything is shifting. It's just so splintered and everything. I don't quite get how it is possible to evade what is going on vis-à-vis the individual and what is left of nature.

I think postmodernism is a great accomplice to technology, and often explicitly so, often as an explicit embrace of it. Lyotard also said that "data banks are the new nature." Of course, if he rules out origins, how does he know what nature is? They have their own set of really totality-type assumptions, but they don't cop to it. It's only the old-fashioned people, I guess, who don't want to play that game.

One more quote: this is from a Professor Escobar in the June 1994 issue of *Current Anthropology*. It really has a lot to do with how technology defines what is the norm and what is ruled out. He said, "Technological innovations in dominant world views generally transform each other so as to legitimate and naturalize the technologies of the time. Nature and society come to be explained in ways that reinforce the technological imperatives of the day." I think that's really well put.

So I started with one basic fallacy—I think it's a basic fallacy—about technology. That is the point that technology is not neutral, not a discrete tool somehow separate from its social placement or development as a part of society. I think the other one, or another one, is that okay, you can talk all you want about technology, but it's here, it's inexorable, and what's the point of talking about it? Well, it isn't inevitable. It's only inevitable if we don't do anything about it. If we just go along, then it is inevitable. I think that's the obvious challenge. The unimaginable will happen. It's already happening. And if we have a future it will be because we stand up to it and have a different vision and think about dismantling it.

I also think, by the way, that if we have a future, we may have a different idea about who the real criminals are, and who, like John Brown perhaps, the Unabomber might be seen to resemble. Who, like John Brown, tried to save us.

1997

THAT THING WE DO

From the Latin *re*, or thing, reification is essentially thingification. Theodor Adorno, among others, asserted that society and consciousness have become almost completely reified. Through this process, human practices and relations come to be seen as external objects. What is living ends up treated as a non-living thing or abstraction, and this turn of events is experienced as natural, normal, unchallenged.

In *Tristes Tropiques*, Claude Lévi-Strauss provides an image of this reifying process, in terms of the atrophy of European civilization: ". . . like some aging animal whose thickening hide has formed an imperishable crust around its body and, by no longer allowing the skin to breathe, is hastening the aging process."[1] The loss of meaning, immediacy, and spiritual vibrancy in Western civilization is a major theme in the works of Max Weber, and also bears on the reification of modern life. That this failing of life and enchantment seems somehow inevitable and unchangeable, largely just taken for granted, is as important as the reified outcome, and is inseparable from it.

How did human activities and connections become separate from their subjects and take on a thing-like "life" of their own? And given the evident waning of belief in society's institutions and categories, what holds the "things" in thing-ified society together?

Terms like reification and alienation, in a world more and more comprised of the starkest forms of estrangement, are no longer to be found in the literature that supposedly deals with this world. Those who claim to have no ideology are so often the most constrained and defined by the prevailing ideology they cannot see, and it is possible that the highest degree of alienation is reached where it no longer enters consciousness.

Reification became a widely employed term as defined by the marxist Georg Lukacs: namely, a form of alienation issuing from the commodity fetishism of modern market relations. Social conditions and the plight of the individual have become mysterious and impenetrable as a function of what we now commonly refer to as consumerist capitalism. We are crushed and blinded by the reifying force of the stage of capital that began in the 20th century.

I think, however, that it may be useful to re-cast reification so as to establish a much deeper meaning and dynamic. The merely and directly human is in fact being drained away as surely as nature itself has been tamed into an object. In the frozen universe of commodities, the reign of things over life is obvious, and that coldness that Adorno saw as the basic principle of bourgeois subjectivity is plumbing new lows.

But if reification is the central mechanism whereby the commodity form permeates the entire culture, it is also much more than that. Kant knew the term, and it was Hegel, soon after, who made major use of it (and objectification, its rough equivalent). He discovered a radical lack of being at the heart of the subject; it is here that we may fruitfully inquire.

The world presents itself to us—and we re-present it. Why the need to do that? Do we know what symbols really symbolize? Is truth that which must be possessed, not re-presented? Signs are basically signals, that is, correlative; but symbols are substitutive.

As Husserl put it, "The symbol exists effectively at the point where it introduced something more than life. . . "[2] Reification may be an unavoidable corollary or by-product of symbolization itself.

At a minimum, there seem to be reified fundamentals in all networks of domination. Calendars and clocks formalize and further reify time, which was likely the first reification of all. The divided social structure is a reified world largely because it is a symbolic structure of roles and images, not persons. Power crystallizes into networks of domination and hierarchy as reification enters the equation very early on. In the current productionist world, extreme division of labor fulfills its original meaning. Made increasingly passive and meaningless, we endlessly reify ourselves. Our mounting impoverishment approaches the condition in which we are mere things.

Reification permeates postmodern culture, in which only appearances change, and appear alive. The dreadfulness of our postmodernity can be seen as a destination of the history of philosophy, and a destination of a good deal more than just philosophy. History qua history begins as loss of integrity, immersion in an external trajectory that tears the self into parts. The denial of human choice and effective agency is as old as division of labor; only its drastic development or fullness is new.

About 250 years ago the German romantic Novalis complained that "the meaning of life has been lost."[3] Widespread questioning of the meaning of life only began at about this time, just as industrialism made its very first inroads.[4] From this point on, an erosion of meaning has quickly accelerated, reminding us that the substitutive function of symbolization is also prosthetic. The replacement of the living by the artificial, like technology, involves a thing-ification. Reification is always, at least in part, a techno-imperative.

Technology is "the knack of so arranging the world that we need not experience it."[5] We are expected to deny what is living and natural within us in order to acquiesce in the domination of non-human nature. Technology has unmistakably become the great vehicle of reification. Not forgetting that it is embedded in and embodies an ever-expanding, global field of capital, reification subordinates us to our own objectified creations. ("Things are in the saddle and ride mankind," observed Emerson in the mid-19th century.) Nor is this a recent turn of events; rather, it reflects the master code of culture, *ab origino*. The separation from nature, and its ensuing pacification and manipulation, make one ask, is the individual vanishing? Has culture itself set this in motion? How has it come to pass that a formulation as reified as "children are our most precious resource" does not seem repugnant to everyone?

We are captives of so much that is not only instrumental, fodder for the functioning of other manipulable things, but also ever more simulated. We are exiles from immediacy, in a fading and flattening landscape where thought struggles to unlearn its alienated conditioning. Merleau-Ponty failed in his quest, but at least aimed at finding a primordial ontology of vision prior to the split between subject and object. It is division of labor and the resulting conceptual forms of thought that go unchallenged, delaying discovery of reification and reified thought.

It is, after all, our whole way of knowing that has been so deformed and diminished, and that must be understood as such. "Intelligence" is now an externality to be measured, equated to proficiency in manipulating symbols. Philosophy has become the highly elaborate rationalization of reifications. And even more generally, being itself is constituted as experience and representation, *as subject* and *object*. These outcomes must be criticized as fundamentally as possible.

The active, living element in cognition must be uncovered, beneath the reifications that mask it. Cognition, despite contemporary orthodoxy, is not computation. The philosopher Ryle glimpsed that a form of knowledge that does not rely on symbolic representation might be the basic one.[6] Our notions of reality are the products of an artificially constructed symbol system, whose components have hardened into reifications or objectifications over time, as division of labor coalesced into domination of nature and domestication of the individual.

Thought capable of producing culture and civilization is distancing, non-sensuous. It abstracts from the subject and becomes an independent object. It's telling that sensations are much more resistant to reification than are mental images. Platonic discourse is a prime example of thinking that proceeds at the expense of the senses, in its radical split between perceptions and conceptions. Adorno draws attention to the healthier variant by his observation that in Walter Benjamin's writings "thought presses close to the object, as if through touching, smelling, tasting, it wanted to transform itself."[7] And Le Roy is probably very close to the mark with "we resign ourselves to conception only for want of perception."[8] Historically determined in the deepest sense, the reification aspect of thought is a further cognitive "fall from grace."

Husserl and others figured symbolic representation as originally designed to be only a temporary supplement to authentic expression.

Reification enters the picture in a somewhat parallel fashion, as representation passes from the status of a noun used for specific purposes to that of an object. Whether or not these descriptive theses are adequate, it seems at least evident that an ineluctable gap exists between the concept's abstraction and the richness of the web or phenomena. To the point here is Heidegger's conclusion that authentic thinking is "non-conceptual," a kind of "reverential listening."[9]

Always of the utmost relevance is the violence that a steadily encroaching technological ethos perpetrates against lived experience. Gilbert Germain has understood how the ethos forcefully promotes a "forgetfulness of the linkage between reflective thought and the direct perceptual experience of the world from which it arises and to which it ought to return."[10] Engels noted in passing that "human reason has developed in accordance with man's alteration of nature,"[11] a mild way of referring to the close connection between objectifying, instrumentalizing reason and progressive reification.

In any case, the thought of civilization has worked to reduce the abundance that yet manages to surround us. Culture is a screen through which our perceptions, ideas, and feelings are filtered and domesticated. According to Jean-Luc Nancy, the main thing representational thought represents is its limit.[12] Heidegger and Wittgenstein, possibly the most original of 20th century thinkers, ended up disclaiming philosophy along these lines.

The reified life-world progressively removes what questions it. The literature on society raises ever fewer basic questions about society, and the suffering of the individual is now rarely related to even this unquestioned society. Emotional desolation is seen as almost entirely a matter of freely-occurring "natural" brain or chemical abnormalities, having nothing to do with the destructive context the individual is generally left to blindly endure in a drugged condition.

On a more abstract level, reification can be neutralized by conflating it with objectification, which is defined in a way that places it beyond questioning. Objectification in this sense is taken to mean an awareness of the existence of subjects and objects, and the fact of the self as both subject and object. Hegel, in this vein, referred to it as the very essence of the subject, without which there can be no development. Adorno saw some reification as a necessary element in the necessary process of human objectification. As he became more pessimistic about the realization of a de-reified society, Adorno used reification and objectification as synonyms,[13] completing a demoralized retreat from fully calling either term into question.

I think it may be instructive to accept the two terms as synonymous, not to end up accepting them both but to entertain the notion of exploring basic alienation. All objectification requires an alienation of subject from object, which is fundamental, it would seem, to the goal of reconciling them. How did we get to this horrendous present, definable as a condition in which the reified subject and the reified object mutually entail one another? How is it that, as William Desmond put it, "the intimacy of being is dissolved in the modern antithesis of subject and object?"[14]

As the world is shaped via objectification, so is the subject: the world as a field of objects open to manipulation. Objectification, as the basis for the domination of nature as external, alien other, presents itself. Clearer still is the use of the term by Marx and Lukacs as the natural means by which humans master the world.

The shift from objects to objectification, from reality to constructions of reality, is also the shift to domination and mystification. Objectification is the take-off point for culture, in that it is makes domestication possible. It reaches its full potential with the onset of division of labor; the exchange principle itself moves on the level of objectification. Similarly, none of the institutions of divided society are powerful or determinative without a reified element.

The philosopher Croce considered it sheer rhetoric to speak of a beautiful river or flower; to him, nature was stupid compared to art. This elevation of the cultural is possible only through objectification. The works of Kafka, on the other hand, portray the outcome of objectifying cultural logic, with their striking illustration of a reified landscape that crushes the subject.

Representation and production are the foundations of reification, which cements and extends their empire. Reification's ultimately distancing, domesticating orientation decrees the growing separation between reduced, rigidified subjects and an equally objectified field of experience. As the Situationist line goes, today the eye sees only things and their prices. The genesis of this outlook is vastly older than their formulation denotes; the project of de-objectification can draw strength from the human condition that obtained before reification developed. A "future primitive" is called for, where a living involvement with the world, and fluid, intimate participation in nature will replace the thingified reign of symbolic civilization.

The very first symptom of alienated life is the very gradual appearance of time. The first reification and increasingly the quintessential one, time is virtually synonymous with alienation. We are now so pervasively ruled and regulated by this "it" which of course has no concrete existence that thinking of a pre-civilized, timeless epoch is extremely difficult.

Time is the symptom of symptoms to come. The relationship of subject and object must have been radically different before temporal distance advanced into the psyche. It has come to stand over us as an external thing—predecessor to work and the commodity, separate and dominating as described by Marx. This de-presentizing force implies that de-reification would mean a return to the eternal present wherein we lived before we entered the pull of history.

E.M. Cioran asks, "How can you help resenting the absurdity of time, its march into the future, and all the nonsense about evolution and progress? Why go forward, why live in time." [15] Walter Benjamin's plea for shattering the reified continuity of history was somewhat similarly based on his yearning for a wholeness or unity of experience. At some point, the moment itself matters and does not rely on other moments "in time."

It was of course the clock that completed the reification, by dissociating time from human events and natural processes. Time by now was fully exterior to life and incarnated in the first fully mechanized device. In the 15th century Giovanni Tortelli wrote that the clock "seems to be alive, since it moves of its own accord." [16] Time had come to measure its contents, no longer contents measuring time. We so often say we "don't have time," but it is the basic reification, time, that has us.

Fragmented life cannot become the norm without the primary victory of time. The complexity, particularity, and diversity of all living creatures cannot be lost to the standardizing realm of the quantitative without this key objectification.

The question of the origin of reification is a compelling one that has rarely been pursued deeply enough. A common error has been to confuse intelligence with culture; namely, the absence of culture is seen as equivalent to the absence of intelligence. This confusion is further compounded when reification is seen as inherent to the nature of mental functioning. From Thomas Wynn[17] and others we now know that pre-historic humans were our equals in intelligence. If culture is impossible without objectification, it does not follow that either is inevitable, or desirable.

As suspicious as Adorno was of the idea of origins, he conceded that human conduct originally involved no objectification.[18] Husserl was similarly able to refer to the primordial oneness of all consciousness prior to its dissociation.[19]

Bringing this condition of life into focus has proven elusive at best. Lévi-Strauss began his anthropological work with such a quest in mind: "I had been looking for a society reduced to its simplest expression. That of the Nambikwara was so truly simple that all I could find was human beings."[20] In other words, he was really still looking for symbolic culture, and seemed ill-equipped to ponder the meaning of its absence. Herbert Marcuse wanted human history to conform to nature as a subject-object harmony, but he knew that "history is the negation of nature."[21] The postmodern outlook positively celebrates the reifying presence of history and culture by denying the possibility that a pre-objectificational state ever existed. Having surrendered to representation—and every other basic given of past, present, and future barrenness—the postmodernists could scarcely be expected to explore the genesis of reification.

If not the original reification, language is the most consequential, as cornerstone of representational culture. Language is the reification of communication, a paradigmatic move that establishes every other mental separation. The philosopher W.V. Quine's variation on this is that reification arrives with the pronoun.[22]

"In the beginning was the Word . . . " the beginning of all this, which is killing us by limiting existence to many things. Corollary of symbolization, reification is a sclerosis that chokes off what is living, open, natural. In place of being stands the symbol. If it is impossible for us to coincide with our being, Sartre argues in *Being and Nothingness*, then the symbolic is the measure of that non-coincidence. Reification seals the deal, and language is its universal currency.

An exhausted symbolic mediation with less and less to say prevails in a world where that mediation is now seen as the central, even defining fact of life. In an existence without vibrancy or meaning, nothing is left but language. The relation of language to reality has dominated 20th century philosophy. Wittgenstein, for example, was convinced that the foundation of language and of linguistic meaning is the very basis of philosophy.

This "linguistic turn" appears even more profound if we consider the entire species-sense of language, including its original impact as a radical departure. Language has been fundamental to our obligation to objectify ourselves, in a milieu that is increasingly not our own. Thus it is absurd for Heidegger to say that the truth about language is that it refuses to be objectified. The reificational act of language impoverishes existence by creating a universe of meaning sufficient unto itself. The ultimate "sufficient unto itself" is the concept "God," and its ultimate description is, revealingly, "I am Who I am"(Exodus 4:14). We have come to regard the separate, self-enclosed nature of objectification as the highest quality, evidently, rather than as the debasement of the "merely" contingent, relational, connected.

It has been recognized for some time that thought is not language-dependent and that language limits the possibilities of thought.[23] Gottlob Frege wondered if to think in a non-reified way is possible, how it could be possible to explain how thinking can ever be reified. The answer was not to be found in his chosen field of formal logic.

In fact, language does proceed as a thing external to the subject, and molds our cognitive processes. Classic psychoanalytic theory ignored language, but Melanie Klein discussed symbolization as a precipitant of anxiety. To translate Klein's insight into cultural terms, anxiety about erosion of a non-objectified life-world provokes language. We experience "the urge to thrust against language,"[24] when we feel that we have given up our voices, and are left only with language. The enormity of this loss is suggested in C.S. Peirce's definition of the self as mainly a consistency of symbolization; "my language," conversely, "is the sum total of my self," he concluded.[25] Given this kind of reduction, is not difficult to agree with Lacan that induction into the symbolic world generates a persistent yearning that arises from one's absence from the real world. "The speechform is a mere sorrogate," wrote Joyce in *Finnegan's Wake.*

Language refutes every appeal to immediacy by dishonoring the unique and immobilizing the mobile. Its elements are independent entities from the consciousness that utters them, which in turn weigh down that consciousness. According to Quine, this reification plays a part in creating a "structured system of the world," by closing up the "loose ends of raw experience."[26] Quine does not recognize the limiting aspects of this project. In his incomplete final work, the phenomenologist Merleau-Ponty began to explore how language diminishes an original richness, how it actually works against perception.

Language, as a separate medium, does indeed facilitate a structured system, based on itself, that deals with anarchic "loose ends" of experience. It accomplishes this, basically in the service of division of labor, by avoiding the here and now of experience. "Seeing is forgetting the name of the thing one sees," an anti-reification statement by Paul Valéry,[27] suggests how words get in the way of direct apprehension. The Murngin of northern Australia saw name-giving as a kind of death, the loss of an original wholeness.[28] A pivotal moment of reification occurred when we succumbed to names and became inscribed in letters. It is perhaps when we most need to express ourselves, fully and completely, that language most clearly reveals its reductive and inarticulate nature.

Language itself corrupts, as Rousseau claimed in his famous dream of a community stripped of it. The path beyond the claims of reification involves breaking representation's age-old spell.

Another basic avenue of reification is ritual, which originated as a means to instill conceptual and social order. Ritual is an objectified schema of action, involving symbolic behavior that is standardized and repetitive. It is the first fetishizing of culture, and points decisively toward domestication. Concerning the latter, ritual can be seen as the original model of calculability of production. Along these lines, Georges Condominas challenged the distinction that is ordinarily made between ritual and agriculture. His fieldwork in Southeast Asia led him to see ritual as an integral component of the technology of traditional farming.[29]

Mircea Eliade has described religious rites as real only to the extent that they imitate or symbolically repeat some kind of archetypal event, adding that participation is felt to be genuine only to the extent of this identification; that is, only to the extent that the participant ceases to be himself or herself.[30] Thus the repetitive ritual act is very closely related to the depersonalizing, devaluing essence of division of labor, and at the same time approaches a virtual definition of the reifying process itself. To lose oneself in fealty to an earlier, frozen event or moment: to become reified, a thing that owes its supposed authenticity to some prior reification.

Religion, like the rest of culture, springs from the false notion of the necessity for combat against the forces of nature. The powers of nature are reified, along with those of their religious or mythological counterparts. From animism to deism, the divine develops against a natural world depicted as increasingly threatening and chaotic. J.G. Frazier saw religious and magical phenomena as "the conscious conversion of what had hitherto been regarded as living beings into impersonal substances."[31] To deify is to reify, and a November 1997 discovery by archaeologist Juan Vadeum helps us situate the domesticating context of this movement. In Chiapas, Mexico, Vadeum found four Mayan stone carvings that represent original "grandfathers" of wisdom and power.

Significantly, these figures of seminal importance to Mayan religion and cosmology symbolize War, Agriculture, Trade, and Tribute.[32] As Feuerbach noted, every important stage in the history of human civilization begins with religion,[33] and religion serves civilization both substantively and formally. In its formal aspect, the reifying nature of religion is the most potent contribution of all.

Art is the other early objectification of culture, which is what makes it into a separate activity and gives it reality. Art is also a quasi-utopian promise of happiness, always broken. The betrayal resides largely in the reification. "To be a work of art means to set up a world," according to Heidegger,[34] but this counter-world is powerless against the rest of the objectified world of which it remains a part.

Georg Simmel described the triumph of form over life, the danger posed to individuality by the surrender to form. The dualism of form and content is the blueprint for reification itself, and partakes in the basic divisions of class society.

At base there is an abstract and somewhat narrow similarity to all aesthetic appearance. This is due to a severe restriction of the sensual, enemy number one of reification. And remembering our Freud, it is the curbing of Eros that makes culture possible. Can it be an accident that the three senses that are excluded from art—touch, smell, and taste—are the senses of sensual love?

Max Weber recognized that culture "appears as man's emancipation from the organically prescribed cycle of natural life. For this very reason," he continued, "culture's every step forward seems condemned to lead to an ever more devastating senselessness."[35] The representation of culture is followed by pleasure in representation that replaces pleasure per se. The will to create culture overlooks the violence in and of culture, a violence that is inescapable given culture's basis in fragmentation and separation. Every reification forgets this.

For Homer, the idea of barbarism was of a piece with the absence of agriculture. Culture and agriculture have always been linked by their common basis of domestication; to lose the natural within us is to lose nature without. One becomes a thing in order to master things.

Today the culture of global capitalism abandons its claim to be culture, even as the production of culture exceeds the production of goods. Reification, the process of culture, dominates when all awaits naturalization, in a constantly transformed environment that is "natural" in name only. Objects themselves—and even the "social" relationships among them—are seen as real only insofar as they are recognized as existing in mediaspace or cyberspace.

A domesticating reification renders everything, including us, its objects. And these objects possess less and less originality or aura, as discussed by commentators from Baudelaire and Morris to Benjamin and Baudrillard. "Now from America empty indifferent things are pouring across, sham things, dummy life," wrote Rilke.[36] Meanwhile the whole natural world has become a mere object.

Postmodern practice severs things from their history and context, as in the device of inserting "quotations" or arbitrarily juxtaposed elements from other periods into music, painting, novels. This gives the objects a rootless autonomy of sorts, while subjects have little or none.

We seem to be objects destroyed by objectification, our grounding and authenticity leached away. We are like the schizophrenic who actively experiences himself as a thing.

There is a coldness, even a deadness, that is becoming impossible to deny. A palpable sense of "something missing" inheres in the unmistakable impoverishment of a world objectifying itself. Our only hope may lie precisely in the fact that the madness of the whole is so apparent.

It is still maintained that reification is an ontological necessity in a complex world, which is exactly the point. The de-reifying act must be the return to simple, non-divided life. The life congealed and concealed in petrified thingness cannot reawaken without a vast undoing of this ever-more standardized, massified lost world.

Until fairly recently—until civilization—nature was a subject, not an object. In hunter-gatherer societies no strict division or hierarchy existed between the human and the non-human. The participatory nature of vanished connectedness has to be restored, that condition in which meaning was lived, not objectified into a grid of symbolic culture. The very positive picture we now have of pre-history establishes a perspective of anticipatory remembrance: there is the horizon of subject-object reconciliation.

This prior participation with nature is the reverse of the domination and distancing at the heart of reification. It reminds us that all desire is a desire for relationship, at its best reciprocal and animate. To enable this nearness or presence is a gigantic practical project, that will make an end to these dark days.

1998

Footnotes

1. Claude Lévi-Strauss, *Tristes Tropiques* (New York, 1972), p. 382.
2. Edmund Husserl, *Le Discours et le Symbole* (Paris, 1962), p. 66.
3. Novalis, *Schriften*, vol. II (Stuttgart, 1965–1977), p. 594.
4. Iddo Landau, "Why Has the Question of the Meaning of Life Arisen in the Last Two and a Half Centuries?" *Philosophy Today*, Summer 1967.
5. Quote attributed to the playwright Max Frisch. Source unknown.
6. Gilbert Ryle, *The Concept of Mind* (London, 1949)
7. Theodor Adorno, *Prisms* (Cambridge, 1981), p. 240.
8. Eduoard Le Roy, *The New Philosophy of Henri Bergson* (New York, 1913), p. 156.
9. Martin Heidegger, "What is Thinking?" in *Basic Writings* (New York, 1969)

10. Gilbert B. Germain, *A Discourse on Disenchantment* (Albany, 1992), p. 126.
11. Friedrich Engels, *Dialectic of Nature* (Moscow, 1934), p. 231.
12. Jean-Luc Nancy, *The Birth to Presence* (Stanford, 1993), p. 2.
13. Theodor Adorno, *Prisms* (Cambridge, 1983) p. 262, for example.
14. William Desmond, *Perplexity and Ultimacy* (Albany, 1995), p. 64.
15. E.M. Cioran, *On the Heights of Despair* (Chicago, 1990), p. 126.
16. Giovanni Tortelli, *De Orthographia*, 1471.
17. Thomas Wynn, *The Evolution of Spatial Competence* (Urbana, 1989).
18. Theodor Adorno, *Aesthetic Theory* (Minneapolis, 1997), pp. 118, 184.
19. Edmund Husserl, *The Crisis of European Sciences and Transcendental Phenomenology* (Evanston, 1970)
20. Lévi-Strauss, op.cit., p. 358.
21. Herbert Marcuse, *One Dimensional Man* (Boston, 1964), p. 236.
22. W.V. Quine, *From Stimulus to Science* (Cambridge, 1995), p. 27.
23. Maxine Sheets-Johnstone, *The Roots of Thinking* (Philadelphia, 1990)
24. Ludwig Wittgenstein, "Wittgenstein's Lecture on Ethics," *Philosophical Review* 74 (1965), p. 12.
25. C.S. Peirce, *Collected Papers* (Cambridge, 1931-1958), vol. 5, pp. 28, 29.
26. Quine, op.cit., p. 29.
27. Quotation is title of Robert Irwin's autobiographical work (Berkeley, 1982).
28. Bradd B. Shore, *Culture in Mind* (New York, 1996), p. 222.
29. Georges Condominas, *We Have Eaten the Forest* (New York, 1977).
30. Mircea Eliade, quoted in *False Consciousness*, by Joseph Gabel (Oxford, 1975), p. 39.
31. J.G. Frazier, *The Golden Bough: A Study in Magic and Religion* (New York, 1932-36), XLIX, p. 74.
32. Mark Stevenson, "Mayan Stone's Discovery May Confirm Ancient Text" (Associated Press, November 17, 1997).
33. Ludwig Feuerbach, *Lectures on the Essence of Religion* (New York, 1967), p. 209.
34. Martin Heidegger, "The Origin of the Work of Art," in *Basic Writings* (New York, 1969), p. 170.
35. Max Weber, "Religious Rejections of the World and their Directions," in *Essays on Sociology*, Hans Gerth and C. Wright Mills, eds. (New York, 1958), pp. 356-357.
36. Rainer Maria Rilke, *Letters of Rilke*, vol. 2 (New York, 1969), p. 374.

ENEMY OF THE STATE:
AN INTERVIEW WITH JOHN ZERZAN

Interview by Derrick Jensen, published in *The Sun*,
September 1998

*My conversation with John Zerzan was as free-form as I might have
expected of a meeting between two anarchists. (Though I call myself an
anarchist, I'd never before met one outside the covers of a book.) What I
hadn't expected was Zerzan's softspoken character. His writing is so sharp,
uncompromising, and tenacious that I'd halfway feared he would be as
fierce in person as he is on the page. I was pleasantly disappointed: he is
one of the most gracious, courteous, and simply nice people I've ever met. I
shouldn't have been surprised. Anarchism is not only the desire to be free of
domination, but also the desire not to dominate others personally. This
abhorrence to manipulate permeates Zerzan's personality. He is also an
extraordinarily good listener. This latter trait, though desirable in a friend,
made my task as an interviewer much more difficult. Much as I tried to
turn this into a "normal" interview, Zerzan steadfastly refused to play the
role of guru. Finally, I quit trying to place him in a role he clearly did not
want and just let the tape recorder run while we talked.*

DJ: What is Anarchism?

JZ: I would say Anarchism is the attempt to eradicate all forms of domination. This includes not only such obvious forms as the nation-state, with its routine use of violence and the force of law, and the corporation, with its institutionalized irresponsibility, but also such internalized forms as patriarchy, racism, homophobia. Also it is the attempt to expose the ways our philosophy, religion, economics, and other ideological constructions perform their primary function, which is to rationalize or naturalize—make seem natural—the domination that pervades our way of life: the destruction of the natural world or of indigenous peoples, for example, comes not as the result of decisions actively made and actions pursued, but instead, so we convince ourselves, as a manifestation of Darwinian selection, or God's Will, or economic exigency. Beyond that, Anarchism is the attempt to look even into those parts of our everyday lives we accept as givens, as parts of the universe, to see how they, too, dominate us or facilitate our domination of others. What is the role of division of labor in the alienation and destruction we see around us? Even more fundamentally, what is the relationship between domination and time, numbers, language, or even symbolic thought itself?

The place where this definition gets a little problematic is that some Anarchists see some things as dominating, and some don't. For example, some Anarchists don't see the technological imperative as a category of domination. I do, and more and more Anarchists are finding themselves taking this anti-technological position. The further we follow this path of the technicization of both our interior and exterior lives, fewer and fewer Anarchists—and this is true as well of people who don't call themselves Anarchists—valorize technology and production and progress and the categories of modern technological life.

Back to the definition. Most fundamentally I would see Anarchism as a synonym for anti-authoritarianism.

DJ: Isn't all this just tilting at windmills? Has such a condition ever existed, where relations have not been based on domination?

JZ: That was the human condition for at least 99 percent of our existence as a species, from well before the emergence of Homo sapiens, probably all the way back for at least a couple of million years, until perhaps only 10,000 years ago, with the emergence of first agriculture and then civilization.

Since that time we have worked very hard to convince ourselves that no such condition ever existed, because if no such condition ever existed, it's futile to work toward it now. We may as well then accept the repression and subjugation that define our way of living as necessary antidotes to "evil human nature." After all, according to this line of thought, our pre-civilized existence of deprivation, brutality, and ignorance made authority a benevolent gift that rescued us from savagery.

Think about the images that come to mind when you mention the labels "cave man," or "Neanderthal." Those images are implanted and then invoked to remind us where we would be without religion, government, and toil, and are probably the biggest ideological justifications for the whole van of civilization—armies, religion, law, the state—without which we would all live the brutal clichés of Hobbes.

The problem with those images, of course, is that they are entirely wrong. There has been a potent revolution in the fields of anthropology and archaeology over the past 20 years, and increasingly people are coming to understand that life before agriculture and domestication—in which by domesticating others we domesticated ourselves—was in fact largely one of leisure, intimacy with nature, sensual wisdom, sexual equality, and health.

DJ: How do we know this?

JZ: In part through observing modern foraging peoples—what few we've not yet eliminated—and watching their egalitarian ways disappear under the pressures of habitat destruction and oftentimes direct coercion or murder. Also, at the other end of the time scale, through interpreting archaeological digs. An example of this has to do with the sharing that is now understood to be a keynote trait of non-domesticated people. If you were to study hearth sites of ancient peoples, and to find that one fire site has the remains of all the goodies, while other sites have very few, then that site would probably be the chief's. But if time after time you see that all the sites have about the same amount of stuff, what begins to emerge is a picture of a people whose way of life is based on sharing. And that's what is consistently found in pre-neolithic sites. A third way of knowing is based on the accounts of early European explorers, who again and again spoke of the generosity

and gentleness of the peoples they encountered. This is true all across
the globe.

DJ: How do you respond to people who say this is all just nutty
Rousseauvian noble savage nonsense?
JZ: I respectfully suggest they read more within the field. This isn't
Anarchist theory. It's mainstream anthropology and archaeology. There
are disagreements about some of the details, but not about the general
structure.

DJ: But what about the Aztecs, or stories we're told of headhunters or
cannibals?
JZ: Considering that our culture is the only one to ever invent
napalm or nuclear weapons, I'm not sure we're in much of a moral
place to comment on the infinitely smaller-scale violence of other cultures. But it's important to note a great divide in the behavior of
indigenous groups. None of the cannibal or headhunting groups—and
certainly not the Aztecs—were true hunter-gatherers. They had already
begun agriculture. It is now generally conceded that agriculture usually
leads to a rise in labor, a decrease in sharing, an increase in violence, a
shortening of lifespan, and so on. This is not to say that all agricultural
societies are violent, but to point out that this violence is not by and
large characteristic of true hunter-gatherers.

DJ: Can you define domestication?
JZ: It's the attempt to bring free dimensions under control for self-
serving purposes.

DJ: If things were so great before, why did agriculture begin?
JZ: That's a very difficult question, because for so many hundreds of
thousands of years, there was very little change, it was almost frozen.
That's long been a source of frustration to scholars in anthropology
and archaeology: how could there have been almost zero change for
hundreds of thousands of years—the whole lower and middle Paleolithic—and then suddenly at a certain point in the upper Paleolithic
there's this explosion, seemingly out of nowhere? You suddenly have
art, and on the heels of that, agriculture. Virtual activity. Religion.

And what's especially striking, it seems to me, is that now we see that the intelligence of humanity a million years ago was equal to what it is now. Thomas Wynn, for example, argues this very persuasively. Recently there was a piece in Nature magazine of a new finding that humans may have been sailing and navigating around what is now Micronesia some 800,000 years ago. All of this means that the reason civilization didn't arise earlier had nothing to do with intelligence. The intelligence argument has always been both comforting and racist anyway, comforting in that it reduces the role of choice by implying that those who are intelligent enough to build a lifestyle like ours necessarily will, and racist in implying that even those humans alive today who live primitive lifestyles are simply too stupid to do otherwise. If they were just smart enough, the reasoning goes, they too could invent asphalt, chainsaws, and penitentiaries.

We also know that the transition didn't come because of population pressures. Population has always been another big puzzle: how did foraging humanity keep the population so low, when they didn't have technologies? Historically, it's been assumed they used infanticide, but that theory has been kind of debunked. I believe that in addition to the various plants they could use as contraceptives they were also much more in tune with their bodies.

But back to the question: Why was it stable for so long, and then why did it change so quickly? I think it was stable because it worked, and I think it changed finally because for many millennia there was a kind of slow slippage into division of labor. This happened so slowly—almost imperceptibly—that people didn't see what was happening, or what they were in danger of losing. The alienation brought about by division of labor—alienation from each other, from the natural world, from their bodies—then reached some sort of critical mass, giving rise to its apotheosis in what we've come to know as civilization. As to how civilization itself took hold, I think Freud nailed that one when he said that "civilization is something which was imposed on a resisting majority by a minority which understood how to obtain possession of the means of power and coercion." That's what we see happening today, and there's no reason to believe it was any different in the first place.

DJ: What's wrong with division of labor?

JZ: That depends on what you want out of life. If your primary goal is mass production, nothing at all. It's central to our way of life. Each person performs as a tiny cog in this big machine. If, on the other hand, your primary goal is relative wholeness, egalitarianism, autonomy, or an intact world, there's quite a lot wrong with it.

DJ: I don't understand.

JZ: Division of labor is generally seen, when even noticed at all, as a banality, a "given" of modern life. All we see around us would be completely impossible without this cornerstone of production. But that's the point. Undoing all this mess will mean undoing division of labor.

I think that at base a person is not complete or free insofar as that person's life and the whole surrounding setup depends on his or her being just some aspect of a process, some fraction of it. A divided life mirrors the basic divisions in society and it all starts there. Hierarchy and alienation start there, for example.

I don't think anyone would deny the effective control that specialists or experts have in the contemporary world. And I don't think anyone would argue that control isn't increasing with ever-greater acceleration.

DJ: Such as in food production. I recently read that one out of every ten dollars Americans spend on food goes to RJR Nabisco. Four meat packers control ninety percent of meat processing. Eight corporations control half of the poultry industry. Ninety percent of all agrichemical and feed-grain industries are controlled by two percent of the corporations involved. And how many of us know how to raise our own food?

JZ: Exactly. And it's not just food. It wasn't that long ago you could make your own radio set. People used to do that all the time. Even ten years ago you could still work on your car. That is becoming increasingly difficult. So the world becomes more and more hostage to people with these specialized skills, and on the people who control specialized technologies. When you have to rely on others, when you don't have the skills to do what's needed in a general sense, you are diminished.

DJ: But humans are social animals. Isn't it necessary for us to rely on each other?

JZ: I don't want to make it seem like my model is to turn people into monads with no connection to others. Quite the opposite. But it's important to understand the difference between the interdependence of a functioning community, and a form of dependence that comes from relying on others who have specialized skills you don't. They now have power over you. Whether they are "benevolent" in its use is really beside the point.

DJ: This reminds me of something the Russian Anarchist Kropotkin wrote about revolution, that the question taking precedence over all others is that of bread. This is because scarcity of food is the strongest weapon with counterrevolutionary forces: by withholding food or creating a blockade, those in power can force people back into compliance.

JZ: In addition to the direct control by those who have specialized skills, there is a lot of mystification of those skills. Part of the ideology of modern society is that without it, you'd be completely lost, you wouldn't know how to do the simplest thing. Well, humans have been feeding themselves for the past couple of million years, and doing it a lot more successfully and efficiently than we do now. The global food system is insane. It's amazingly inhumane and inefficient. We waste the world with pesticides, herbicides, the effects of fossil fuels to transport and store foods, and so on, and literally billions of people go their entire lives without ever having enough to eat. But few things are simpler than growing or gathering your own food.

DJ: Last year I interviewed a member of the Tupac Amaru Revolutionary Movement, the group that took over the Japanese Ambassador's house in Peru. I asked him what his group wanted for his country. He replied, "We want to grow and distribute our own food. We already know how to do that, we merely need to be allowed to do so."

JZ: Exactly.

DJ: How much division of labor do you believe we should jettison?

JZ: I think the appropriate question is, "How much wholeness for ourselves and the planet do we want?"

DJ: You mentioned earlier you see a relationship between time and domination.

JZ: Two things that come to mind. The first is that time is an invention, a cultural artifact, a formation of culture. It has no existence outside of culture. The second is that time is a pretty exact measure of alienation. And I believe that the present informs the past, or rather gives directions to looking at the origins of modern alienation.

DJ: How so?

JZ: Let's start at the present. Time has never been as palpable, as material, as it is now. It's never existed as a reification with so much presence. Everything in our lives is measured and ruled by time.

DJ: Even dreams, it occurs to me, as we force them to conform to a workaday world of alarm clocks and schedules.

JZ: It's really amazing when you think that it wasn't that long ago that time wasn't so disembodied, so abstract.

DJ: But wait a second. Isn't the tick, tick, tick of a clock about as tangible as you can get?

JZ: It becomes concrete. That's what reification means, when a concept is treated as a thing, even when it isn't really a thing, but just a concept. A second is nothing, and to grant it separate existence is counter to our experience of living. I really like what Levy-Bruhl wrote about this: "Our idea of time seems to be a natural attribute of the human mind. But that is a delusion. Such an idea scarcely exists where primitive mentality is concerned."

DJ: Which means. . . .

JZ: Most simply, that they live in the present, as we all do when we're having fun. It has been said that the Mbuti of southern Africa believe that "by a correct fulfillment of the present, the past and the future will take care of themselves."

DJ: What a concept!

JZ: Of the North American Pawnee it was said that life has a rhythm but not a progression. Primitive peoples generally have no interest in birthdays or measuring their ages. As for the future, they have little desire to control what does not yet exist, just as they have little desire to control nature. That moment-by-moment joining with the flux and flow of the natural world of course doesn't preclude an awareness of the seasons, but this in no way constitutes an alienated time consciousness that robs them of the present.

What I'm talking about is really hard for us to wrap our minds around, because the notion of time has been so deeply inculcated that it's sometimes hard to imagine it not existing.

DJ: You're not talking about just not measuring seconds. . . .

JZ: I'm talking about time not existing. Time, as an abstract continuing "thread" that unravels in an endless progression that links all events together while remaining independent of them. That doesn't exist. Sequence exists. Rhythm exists. But not time. Part of this has to do with the notion of mass production and division of labor. Tick, tick, tick, as you said. Identical seconds. Identical people. Identical chores repeated endlessly. Well, no two occurrences are identical, and if you are living in a stream of inner and outer experience that constantly brings clusters of new events, each moment is quantitatively and qualitatively different than the moment before. The notion of time simply disappears.

DJ: I'm still confused.

JZ: You might try this: if events are always novel, then not only would routine be impossible, but the notion of time would be meaningless.

DJ: And the opposite would be true as well.

JZ: Exactly. Only with the imposition of time can we begin to impose routine. Freud was really clear on this. He repeatedly pointed out that in order for civilization—with alienation at its core—to take place, it first had to break the early hold of timeless and non-productive gratification.

This happened, I believe, in two stages. First the rise of agriculture magnified the importance of time, and specifically reified cyclical time, with its periods of intense labor associated with sowing or reaping, and with the surplus of the harvest going to support those who ran the calendars: the priests. This was true of the Babylonians, and of the Mayans. In the West, the notion of cyclical time, which still maintained at least a bow toward the natural world with its connection to the rhythms of the days and seasons, gave way to linear time. This began with the rise of civilization, and really took hold near the start of the Christian era. And of course once you have linear time, you have history, then progress, then an idolatry of the future that sacrifices species, languages, cultures, and now quite possibly the entire natural world on the altar of some future. Once this was at least the altar of a utopian future, but we don't even have that to believe in anymore. The same thing happens in our personal lives, as we give up living in the moment in exchange for the hope of being able to live in the moment at some point in the future, perhaps after we retire, or maybe even after we die and go to heaven. This otherworldly emphasis on heaven, too, emerges from the unpleasantness of living in linear time.

DJ: It seems to me that linear time not only leads to habitat degradation, but also springs from it. If everything is in reasonable balance, you are still on cyclical time, or as you mention, not on time at all, but as soon as you begin degrading your habitat such that there are perceptible changes, you've entered historical time. When I was young, there were many frogs. Now there are fewer. There were many songbirds. Now there are fewer. That's linear time. I can count the passage of years by counting clearcuts. Historical time will only cease once the last vestiges of our civilization cease to be, once the last steel beams of the last skyscrapers rust into dust, and once this current spasm of extinctions abates, and once again those who remain can enter a rhythm, a peace.

JZ: Yes.

Linear time then transformed itself with the introduction of the clock into mechanical time. All connection to the natural world or to the present was lost, subsumed to the tyranny of the machine and of production. The Church was central to this endeavor. The Benedictines, who ruled 40,000 monasteries at their height in the Middle Ages, helped to yoke human endeavor to the regular, collective beat and rhythm of the machine by forcing people to work "on the clock."

The fourteenth century saw the first public clocks, and also the division of hours into minutes and minutes into seconds. The increments of time were now as fully interchangeable as the standardized parts and work processes necessary for capitalism.

At every step of the way this subservience to time has been met with resistance. For example, in early fighting in France's July Revolution of 1830, all across Paris people began to spontaneously shoot at public clocks. In the 1960s, many people, including me, quit wearing watches.

DJ: For a while in my twenties, I asked visitors to take off their watches as they entered my home.

JZ: Even today children must be broken of their resistance to time. This was one of the primary reasons for the imposition of this country's mandatory school system on a largely unwilling public. School teaches you to be at a certain place at a certain time, and prepares you for life in a factory. It calibrates you to the system. Raoul Vaneigem has a wonderful quote about this: "The child's days escape adult time; their time is swollen by subjectivity, passion, dreams haunted by reality. Outside, the educators look on, waiting, watch in hand, till the child joins and fits the cycle of the hours."

Time is not only important sociologically and ecologically, but personally. If I can share another quote, it would be Wittgenstein's: "Only a man who lives not in time but in the present is happy."

DJ: You mentioned also that number alienates. . . .

JZ: You count objects. You don't count subjects. When members of a large family sit down to dinner, they know immediately without counting whether someone is missing without counting. Counting only becomes necessary when you have homogenized things.

Not all peoples use systems of numbers. The Yanomami, for example, do not count past two. Obviously they are not stupid. But just as obviously, they have a different relationship with the natural world.

The first number system was almost undoubtedly used to measure and control domesticated flock or herd animals, as wild creatures became products to be harvested. We next see mathematics being used in Sumer about 5000 years ago to facilitate business. Later, Euclid developed his geometry, literally meaning "land measuring," explicitly to measure fields for reasons of ownership, taxation, and slave labor. Today the same imperative drives science, only now it is the entire universe we are trying to measure and enslave. Once again, this isn't obscure Anarchist theory. Descartes himself, considered by many to be the father of modern science, declared that the aim of science is "to make us as masters and possessors of nature." He also declared the universe a giant clockwork, tying these two forms of domination—numbers and time—back neatly together.

DJ: I've read that Nazi death camps often had quotas to fill as to how many people they were to kill each day. Today National Forests have deforestation quotas, as they must "produce" a certain number of board feet. It's long been clear to me that it's easier to kill a number than an individual, whether we are talking about boxcars of *untermenschen*, millions of board feet of timber, or tons of fish. Where does this leave us?
JZ: In a dying world. Alienated.

DJ: Alienated?
JZ: Marx defined alienation as being separated from the means of production. Instead of producing things to use, we are used by the system. I would take it a step further and say that to me it means estranged from our own experiences, dislodged from a natural mode of being. The more technicized and artificial the world becomes, and as the natural world is evacuated, there's an obvious sense of being alienated from a natural embeddedness.

To refer again to a pre-domesticated state, I think people once were in touch with themselves as organisms in ways we can't even comprehend. On the level of the senses, there are credible accounts of San hearing a single-engine plane seventy miles away, and seeing four of the moons of Jupiter with the unaided eye. And this connection of course extended to those around them: Laurens Van der Post stated that the San seemed to know what it actually felt like to be an elephant, a lion, an antelope, and so on. This connection was then reciprocated. There are scores if not hundreds of accounts by early European explorers describing the lack of fear shown by wild animals toward humans.

DJ: Just last year I came across an account by the eighteenth-century explorer Samual Hearne, the first white man to explore northern Canada. He described Indian children playing with wolf pups. The children would paint the pups' faces with vermilion or red ochre, and when they were done playing with them return them unhurt to the den. Neither the pups nor the pups' parents seemed to mind at all.

JZ: Now we gun them down from airplanes. That's progress for you.

DJ: More broadly, what has progress meant in practice?

JZ: Progress has meant the looming specter of the complete dehumanization of the individual and the catastrophe of ecological collapse. I think there are fewer people who believe in it now than ever, but probably there are still many who perceive it as inevitable. We're certainly conditioned on all sides to accept that, and we're held hostage to it, too. The idea now is to have everybody dependent on technology in an increasingly immiserated sense. In terms of human health, it means increasing dependence on technologies, but what we're supposed to forget is that the technologies created these problems in the first place. Not just cancers caused by chemicals. Nearly all diseases are diseases either of civilization, alienation, or gross habitat destruction.

DJ: I have Crohn's Disease, which is virtually unheard of in nonindustrialized nations, only becoming common as these nations industrialize. In all literal truth industrial civilization is eating away at my guts.

JZ: I think people are really starting to understand how hollow the progress myth has been. Maybe that's too sanguine. But the fruits of it are too hard to miss. In fact the system doesn't talk so much about progress anymore.

DJ: What new word has replaced it?

JZ: Inertia. This is it. Deal with it, or else get screwed. You don't hear so much now about the American Dream, or the glorious new tomorrow. Now it's a global race for the bottom as transnationals compete to see which can most exploit workers, most degrade the environment. That competition thing works on the personal level, too. If you don't plug into computers you won't get a job. That's progress.

DJ: Where does that leave us?

JZ: I'm optimistic, because never before has our whole lifestyle been revealed as much for what it is.

DJ: Having seen it, what is there to do?

JZ: The first thing is to question it, to make certain that part of the discourse of society—if not all of it—deals with these life and death issues, instead of the avoidance and denial that characterizes so much of what passes for discourse. And I believe, once again, that this denial can't hold up much longer, because there's such a jarring contrast between reality and what is said about reality. Especially in this country, I would say.

Maybe, and this is the nightmare scenario, that contrast can go on forever. The Unabomber Manifesto posits that possibility: people could just be so conditioned that they won't even notice there's no natural world anymore, no freedom, no fulfillment, no nothing. You just take your Prozac everyday, limp along dyspeptic and neurotic, and figure that's all there is.

But the way to break through that, the way to break the monopoly of lies, is simply to break the monopoly of lies, and bring out the old emperor has no clothes bit in its reality, its fullness, in how awful it really is, and what is at stake. To contrast what is possible—what has been, and what could again someday be—with how miserable the present is and what the immediate future will bring.

Clearly if we don't break the monopoly of lies, in a few decades there won't be much left to fight for. Especially when you consider the acceleration of environmental degradation and personal dehumanization.

So it's doubly crucial that dialog includes these off-limits subjects of how bad things really are. We need to redefine the acceptable discourse of this society. To refer to the Unabomber again, he decided he had to kill people to bring up this suppressed point of view. And he forced them to publish it. The point here is not whether he was justified or not, but merely to reveal the level of denial. This denial is not going to be changed by little reforms, and the planet is not going to be saved by recycling. To think it will is just silly. Or no, it's not silly, it's criminal. We have to face what's going on. Once we've faced reality, then we can together figure out how to change it, how to completely transform it.

You asked, "What's progress?" Take a look.

We need to talk about alienation. That's the number one problem. Two days ago I read in the paper that the young have never smoked as much as they do now. All the anti-smoking programs in the world aren't going to overcome the alienation at the root of this and other addictions. Take the war on drugs. All the billboards and flashy videos and all that shit aren't going to help one bit, because we aren't doing anything about the conditions that produce it. So we're in this never-never land where at least some people think if you produce some hip stuff about smoking or dope you can change something. But it's more of the avoidance and denial. It's more of the problem.

What is the system that generates these malignant things? Let's talk about that, even though it's forbidden. Still it's forbidden to talk about the fundamental nature of the global system. Before we jump to what are the specific answers, the very first thing, the essential thing is just to face it as a question, to pose it as a question, to talk about it as a question. Otherwise it's pointless to talk about the tactics.

There's a debate going on in Earth First! now about the question of violence versus nonviolence. But I think even Earth First! is missing the point. I think people get so exercised about tactics because they haven't faced the more fundamental questions: what are we really trying to do? What's the overview? What's our grasp on things? What is the meaning of our work? Tactics arise organically in large part from your starting position. But if you don't want to talk about where you are, your talk of tactics is meaningless.

The place to start is by asking questions like: how can we make a radical break? Is what we're doing contributing to a radical break? Do we even want a radical break? Do we want to have a few more liberals, who will chop down a few fewer trees? Is that all we want?

DJ: I just wrote an article for Earth First! surrounding that same question: when is violence appropriate? My belief also is that this isn't the most basic question. The question I would ask is: to what depth do we feel the destruction in our bodies?

I have on my wall a news clipping headlined "Mother bear charges

trains." I keep it because if we're able to perceive the situation deeply
enough in our bodies—like the mother grizzly who charges the train
that killed her sons—we will know precisely what to do. She didn't go
into theoretical discussions of right and wrong; her response was
embodied.

JZ: And it's the same for people who hate their jobs. If they would
just reenter their bodies, they would know what they need to do.

DJ: I read accounts of the lives some people have—for example,
miners who are underground from dawn to dusk day after day—and I
wonder how they survive. So far as we know, we only get one life, and
what the hell are you gonna do spending it all breaking your back?

JZ: Or causing others to break their backs. I was having a discussion
about technological society with a few friends, and some of them were
saying, "Well, we've got to have phones. We can't do away with them."
And another friend responded, "Are you going to go down in the
mines? Are you going to do that?" Because our whole lifestyle is predicated on someone having to slave his or her life away, or rather millions and millions of someones.

I wouldn't go down there unless you put a gun to my head. And
of course some people do have guns to their heads, because they don't
have as much flexibility as you or I do so far as surviving. But those of
us who don't have guns to our heads need to be aware of the bargains
we make in order to live the way we do.

DJ: Let's talk more about technology. Isn't technology just driven by
curiosity?

JZ: You hear people say this all the time: "You can't put the genie
back in the bottle"; "You're asking people to forget." Stuff like that.
But that's just another attempt to naturalize the craziness. And it's a
variant of that same old racist intelligence argument. Because the Hopi
didn't invent backhoes, they must not be curious. Sure, people are naturally curious. But about what? Did you or I aspire to create the
neutron bomb? Of course not. That's crazy. Why would people want
to do that in the first place? They don't. But the fact that I don't want
to create a neutron bomb doesn't mean I'm not curious. Curiosity is
not value free. Certain types of curiosity arise from certain types of

mindsets, and our own "curiosity" follows the logic of alienation, not simple wonder, not learning something to become a better person. Our "curiosity," taken as a whole, leads us in the direction of further domination. How could it do any other?

DJ: We may try to make better mousetraps—more efficient ways to kill small rodents—but I don't see us working real hard to stop rape, child abuse, or global warming. Strange the things we apply this much-vaunted curiosity to.

Also, I think about friends. I want to learn about them so we can be better friends, not so I can utilize them more efficiently. That is true for humans and nonhumans alike.

JZ: We gotta hope this thing collapses.

DJ: Speaking of collapse, how do you see the future playing out?

JZ: I was talking to a friend about it this afternoon, and he was giving reasons why there isn't going to be a good outcome, or even an opening toward a good outcome. I couldn't say he was wrong, but as I mentioned before, I'm kind of betting that the demonstrable impoverishment on every level goads people into the kind of questioning we're talking about, and toward mustering the will to confront it. Perhaps now we're in the dark before the dawn. I remember when Marcuse wrote *One Dimensional Man*. It came out in about 1964, and he was saying that humans are so manipulated in modern consumerist society that there really can be no hope for change. And then within a couple of years things got pretty interesting, people woke up from the '50s to create the movements of the '60s. I believe had he written this book a little later it would have been much more positive.

Perhaps the '60s helped shape my own optimism. I was at the almost perfect age. I was at Stanford, in college, and then I moved to Haight-Ashbury, and Berkeley was across the Bay. I got into some interesting situations just because I was in the right place at the right time. I agree with people who say the '60s didn't even scratch the surface, but you have to admit there was something going on. And you could get a glimpse, a sense of possibility, a sense of hope, that if things kept going, there was a chance of us finding a different path.

They didn't, but I still carry that possibility, and it warms me, even though thirty years later things are frozen, and awful.

Sometimes I'm amazed that younger people can do anything, or have any hope, because I'm not sure they've seen any challenge that has succeeded even partially.

DJ: Certainly none coming from the environmental movement.

JZ: I have that amazing boost in my life and my psyche that younger people don't. And I am so very impressed at the capacity for hope among the young.

DJ: Some say that the '60s were the last big burst, the last gasp, and from then on it's been downhill.

JZ: I sometimes think of it that way, like it was the Big Bang, and everything's been cooling ever since. Or like an earthquake, followed by aftershocks. I was in San Francisco in '76 and '77 during the punk explosion, and that was very exciting, but there was no sense this was going to kickstart a new round of change. We hoped so, but didn't think so.

But I think we're coming to a big one, something much bigger than the '60s. Not only because we have to, if we are to survive, but also because back then we had a tremendously high level of illusion. Much of our idealism was misplaced, and we believed it wouldn't take that much to effect significant change. We had a certainly unwarranted faith in institutions, and we didn't think things through far enough. We weren't grounded enough, tied tightly enough to reality. Now if that revolutionary energy comes back it's going to be far more total.

DJ: I used to teach at Eastern Washington University, and I would ask my students if we live in a democracy. They wouldn't bother to answer, but would just laugh. I would ask if the government cares more for the rights of corporations or individuals. Same response. That filled me with hope.

JZ: I first really saw that when I moved back to Oregon from California in 1981. It was the day Reagan was shot. It was a total contrast to the killing of Kennedy. In 1963 people cried and mourned. It was a trauma. But in 1981 that wasn't the case. I had delivered a car to Eugene, and then had to take a bus to my parents' home. As I walked into the bus station, there were a bunch of people huddled around this little portable TV set. It was coverage of the assassination attempt. They didn't know yet if Reagan was dead. There had been some sort of event, and the people waiting for the bus were primarily students from Oregon State, which is, as I suspect is the case for Eastern Washington, a conservative school. Anyway, everyone was laughing and chuckling and carrying on. They were scathing. I just listened the whole way, and really noticed the total lack of faith in the government. So this time when things blow, they're going to blow for real.

DJ: In *Elements of Refusal* you go into great detail about how in the early part of this century, there was a tremendous amount of revolutionary energy in the air, and that in many ways World War I was an explicit attempt to destroy that energy through the carnage of state-sponsored violence.

JZ: War, of course, always requires a good excuse, especially when the state's real enemies are, more clearly than usual, its own citizenry. The assassination of Archduke Ferdinand well-suited the needs of a dying regime. But by no means did it cause the war. First, the assassination was not atypical. Many European heads of state or upper level administrators were killed in the years just previous. Next, the immediate reaction all through Europe to the news of the assassination was indifference. The people took little notice, and the stock market didn't really respond at all.

We've also been told that the war came because an intricate series of treaties guaranteed that any localized conflict would quickly spread. That's nonsense. After the assassination Austria-Hungary delivered an ultimatum to Serbia. But Serbia capitulated! There was no reason for war! Nonetheless, Austria-Hungary needed a war, and a big one, so war was declared anyway. And why would Russia defend an already-capitulated Serbia? Because it, too, needed a war to stave off its own imminent collapse.

The real reason for the war, I believe, had to do with the tremendous unrest in all of Europe. 1913 and 1914 had seen immense strikes all across Russia. Austria-Hungary was on the verge of civil war. Revolutionary movements and radical unions were on the ascent in the United States, Germany, France, Italy, England. Even George V acknowledged this when he said in the summer of 1914, just before the war, "The cry of civil war is on the lips of the most responsible and sober-minded of my people." Things had to explode.

But how would things explode, and at whom would this explosion be directed? What better way to destroy hope than through a long and pointless war? And it worked. Most unions and left-wing parties backed the war, and those that didn't—like the Wobblies here in the US—the state simply destroyed. After the war not many people had the heart anymore to pursue revolution, and those who did, like Mussolini or the Bolsheviks, were not true revolutionaries in terms of overturning the social order, but instead opportunists who turned the power vacuums to their own advantage.

DJ: Does that parallel make you think there will be another big war?
JZ: Sure, but this one can only last 24 hours, because people won't support it any longer than that. . . .

DJ: Where do you think all this energy—it seems odd to call alienation energy—is going to go?
JZ: Is it piling up? I don't know. I definitely know we aren't the happy mindless consumers we're supposed to be. Or even if we believe we are, our bodies know better. I recently wrote a short review of the new book by Ellen Showalter, called *Hysterias*. In this she talks about what she calls six different hysterias of the '90s: Chronic Fatigue Syndrome, Gulf War Syndrome, recovered memory, satanic cults, and so on. Some people are very offended because it sounds like she's saying it's all in your head.
DJ: Even her choice of title is very revealing in that manner. Freud chose the term hysteria to describe his patients' descriptions of childhood sexual abuse at the hands and genitals of their fathers. At first he believed these accounts, and began to uncover a tremendous epidemic of incest, an epidemic that continues unabated to this day. But when he began to go public with these findings, they were so ill-received that he found himself quickly backing away, and created an entire philosophy around his denial of this evidence. To allow himself to disbelieve these accounts, he called the women hysterical.
JZ: I hear what you're saying, and that's a very good point. Where I'm taking this, however, is in a slightly different direction. It seems to me,

and I have to say the book is very undeveloped, that the point of her book is that we are all so miserable, and so deeply in denial, that these crises will keep arising, whether or not they have physical geneses: once each "hysteria" passes by, another will arise. And you'll never find any cures. You might say that in the case of Gulf War Syndrome this takes the government off the hook by suggesting the government didn't poison or irradiate American troops. But it seems to me more radical to say that not only may the government have poisoned Americans—which it's done so many times as to almost be banal—but that no matter what you are doing or where you live, life now is so crippling, alienated, bizarre, and fucked as to spawn all these potentially psychogenic problems. Of course we all know that's the case, with little kids mowing each other down in school—four cases of it in four months—and all sorts of other outrages unimaginable even ten years ago. And now they're commonplace. Expected even. What the hell does that say about our way of living? No longer can anyone get away with particularizing any of these problems. It's all just so fundamentally rotten and pathological that it indicts the whole system.

Sure the government is capable of and willing to poison its own citizens. Happens all the time. But it's even worse. . . .

DJ: No matter how you look at it, it's damning. If the government didn't poison the soldiers in this case, what's the psychogenic cause of the syndrome? And if it did, which I believe is the case, what the hell does that mean? What does it mean that our own "elected" government would poison us?

This leads to a difficulty I have with this whole discussion. It's something I've not yet answered in my own work. Not only do we have to remember or relearn how to live sustainably, but we have to figure out how to deal with those forces that right now are destroying all those who do live sustainably. It's all very good for us to talk about living sanely and without domination, but we all know what would happen if we in our communities developed sustainable ways to live, and members of the dominant culture wanted our resources. We and our community would be destroyed, and our resources would be stolen.

JZ: That's just a reality. We'd like to think that violence isn't necessary in response, but I'm not sure if that's the case.

Now, you can say that if upheavals are large enough, actually there isn't very much violence.

DJ: Tell me more.

JZ: The first example that comes to mind is the May 1968 uprising in France, in which ten million people, in a wildcat strike, just began to occupy their workplaces. Astronomers, factory workers, you name it. Students provided the trigger, but after that all these grievances came out in a rush. The police and the army were completely useless to the state, because the whole country was involved. For a time they considered sending in NATO. Unfortunately, the uprising didn't last very long before it was brought under control, mainly by the leftists and unions who wanted to co-opt the revolutionary energy for their reformist demands. But for a time the people really had control of the entire country. And it was totally nonviolent. Violence wasn't necessary.

DJ: But the uprising created no long-term change, did it?
JZ: No. But it did expose how really fragile are the powers of coercion that the state has. In that kind of mass uprising the state is helpless.

We saw that again in the collapse of state capitalism in the USSR and the East Block. There was not much violence. It just all fell apart. I'm not saying that's going to happen, nor am I saying that collapse led to any sort of radical shift, but it does point out there have been bloodless upheavals in history.

DJ: Maybe one of the things that can help us through this is the natural world. The system is already beginning to collapse, and I think one of the things we can do is try to make sure that grizzly bear and salmon stay alive through the crash. Another thing we can do is attempt to articulate these alternatives.
JZ: Which is what I believe we are trying to do here.

DJ: I want to come back to the question of what one does with the knowledge that those in power have tanks and guns and airplanes. This seems to me one of the fundamental questions of our time, if not the fundamental question. How does one respond sanely and effectively to outrageously destructive behavior? How does a fundamentally peaceful person respond to violence? How do you make peace with the fact that in order to end coercion, you may have to coerce? You may have to coerce the coercers.

JZ: That is a tough one. You read the journals of Columbus—and there are hundreds of examples of this type of thing—where the peaceful indigenous people greeted the invaders with open arms. The smart thing to have done, I suppose, would have been to cut the throats of the invaders. I don't think many people would argue with that, or if they would, they have probably not been the subject of violence in their own person, their own family, their own community. But the question arises, among these peaceful people, where would the imperative to cut the invaders' throats have come from? Not only the knowledge of what was going to happen to them, but also the moral knowledge to commit that violence. It was not their way.

DJ: Sherman Alexie tells this great story about how he wishes he would have been alive when Columbus landed. He proceeds through all manner of violence he would have done to Columbus and his troops, then stops and says, "No, we couldn't have done that. That is not who we are."

JZ: Maybe you just have to say that the second time around it isn't going to be that way. We didn't make this culture. We didn't turn the world into the battleground and cemetery it has become. We didn't turn human relations into the parody they have become. But now it is our responsibility to overcome what our culture has created. Maybe you could say that now we must be what we must be to overcome it. Adorno talks about that, about overcoming alienation with alienation. How does that work? I don't know, but I think about it. Anybody who cares about the continuation of life on the planet really has to, at this point. To take it to the most personal level, could you kill somebody, if you knew that to do so would save other lives?

DJ: Lately I've been reading a lot about German resistance to Hitler, and I have been struck by the fact that despite knowing Hitler had to be removed before a "decent" government could be installed, they spent more time creating paper versions of this theoretical government than attempting to remove him from power. It wasn't a lack of courage that caused this blindness but rather a misguided sense of morals. Karl Goerdeler, for instance, though tireless in attempting to create this new government, staunchly opposed assassinating Hitler, believing that if only the two could sit face to face Hitler might relent. How do you wrap your mind around that, and how do you personalize it, as you said?

JZ: This ties back to the Showalter book. Maybe these "hysterias," if that is what they are, are the result of our turning anger inward instead of turning it against the system.

We also know what happens to those who turn violent against the system, even if their violence is justified. The ones I know are either dead or in prison. I have a friend in prison who was once a member of the Symbionese Liberation Army. I once asked what made him cross the line into violence, and he said, "I just had to do it. It was absolutely unavoidable."

DJ: I asked the Tupacamarista what caused him to cross that line, and he said it was seeing the futility of civil resistance, and also seeing friends and fellow nonviolent activists murdered by state police.

JZ: I've thought a lot about how I can best serve—and I realize that at least part of this answer is based on class privilege, on a wider set of options being open to me than to many others—but for right now I'm OK with my form of resistance, which is through cultural critique. For me, words are a better weapon to bring down the system than a gun would be. This is to say nothing of anybody else's choice of weapon, only my own. So that's why I do what I do. But my words are nothing but a weapon.

DJ: Obviously the same is true for me. But even having made that decision for now, I still revisit the question. Every morning when I awake, for example, I ask myself whether I should write or blow up a dam. I tell myself I should keep writing, though I'm not sure that's right, because it's neither a lack of words nor activism that's killing salmon here in the Northwest, but the presence of dams. Anyone who knows anything about salmon knows the dams must go. Anyone who knows anything about politics knows the dams will stay. Scientists study, politicians and business people lie and delay, bureaucrats hold sham public input meetings, activists write letters and press releases, I write books, and still the salmon die. It's a cozy relationship for all of us but the salmon.

Or to take another example, I recently read that Gandhi wrote a letter to Hitler appealing to his conscience, and was amazed that it didn't work.

JZ: Gandhi's failure doesn't mean words must always fail. He was obviously directing his words at the wrong place. Had he spoken more radical and effective words to his fellow Indians, things might be different there now.

DJ: Right! Or if he was going to get involved in Germany, he should have written not to Hitler, who was obviously a lost cause, but instead perhaps an open letter to members of the resistance, letting them know they were not alone.

JZ: Yes.

DJ: But the question of violence is even more complex than we've made it so far. I know also we kill by inaction as surely by action. I came to that understanding a year ago. I had a goose who was killing chickens, and because I don't like to kill I didn't kill him. Finally he killed one too many, and so I killed him and ate him for dinner. Here's the point: that evening I was noticing my existential depression at having ended a life, when a friend pointed out that I was responsible that day not just for one death, but for many more. I was responsible as well for the chickens I allowed him to kill because I myself was not willing to stop him.

JZ: I recently saw a quote by Exene Cervenkova, the lead singer in the band X, in which she said, "I've killed way more people than Kaczynski, because I've been paying a lot of taxes in the last fifteen years, and he hasn't." I was really struck by what an effective point that is. It reminds us we're all implicated.

DJ: Let's go back to the notion of anti-authoritarianism. Can there be leaders without domination?

JZ: I think persuasion isn't domination, as long as it isn't manipulative, and as long as it's transparent. That's exactly how the Anarchist troops in the Spanish Civil War were led. Decisions were largely made

by discussion, and once decisions were made then whomever was
going to lead the troops decided how it was to be done. He was given
authority on a case by case basis. This worked well for a time, but then
as happens so often, so-called allies—in this case the Communist party
and the Soviet Union, along with other conservative pressures in
Spain—weeded out the anti-authoritarianism. The Anarchist units
ended up becoming regular units in the army, and the passion for the
revolution was sacrificed.

This whole question of leadership, by the way, is the reason I
stopped being an organizer. For a time I was in this sort of do-it-yourself union in San Francisco. It was opposed to all of the corrupt bureaucratic Organized Labor unions, and it was very Anarchist, though we
didn't use that term. Our general tactic was to help everybody with all
of their issues, all of their grievances, defend everything, dispute everything. We were following a theory prevalent in the '60s called "The
Long March Through the Institutions," which held that the only way
to topple the system is from within. I no longer believe that, of course.
But the thing that finally dawned on me was that I wasn't doing the
work for the right reason. I wasn't specifically trying to help this person
get her job back, or that person change this policy—although I did
help with these situations—so much as I was using the work as an
avenue to overturn the institutions. I didn't say, "I'm doing this because
I want to destroy the system," nor did I say, "My perspective goes way
beyond this union," because I didn't think a lot of people could relate
to that. They just wanted their jobs back, or higher wages, or whatever.
And they came to me because I could help with that. I eventually realized that this lack of transparency was manipulative. So I had to stop.

That's why now I depend more on critique, because I couldn't
figure out how to not have a hidden agenda and still be an effective
organizer. I don't run into that problem as a writer. No one is forced to
read my stuff, and so we—the readers and I—enjoy a nonhierarchical
relationship.

DJ: So persuasion isn't domination?
JZ: Not at all. Not so long as it's honest.

DJ: What do you want from your work and your life?

JZ: I would like to see a face to face community, an intimate existence, where relations are not based on power, and thus not on division of labor. I would like to see an intact natural world, and I would like to live as a fully human being. I would like that for the people around me.

DJ: Once again, how do we get there from here?
JZ: I have no idea. It might be something as simple as everybody just staying home from work. Fuck it. Withdraw your energy. The system can't last without us. It needs to suck our energy. If people stop responding to the system, it's doomed.

DJ: But if we stop responding, if we really decide not to go along, aren't we doomed also, because the system will destroy us?
JZ: Right. It's not so easy. If it were that simple, people would just stay home, because it's such a drag to go through these miserable routines in an increasingly empty culture. But a question we always have to keep in mind is this: we're doomed, but in which way are we more doomed? I recently gave a talk at the University of Oregon in which I spoke on a lot of these topics. Near the end I said, "I know that a call for this sort of overturning of the system sounds ridiculous, but the only thing I can think of that's even more ridiculous is to just let the system keep on going."

DJ: How do we know that all the alienation we see around us will lead to breakdown and rejuvenation? Why can't it just lead to more alienation? I know I've spent the last twenty years working as hard as I can to understand all this and extricate myself as much as I can from it. But I've no family to support. I've no wage job. Alienation can lead to understanding, but it can also lead to just passing on the damage to those around us.
JZ: It's a question of how reversible the damage is. Sometimes—and I don't believe this is too much avoidance or denial—sometimes in history things are reversed in a moment when the physical world intrudes enough to knock us off balance. Vaneigem refers to a lovely little thing that gives me tremendous hope. The dogs in Pavlov's laboratory had been conditioned for hundreds of hours. They were fully

trained and domesticated. Then there was a flood in the basement. And you know what happened? They forgot all of their training in the blink of an eye. We should be able to do at least that well. I am staking my life on it, and it is toward this end that I devote my work.

Julie Mayeda was present for and contributed to this interview.

1998

ABSTRACT EXPRESSIONISM: PAINTING AS VISION AND CRITIQUE

Also known as Heroic Abstraction, the New York School, Gesture Painting, and Action Painting, Abstract Expressionism was modernism's last, great assault on the dominant culture, the finale for painting as opposition or breakthrough.

Abstraction and expressive power had hitherto been considered mutually exclusive, but by the end of 1947 a few artists had abandoned all traces of figural representation, and a definite, if widely varying tendency emerged. This paradoxical combination of elements found potent resolution in works as diverse as the allover "drip" canvases of Jackson Pollock, the black gestures of Franz Kline and Robert Motherwell, and the extremely flat, open color-field paintings of Clyfford Still, Mark Rothko, and especially Barnett Newman. All "so revolutionary," according to critic Irving Sandler (1978), "that all links to the past seemed severed."

In the late 1940s American art was dominated by a mediocre, academic style, which only occasionally went so far as to incorporate suitably tamed aspects of no longer current European styles. Abstract Expressionism was very definitely not about comfortable evocations of beauty or harmony, and the radical break it represented was very distasteful to many. The more traditional painter Ethel Schwabacher, in her *Hungry for Light* memoir (1993) recalls the antipathy she felt to Pollock's "uneasiness" and "demolition quality"; characterizing his efforts as "storm voltage in the wake of which comes wild destruction."

I find, particularly in his huge, signature-style paintings, a volcanic energy in Pollock that seeks to blow away this sham life, that points toward a utopian renewal. People have been known to weep before the shimmering color rectangles of Rothko at his best. It is clear that the AE painters went all-out, united somehow in a common search for an absolute. As Frank O'Hara (1959) observed about them, "In the state of spiritual clarity there are no secrets. The effort to achieve such a state is monumental and agonizing."

By 1950 or so, aided by sensationalist stories in *Life* magazine and elsewhere, awareness of this New York School moved from the art world to the general public. Not surprisingly, the conventional image was that of young, probably talentless know-nothings engaged in tantrums with oil paints. In fact, the arrival of abstract expressionism was the culmination of long, arduous evolution. A fair number of these painters were born within the two or three years prior to 1905 and had been painting for decades, mastering various styles and working through stages of formal development. It was at the peak of their powers and maturity that a number of artists, rather independently, achieved the AE breakthrough. When asked by a reporter how long it had taken him to paint a large work, Rothko replied (1961), "I am 57 years old and it took me all that time to paint this picture."

Of course, a conformist media virtually guaranteed that the public response would be largely one of shock and anger. Probably the only surprise for the painters in question was the intensity of the hostility, and its duration. And how many could have been ready for an art that refused all fixed systems, ideologies, and pigeonholes—anything that might deny expressive possibilities? David and Cecile Shapiro (1990) noted that the new current was "programmatically divorced from anything in the entire history of art East or West."

The AE attitude or orientation was captured, in its utopian aspect, in this line by critic Harold Rosenberg (1948): "The modern painter is not inspired by anything visible, but only by something he hasn't seen yet." In the estimation of Kim Levin (1986), "During the

1950s, New York artists produced some of the most difficult—and violent—painting in the history of art. . . ."

And yet this American vanguard painting made New York the foremost source of aesthetic ideas and energies in the world, definitively surpassing Paris in this regard. Perhaps more importantly, there was an aspect of popular resonance—despite the orchestrated vilification—with Abstract Expressionist intransigence and non-conformism. In an era of mass-produced being and thinking, at least some fraction of society was inspired by the Action Painters.

Europe, by the way, had its own versions of the new painting. The work of the Cobra Group of 1948–1950, so named for its locations in Copenhagen, Brussels, and Amsterdam, was similar in many respects to what the intrepid Americans were up to. Equally dissatisfied with lifeless abstraction and depthless Socialist Realism, the Cobras, albeit briefly, were blazing new paths. Likewise, the Tachist movement in France had ties to New York and a defiant spirit of innovation and profound challenge; to quote Tachist painter Georges Mathieu (1958), "The question is posed: it does more than put the basis of Western civilization at stake . . ."

In the U.S. 1950 saw production beginning in the areas of hydrogen bombs and Miltown tranquilizers, as Cold War repression and consumerist emptiness began to define post-World War II society. In this depersonalized age the Abstract Expressionists put forth their desperate assertions in favor of spontaneity, freedom, and discovery of self and context. It was their romantic anti-capitalist hope, complete with weaknesses and contradictions, that the values embodied in their art could supersede the artistic and transform society. Behind the energy of the immediate impulse was a rigorous way of life demanding total dedication. Pollock summed it up best, simply, when he said, "Painting is my whole life." Hard to imagine a starker contrast to the cowardly cynicism of today's postmodern art-world cadaver.

For a radical art whose purpose was to venture into the unknown, to attempt painting as the yet indefinable, key components were risk, passion and adventure. For such intensity of purpose against such great odds, only extremists need apply. Little wonder that even before 1950 Philip Guston, Mark Rothko, and David Smith, leading AE sculptor, had already suffered serious depression or nervous collapses.

Arshile Gorky had hanged himself in 1948; Pollock, following years
of torturous alcoholism, killed himself in a drunken car crash in
1956; Franz Kline drank himself to death in 1962; Smith died in a
car crash in 1965, and Rothko slashed his arms and died in his studio
in 1970. In fact, alcoholism, if not madness, haunted most of the
twenty or so most visible New York painters of this movement. April
Kingsley (1992) judged that "Not since the Renaissance has there
been a group of artists whose real lives have been so fascinating." Fascinating may be too gentle a word.

Malcolm Lowry once said, "The real cause of alcoholism is the
complete baffling sterility of existence as sold to you." The Abstract
Expressionists were acutely aware of that sterility and believed that art
should reveal and challenge the barrenness and oppression of modern
capitalist society. Sam Francis (1959) rendered this with a poetic precision: "What we want is to make something that fills utterly the sight
and can't be used to make life only bearable."

A large number of the Action painters had radical credentials.
Pollock, Newman, Rothko, Robert Motherwell, and Ad Reinhardt,
among others, made persistently anti-nationalist and anti-capitalist
statements. David and Cecile Shapiro (1977) offered this formulation:
their politics might best be described as "anarchist or nihilist, both
antipodes of authoritarianism, in its drive to jettison rules, tradition,
order, and values." Clearly, there was no accommodation with the prevailing political and social ethos. Newman, Rothko, and Adolph Gottlieb were, in fact, life-long anarchists; once when asked about his,
Rothko answered, "What else?"

Cubism and surrealism were influences in the development of the
painters who became the New York School, but fundamentals of the
two major twentieth century orientations were rejected for characteristically AE reasons. At base, the new painters emphasized (in addition
to expressiveness) flatness and literalness. As early as 1943, in a group
New York Times statement, they declared, "We are for flat forms
because they destroy illusion and reveal the truth." More specifically,
they condemned surrealism, still reigning in modern art at the time of
the statement, for its very conservative representationalism.

Abstract Expressionism, despite its abstraction, upheld concrete-
ness. Action paintings do not "stand for" anything outside themselves,

and in the autonomy of the artistic act imply an autonomy in the world. The struggle to overcome mediation and non-transparency aesthetically looks past the goal of personal wholeness to that of the social order. Many of these "Irascibles" (a *Life* magazine term) were attempting, by the late 1940s, "to eliminate all traces of existing symbol systems." Frank O'Hara (1959) understood their aim as "a oneness which has no need for the mediation of metaphor or symbol."

The action in the picture became its own representation, and paintings tried to convey their full meaning through direct sensation. Clifford Still, Rothko, Newman and others used color to evoke the sublime directly. A related method involved an unprecedented use of black as a color, for its lack of ambiguity and potential expressive force; black and white paintings were often used to try new approaches, in stark, non-chromatic gambles.

Although certainly not new to art, the use of the primitive was a powerful element in much Action painting, as suggested by "Art has been in decadence since the caveman," a sentiment from Miró. These painters were interested in a spirit of communion with the primitive, heeding the call of David Smith, sculptor and radical, for a "return to origins, before purities were befouled by words." But in drawing from this source, one sees a contradiction: the primitive represented not only optimism and community, but also a state of brutality, helplessness, and fear of nature. We now understand this ambivalence to have been unnecessary, given the distinctly positive view that recent decades of scholarship have disclosed of life in pre-civilization.

Art is predicated on its formal strategies and development. Even an art that sought to embody impulses which are not primarily aesthetic finds its success or failure, at bottom, in formal terms. Robert Motherwell gave his reason for this in a 1944 talk, the estimation that "so long as modern society is dominated by the love of property—and it will be, so long as property is the only source of freedom—the artist has no alternative to formalism."

One obvious aspect of this, as already noted in passing, is the rejection of representation. The Abstract Expressionists had come to the conclusion that through thousands of years of exposure, representational images were worn out. As Rothko (1958) disclosed, "a time came when none of us could use the figure without mutilating it."

To come more to the heart of the formal means involved, it is plausible to assert not only that these works were new in the history of Western civilization, but that they are the final evolution of painting. There is an extreme, reductivist purification underlying them, prompting some to refer to the "abolitionist" nature of Abstract Expressionism.

In their quest for critical revelation and the visionary, the Action painters, in their varying styles, went after everything that was dispensable and rejected it. Harold Rosenberg (1972) referred to their conceptions of painting as "a kind of marathon of deletion." They were going for broke, throwing out virtually every last convention in art to get to the irreducible essentials.

In a reference to Cézanne's famous still lifes that were so influential for modern art, Rosenberg had noted earlier (1959), "the apples weren't swept off the table in order to make room for perfect relations of space and color. They had to go so that nothing would get in the way of the act of painting." This was the grand gesture of those who fought desperately for a coherence possessed of supra-aesthetic potency, in the face of an increasingly alienated and divided society. Small wonder that few could follow the extremist paths of such aesthetic dialecticians.

The turbulent lives of the Abstract Expressionists constitute one aspect of this demanding, ground-breaking project, and the limitations of the aesthetic itself, a subject beyond the scope of this offering, is another, more general question. It becomes hard to resist concluding, let me concede, that the heroic AE enterprise was destined to be a dead end, inspiring to some, but unrealizable. Max Horkheimer (1959) was referring to the overreachings of Abstract Expressionism when he judged, sadly, "As it becomes coherent in itself, it also becomes mute, and that it requires commentary is proof of that fact."

In discarding the non-essentials to get at new heights of expressive coherence, it was Jackson Pollock who went furthest. He realized how little was left to work with and yet persisted in trying to force art to make good on its never-delivered promise of revelation, to show us truth that would truly make a difference.

Pollock's huge "drip" or poured canvases—their very size a rebuff to market considerations—are unequalled in their immediacy, wildness and epic qualities. Continually more inventive and radical, his project, his life, was that of a total engagement of the spirit in the expression of meaning.

The poured technique, arrived at in 1947, was a daring formal solution of dripping or even throwing paint in long, looping rhythms. Michael Fried (1965) felt that Pollock had "managed to free line from its function of representing objects in the world, but also from its task of describing or bounding shapes and figures. . . ." He advanced past symbols, shapes and forms altogether, employing line as trajectory rather than as a form-defining device. Not surprisingly, this break-through was seen by not a few as the destruction of art.

Allan Kaprow in 1958, two years after Pollock's drunken end, referred to him as "the embodiment of our ambition for absolute liber-ation and a secretly cherished wish to overturn old tables of crockery and flat champagne." A reminiscence of his work by Paul Jenkins (1985) declared, "He awakens us like a flash of light, and his presence was something that had gone through fire and existed in fire. . . ."

There is often a violent, terrible energy to Pollock's paintings which at times have a raw, unfinished feel to them. In fact, he tried precisely to move beyond beauty, beyond the usual pictorial ambition. The "well-made" picture, the notion of painting as some kind of haute cuisine was just what he and the other Abstract Expressionists were out to demolish. There was an undeniable sense of freedom to all this, an exhilaration. At times it was "so delicious," recalled Willem DeKoon-ing. "Like children we broke all the windows."

And this iconoclastic nihilism, again, was the bane of many critics. Hilton Kramer, for instance, never tired of railing against Pollock's "anar-chic" impulses, his "anarchic" sensibilities, the "vehemence of his anar-chic energy, " etc. (e.g. 1957). Even some of his fellow Action painters could be shocked by the violence of Pollock's approach. Hans Hoffman, older and a significant influence on the New York School in general, visited Pollock's studio and was appalled by the disorder he found there. Picking up a dried-out brush that had stuck to a palette, he said, "With this you could kill a man." Jackson's reply was "That's the point."

An earlier encounter with Hoffmann, as recounted by Lee Krasner, Pollock's wife and a considerable painter in her own right, is also telling:

I brought Hoffmann up to meet Pollock for the first time and Hoffmann said, after looking at his work, "You do not work from nature." Pollock's answer was, "I am nature."

This seemingly bombastic statement had less to do, I would say, with megalomania than with Pollock's rejection of the usual expedient of symbolizing nature. Pollock was very much interested in nature all the way along, and the rhythms of nature are readily recognized in many of his pictures.

The movement, energy, and surprise of Pollock's major (1947–50) works tend to make the eye of the viewer move constantly and thus apprehend the image as a whole. A universal dimension is suggested, in fact, an evocation of the totality precisely because nothing is represented. Primal vitality, dionysiac energy testify to how much he longed "to escape from American ordinariness, its lure of banality." Pollock displayed elements of an "apocalyptic mentality, of a social contract with a future world and, simultaneously, a falling one," in the words of Donald Kuspit (1979, 1980). His utopian vision is also about origins, about what has disappeared from the world, and is thus "partly a project of retrieval" (T.J. Clark 1990). The promise of the past as well as of the future— "memories arrested in space," his phrase—is what he tried to convey, and what I think is told best by the sense of unlimited freedom of his poured paintings. Pollock offers, as David Anfan (1990) phrased it very well, "a foretaste of the reign of wonder."

As compared to Pollock's line and energy, Mark Rothko utilized fields of color and repose; aside from their commitment to total abstraction, the two are stylistic opposites. But Rothko, in another approach to shared values, made almost as large a contribution to pictorial heresy as his slightly younger colleague. Early on, around 1945, he made some of his strongest, defining statements for emerging Abstract Expressionism and in time reached such levels of the sublime in painting as to go, according to Dore Ashton (1958), "almost beyond the reach of the word."

Two or three centrally aligned rectangles, floating in layers of vibrant light and color, were a characteristic picture, by which he gave materiality to his redemptive vision. A secret, inner harmony underlies these works, a pulsating presence, what he termed "the impact of the unequivocal." He aimed at a distilled content that, like that of other Action painters, had jettisoned such components as recognizable subject matter, spatial illusion, complex formal relationships, even titles.

It was out of fear of being assimilated by society that Rothko purged his art of any precise images. As he wrote in 1947, "The familiar identity of things has to be pulverized in order to destroy the finite associations with which our society increasingly enshrouds every aspect of our environment." The "look" of the everyday only gets in the way of seeing what is really there and what really could be there.

Like his friends Barnett Newman, and Clyfford Still, Rothko was something of an absolutist, morally and politically. He was also an anarchist during his entire adult life, and the anti-authoritarian foundation of his outlook was always present. This comes through even in a remark about the size of paintings, in favor of big canvases: "However you paint the larger picture, you are in it. It isn't something you command."

Growing up in Portland, Oregon, he listened to IWW orators and once heard Emma Goldman speak. His ill-fated Seagram murals experience in the late 1950s is a colorful testimony to an anarchist, anti-commodity, and anti-art world perspective. Rothko accepted a commission to paint several murals for the restaurant in the New York headquarters of the Seagram liquor corporation, but later changed his mind on the subject of adorning space mainly frequented by a ruling class clientele. He had hoped "to paint something that would ruin the appetite of every son of a bitch who ever ate in that room." Reconsidering the soundness of this tactic, as Breslin (1993) tells it, he returned the commission in disgust, raging that "Anybody who will eat that kind of food for those kinds of prices will never look at a painting of mine."

Rothko's paintings often evoke strongly emotional responses, including great sadness. It was a mark of his courage to struggle so long and so well with his glowing color fields, against the sterility of society and encroaching depression and despair. An almost obsessional darkness began to creep into his vision by 1957, and his late works, largely grey negativities, move toward a dimming invisibility.

Barnett Newman was one of the main whipping boys of Abstract Expressionism.

When in 1950 he first showed his remarkably simple color-field paintings, generally consisting of a huge expanse of one color divided by a couple of thin vertical stripes, even his outlaw colleagues rejected them. Many consider his works to be the most radical of all Abstract Expressionist art.

A Newman picture overwhelms the eye with one main color, providing the immediate sensation of an all-pervading forcefulness. Newman's thrust was the primal unity, wholeness, harmony between humanity and nature, and the potential greatness of the human spirit.

He strove for the highest in discourse and momentous meaning, and while the means were drastically simplified, content was amplified. In a July 1950 letter from Still, one of his few supporters at the time, the "magnitude" and "intensity" of Newman's color were linked to a total rejection of contemporary culture and those behind it. In response to the question of what his art could mean to the world, he pointed to a canvas from his inaugural 1950 exhibition and said, "You know, that painting, if read correctly, means the end of the capitalist system!"

Newman was a utopian primitivist who advocated a return to the first, communal forms of human society. He upheld a vision of life based on voluntary cooperation, free of antagonism and repression. Never sympathetic to the Communist Party, from the 1920s he was an active anarchist, and taught himself Yiddish in order to read the only anarchist newspaper then available in New York. In 1933 Newman ran for mayor of New York on a platform of free housing, public galleries and orchestra spaces, the closing of streets to private automobiles, and playgrounds for adults.

Looking back at Abstract Expressionism (1966), he claimed that "we actually began, so to speak, from scratch, as if painting were not only dead but had never existed." But Newman was definitely influenced, as were 19th century figures like Pisarro and Seurat, by Kropotkin's ideas of artistic autonomy and mutualist spontaneity. Indeed, in the late 1960s, not long before he died, he persuaded a publisher who wanted to bring out a book of Newman's own collected writings to instead publish Kropotkin's *Memoirs of a Revolutionist*, for which he wrote a preface.

Barnett Newman's friend and fellow anarchist Clyfford Still drew less on Kropotkin's critique of society, than from Bakunin's demand for its violent abolition. In fact, the uncompromising vehemence and intensity of his approach almost make Newman look like a genial middle-of-the-roader.

For starters, no other artist had ever loathed the art world as a system with such an undying passion. Critics were "venomous scribblers," galleries were "brothels," the Museum of Modern Art in particular was a "gas chamber." He rejected all constraints and demanded that art work assume the most momentous of empancipatory responsibilities.

His style was that of rough and craggy fields of color, usually suggesting turbulence and cataclysm. These generally large, raw pictures refused comfortable confinement within edges. He wrote in 1963 that "to be stopped by a frame's edge was intolerable; a Euclidean prison had to be annihilated, its authoritarian implications repudiated. . . ."

His all-or-nothing outlook placed enormous faith in the inherent autonomy of engagé art as an instrument of freedom. Blake and Nietzche were influences; even more so he emphasized the reassertion of human beginnings to show the way toward clearing away the weight of accumulated imprisonment. Donald Kuspit (1977) pondered "this grand primitivist negation, this grand return to origins" in the service of a radical freedom, and understood its underlying affirmation.

Still rejected what he called the "totalitarian hegemony" of art's history. The "security" that comes from tradition, he wrote in 1952, is "an illusion, banal, and without courage." The alienated, technological essence of the Bauhaus school, "I rejected out of hand as an abdication to systems of power and mass control with their underpinnings of political and economic reactionary theses. . . ." His critical acumen and acerbic style are, I think, worth quoting further in this regard:

> The manifestoes and gestures of the Cubists, the Fauves, the Dadaists, Surrealists, Futurists or Expressionists were only evidence that the Black Mass was but a pathetic homage to that which it often presumed to mock. And the Bauhaus herded them briskly into a cool, universal Buchenwald. All the devices were at hand, and all the devices had failed to emancipate.

For the severe Still, painting was really a life and death affair on both personal and social levels; its potential was boundless. He reflected in 1963 on his role in the 1940s: "I had made it clear that a single stroke of paint, backed by work and a mind that understood its potency and implications, could restore to man the freedom lost in twenty centuries of apologies and devices for subjugation." As he had said in 1952, "We are now committed to an unqualified act, not illustrating outworn myths or contemporary alibis."

If Abstract Expressionism had an organizer, it was the articulate internationalist, Robert Motherwell. Somewhat like Barnett Newman, he facilitated and promoted the movement and its basic orientation. He saw at its heart "a rejection of nearly everything that seems to interest nearly everyone, a protest against what goes on and the art that supports it" (1950), and was most impressed by "the radiance and subtlety with which this attitude of protest is expressed."

He found the whole point of existence, in fact, to be opposing the established order, but his work, while strongly radiant, does not strike one as subtle. For 30 years he painted his Elegies to the Spanish Republic: thick, black and brooding forms, rough-edged, dripping and full of emotional intensity. He executed over 140 pictures in this long series of a similar black and white style, possessing inescapable physical presence and urgency. As with so many other Action painters, he dared to drastically simplify the number of elements and thereby achieved a greatly magnified expressive power.

Motherwell wrote in 1948 of a projected Abstract Expressionist goal of "ridding us of the glory of conquerors and politicos," of "defending [human] values with intelligence and ingenuity against the property-loving world." More specifically, he saw the new school as deeply critical of standardization and instrumentalism, later sadly concluding (1977) that "Western man, in choosing centuries ago to exploit nature rather than marry her, has doomed himself . . . with an industrial technology" out of his control. "One can only guess," he had written in 1959, "if there were something more deeply and humanly inspiring, at what we might be, what all mankind might be capable of."

Franz Kline, Willem deKooning, Helen Frankenthaler, Adolph Gottlieb, Phillip Guston, so many important others, too many for even brief commentary here. The spirit of inspired antagonism of that whole heroic and diverse group was perhaps best captured in 1949 by

William Baziotes: "when the demagogues of art call on you to make the social art, the intelligible art, the good art—spit on them and go back to your dreams."

After a brief period of critical success and just as some of its partisans were finally able to sell a few paintings and wonder if they were selling out, by the late '50s, Abstract Expressionism was on the wane. The Italian critic Marco Valsecchi wrote in 1950 of its basis in "the necessity of surviving as individuals without being crushed by the conformism of industrialized life," and that AE paintings give the sense of "witnessing a shipwreck and the fight for survival." Very similar was Gottlieb's 1963 statement, "Everything seemed hopeless and we had nothing to lose, so that in a sense we were like people condemned to life imprisonment who make a dash for freedom."

Though based on resistance and refusal, their desperate initiative was widely misunderstood and steadily assimilated into the prevailing cultural, political, and social ethos. Nonetheless, Action painting was not only the evident end of formal development in art, it was the highest point, in its sphere, of the whole modernist project. And because of what David Craven (1990) recognized as its "unequivocal opposition to scientism, technologism, and wage labour alienation," Abstract Expressionism superseded the non-radical Enlightenment belief in progress usually found near the heart of modernism.

By the late '50s, Pop Art, which represents a sweeping transition from modernism to postmodernism, was in full swing. Martha Rosler (1981) perceived the postmodern renunciation of purity and celebration of pluralism as "a pretend triumph of egalitarian tolerance." At base, and seen most clearly in Pop Art, it simply reflects the enormous consequences of mounting post-war commodity production and consumption. Shallow, banal, indiscriminate, Pop Art exalts the standardized and makes no demand upon the viewer except his or her money. It has exactly nothing of the inner necessity or passionately sought authenticity of its immediate artistic predecessor. The triumph of Pop Art over Abstract Expressionism is inseparable from "the feeling of bankruptcy that permeates our art and culture," that Kim Levin referred to in 1986.

True to the postmodern canon, Pop Art renounces any grasp of the whole, and in so doing ends up with just what the system gives it.

As Octavio Paz saw in 1973, Pop Art is not a figure in a vision, but a mannequin in a department store. The commercial images of Warhol and the rest are unmistakably tied to the oppressive set-up whose understanding it rules out. It is their objective of totality that gave Action painting, according to T.J. Clark (1990), both its fierceness and its sensuousness. While the likes of Pop Art come and go as trivial consumption, the valiant, life-affirming effort of Abstract Expressionism will endure and inspire.

1999

THE AGE OF NIHILISM

Technological mediation and separation continue on their emptying ascendancy, embodying so well capital's impoverishing penetration of every level of life on this planet. But there are signs that an era of unchecked cynicism, engendered by this rampant advance of techno-capital, is finally being challenged. The challengers, moreover, are quickly deepening their understanding of how fundamental the challenge must be if it is to succeed.

With this in mind, the following comments on nihilism may well be less apropos than they would have been even a year or two ago. For the focus of this essay is passive nihilism, rather than the probing, critical variety, which is the active nihilism now emerging as a force to be reckoned with. Nonetheless, the question of how and why an enfeebling ethos of meaninglessness and indifference came to predominate may still be of some interest.

In *Fathers and Sons*, Turgenev described the nihilist as one "who looks at everything critically . . . who does not take any principle for granted, however much that principle may be revered." But during the same period, Dostoevsky portrayed modern, passive nihilism in *Notes from Underground*. Its protagonist was merely disgruntled, and lacked the passion and conviction necessary to hold convention to the flame of critique.

During the following century, it appears, the sense that nothing matters became widespread. One current among others, quite obviously, but a growing one. Nothing counts more than anything else, so nothing really counts. Nietzsche had said that nihilism "stands at the door" of modern civilization, and that door opened wider as the important sources of meaning and value steadily revealed themselves as inconsequential and irrelevant, unequal to the rigors of modern life.

Heidegger found in nihilism "the fundamental movement of the history of the West," and what was the bane of the nineteenth century became, by the 1990s, a banality. Nihilism, in the current postmodern clime, is simply the matter-of-fact state of mind of our period—so widespread today is the attitude that little or nothing is compelling, authentic, or makes a difference. Distinctions of value or meaning and the value or meaning of distinctions are less and less persuasive. There is a cultural exhaustion in the movement through decadence into nihilism. According to John Gray, nihilism constitutes modernity's "only truly universal inheritance to humankind."

That inheritance has accelerated, it seems, since the failure of the movement of the 1960s, when belief in continuous Progress had reached its peak. As utopian oases dried up, a desert of inertia and pointlessness spread. By the '80s, with nothing to look for and nowhere to go, youth were tagged as slackers, Generation X, etc. In the summer of 1990, the *New York Times* called kids the generation "that couldn't care less."

With young people looking ahead to a lifetime of strain and empty consumerism, it should surprise no one that teens' suicide rate has tripled in the past 30 years. Or that network television now offers what amount to "snuff" programs for the jaded and bored, as the population in general experiences its life-world as more and more of a vacuum in every way. A melancholy escapism flowers in this Dead Zone, this Nowhere.

Development is a given; this cancer of a system would soon collapse without its steady onslaught. It continues its onrush into the hypermodern vista of high-tech unreality. Nietzsche saw nihilism as a consequence of the erosion of the Christian world view. But this is a superficial judgment, in many ways confusing effect with cause.

A deeper causative factor is the march of technology, in the direction of the complete industrialization of society. From the present apex of cultural homogenization and standardized life, this is easier to see than it was for Nietzsche more than a century ago. The hollowing out of the substance and texture of daily existence is being completed, a process intimately related to the near impossibility of experiencing the world without technological mediation. The overall destruction of experience speaks to the deprivation at the heart of both technology and nihilism.

With this absence of unmediated personal experience at the heart of technological progress, skyrocketing levels of stress and depression cannot be surprising. Technology mediates between individuals and nature, ultimately abolishing both. With the triumph of technology, autonomy regresses and negates itself. The promises have all been lies. One is the promise of connection, so mercilessly (though inadvertently) mocked in a recent TV commercial: "I've got gigabytes. I've got megabytes. I'm voice-mailed. I'm e-mailed. I surf the Net. I'm on the Web. I am Cyber-Man. So how come I feel so out of touch?"

A set-up whose essence is efficiency is already fundamentally nihilist. Technical rules are rapidly supplanting ethical norms by making them irrelevant. What is more efficient or less efficient holds sway, not some moral consideration, even as the systemic goals of techno-capital are shaped by the evolution of its technology. Production, based on mastery and control, becomes more visibly a process of humanity devouring itself.

When powerlessness prevails, a generalized sense of paranoia is not an illogical symptom. Similarly, a current and telling form of cynicism is technological fatalism ("There's nothing we can do about it"), further exposing the tendency of cynicism to shade into conformity. As Horkheimer and Adorno observed, "technological rationale is the rationale of domination itself."

Understanding and responsibility succumb to an ever-increasing fragmentation, a division of labor that is always unequal and alienating. The only wholeness resides in the fundamental system that turns all else into parts. As the moral self recedes, it becomes harder to grasp the relationship of these parts to one another and to see what they are part of. Domination and nihilism's crisis of meaning are inseparably entwined.

For Heidegger, technology constitutes the final phase of nihilism.

Under its sign all talk of freedom, happiness, emancipation becomes a mockery. In fact, technology itself becomes the ideological basis of society, having destroyed the possibility of other, overt forms of justification. Engagement or belief are hardly necessary for technology's effective rule. In this way the nagging problem of declining participation in the system can be mitigated, or deferred.

Technology is the embodiment of the totalizing system of capital, and media is an indispensable, ever more defining bridge between technology and the commodity system. If the high-tech information explosion cancels all meaning in a meaningless noise, the mass-entertainment industrial complex pumps out increasingly desperate diversions to a society of relentless consumerism.

"Infotainment" and McJournalism are the latest pop culture products of nihilism. Why bother with truth if nothing can be done about reality anyway? And yet media, like technology, is always promising solutions to problems it has created, or worsened. One example among many is the significant rise in teen smoking in the 1990s despite an enormous media campaign aimed at reducing teen smoking. Strangely enough, beefing up the media does not combat alienated behaviors.

In the United States, and soon to spread elsewhere as not less than a function of development, we witness the recent transition to an amusement society of commodified spectacles and simulations. The eclipse of non-mediated reality feeds still greater urges to escape an emptied everyday life. Massified culture works in favor of distraction, conformity, and culturally enforced stupidity. The consequent lack of authenticity produces a mass turn-off, not unrelated to the decline of literacy.

The collapse of the distinction between reality and simulation in the world of representation can be seen as the ultimate failure of the symbolic. Art, music, and other forms of symbolic culture are losing their power to pacify and console us. Simulation technologies are just the most recent steps away from lived life, toward represented life. Their failure to satisfy means that the system must turn, increasingly, to containment and control.

To protect the desolate society an alternative to that society is safely set up, by means of image technologies. As the social dimensions of human life disappear along with meaning and value, a consumer

society in cyberspace becomes the next stage of human existence. We
are moving steadily toward the goal of complete illusion—virtual life
in a virtual reality.

Under the Juggernaut, the subject is not supposed to have any
sense of social causality, structure, coherence, or motive. Virtual
Reality's merely surface experience is exactly mirrored by postmodernism's fascination with surfaces. As the culture that can just barely
still be called one, postmodernism celebrates its own depthlessness,
and is thus nihilism's essential accomplice. It comes to pervade society
when too many have given up hope that they can plumb the depth
and roots of the whole. Postmodern perspectives are grounded in the
incapacity to specify why change might be desirable or how it might
come about.

Postmodernism is fundamentally the collapse and refusal of the
chance to understand the totality. This indeed is the postmodern
boast, mirroring the fragmentation of life instead of challenging it. Its
"politics" is that of pragmatism, the tired liberalism that accommodates
to the debased norm.

Deconstruction, for example, treats every moral statement as an
endlessly manipulable fragment that possesses neither meaning nor
intrinsic worth. Rem Koolhaus formulates the overall PM subjugation
as follows: "According to Derrida we cannot be Whole, according to
Baudrillard we cannot be real, according to Virilio we cannot be
There."

Postmodernism, it might be argued, expresses fewer illusions, but
the basic ones remain unchallenged. Its exhausted, ironic cynicism is
prostrate before the nihilist ascendancy. What could be more passive
than critique-less postmodernism double talk—an ideology of acquies-
cence.

Falsely laying claim to the protection of the particular as against
the universal, postmodernism presents no defense whatsoever against
the most universalizing force of all, technology. In the guise of particularity it incarnates nothing less than the realization of technology's universalizing Midas touch.

Postmodernism emphasizes plurality, accessibility, absence of
boundaries, endless possibility. Just as consumerist society does. And
just as speciously. Where culturally a glut of meaningless information

and incoherent fragments hold sway, the glut of ersatz commodities provides a perfect economic parallel. The liberty that remains to us is essentially the freedom to choose among brands A, B, and C, and the KFC in Tienanmen Square expresses domination as surely as the suppression of human rights protesters there in 1989.

"Systematic consumer segmentation and micro-marketing" is the dominant model of individualism today in the nihilist ethos of listless yet restless buyers. In fact, in an overwhelmingly commodified existence, consumption becomes the number one form of entertainment. Little wonder that academic journals now seriously discuss not only the McDonaldization of society but also its Disneyization, while life is largely defined in terms of consumer styles. The cognitive and moral focus of life becomes that of consumer behavior—including, it should be noted, voting and recycling.

Nihilism has effectively leached out the substance and texture from the life-world in the painful progression by which capital and technology have reduced and debased everything in their way. There is no exit from the closed system except by the elimination of that system.

Civilization begins by myth and ends in radical doubt, to paraphrase E.M. Cioran. This may remind us that cultural radicalism, which has become such a convention, feeds the dominant system rather than undermining it. Culture, born of alienation, needs alienation to go on. We must challenge the idea of symbolic culture as well as the reality of high-tech barbarism.

Nihilism is not a one-way street with no return, rather a route that has revealed the ensemble of domination for what it is. There are now very visible signs of the possibility of breaking its hold, redeeming its long, dark night.

2000

POSTSCRIPT TO *FUTURE PRIMITIVE*
RE: THE TRANSITION

"Yeah, the critique is impressive and everything, but just how might we actually get from this ghastly world to some healed, whole existence?"

I think we should not doubt that such a journey is possible, nor that the explosion necessary to begin it may be approaching.

The thought of the dominant culture has, of course, always told us that alienated life is inescapable. In fact, culture or civilization itself expresses this essential dogma: the civilizing process, as Freud noted, is the forcible trading of a free, natural life for one of unceasing repression.

Today culture is in a dispirited, used-up state wherever one looks. More important than the entropy afflicting the logic of culture, however, is what seems to be the active, if inchoate resistance to it. This is the ray of hope that disturbs the otherwise all-too-depressing race we witness to determine whether total alienation or the destruction of the biomass will happen first.

People are being stretched and beaten on the rack of everyday emptiness, and the spell of civilization is fading. Lasch referred to a near-universal rage abroad in society, just under the surface. It is growing and its symptoms are legion, amounting to a refusal to leave this earth unsatisfied.

Adorno asked, "What would happiness be that was not measured by the immeasurable grief at what is?" Certainly, the condition of life has become nightmarish enough to justify such a question, and perhaps also to suggest that something started to go deeply wrong a very long time back. At least it ought to be demonstrating, moving on toward specifics, that the means of reproducing the prevailing Death Ship (e.g. its technology) cannot be used to fashion a liberated world.

Saul Bellow's Mr. Sammler wondered, "What is 'common' about the common life? What if some genius were to do with 'common life' what Einstein did with 'matter'? Finding its energetics, uncovering its radiance." Of course, we must all be that "Einstein," which is exactly what will unleash a creative energy sufficient to utterly refashion the conditions of human existence. Ten thousand years of captivity and darkness, to paraphrase Vaneigem, will not withstand ten days of full-out revolution, which will include the simultaneous reconstruction of our inner selves. Who doesn't hate modern life? Can what conditioning that remains survive such an explosion of life, one that ruthlessly removes the sources of such conditioning?

We are obviously being held hostage by capital and its technology, made to feel dependent, even helpless, by the sheer weight of it all, the massive inertia of centuries of alienated categories, patterns, values. What could be dispensed with immediately? Borders, governments, hierarchy, what else? How fast could more deep-seated forms of authority and separation be dissolved, such as that of division of labor? I assert, and not, I hope, in the spirit of wishing to derive blueprints from abstract principle, that I can see no ultimate freedom or wholeness without the dissolution of the inherent power of specialists of every kind.

Many say that millions would die if the present techno-global fealty to work and the commodity were scrapped. But this overlooks many potentialities. For example, consider the vast numbers of people who would be freed from manipulative, parasitic, destructive pursuits for those of creativity, health, and liberty. At present, in fact, very few contribute in any way to satisfying authentic needs.

Transporting food thousands of miles, not an atypical pursuit today, is an instance of pointless activity, as is producing countless tons of herbicide and pesticide poisons. The picture of humanity starving if a transformation were attempted may be brought into perspective by reference to a few other agricultural specifics, of a more positive nature. It is perfectly feasible, generally speaking, that we grow our own food. There are simple approaches, involving no division of labor, to large yields in small spaces.

Agriculture itself must be overcome, as domestication, and because it removes more organic matter from the soil than it puts back. Permaculture is a technique that seems to attempt an agriculture that develops or reproduces itself and thus tends toward nature and away from domestication. It is one example of promising interim ways to survive while moving away from civilization. Cultivation within the cities is another aspect of practical transition, and a further step toward superseding domestication would be a more or less random propagation of plants, à la Johnny Appleseed.

Regarding urban life, any steps toward autonomy and self-help should be realized, beginning now, so that cities may be all the more quickly abandoned later. Created out of capital's need to centralize control of property transactions, religion, and political domination, cities remain as extended life-destroying monuments to the same basic needs of capital. Something on the order of what we know now as museums might be a good idea so that post-upheaval generations could know how grotesque our species' existence became. Moveable celebration sites may by the nearest configuration to cities that disalienated life will express.

Along with the movement out of cities, paralleling it, one might likely see a movement from colder climes to warmer ones. The heating of living space in northern areas constitutes an absurd effort of energy, resources, and time. When humans become once again intimate with the earth, healthier and more robust, these zones would probably be peopled again, in altogether different ways.

As for population itself, its growth is no more a natural or neutral phenomenon than is technology. When life is fatally out of balance, the urge to reproduce appears as compensation for impoverishment on various levels. In the absence of such impoverishment, as with the non-civilized gatherer-hunters surviving today, population levels would be relatively quite low.

Enrico Guidoni pointed out that architectural structures necessarily reveal a great deal about their social context. Similarly, the isolation and sterility of shelter in class society is hardly accidental, and deserves to be scrapped in toto. Rudofsky's *Architecture Without Architects* deals with some examples of shelter not produced by specialists, but by spontaneous and evolving communal activity. Imagine the inviting richness of dwellings, each unique not mass produced, and a part of a serene mutuality that one might expect to emerge from the collapse of boundaries and artificial scarcities, material and emotional.

Probably "health" in a new world will be a matter even less recognizable that the question of shelter. The dehumanized industrial "medicine" of today is totally complicitous with the overall processes of society which rob us of life and vitality. Of countless examples of the criminality of the present, direct profiting from human misery must rank near the top. Alternative healing practices are already challenging the dominant mode, but the only real solution is the abolition of a setup that by its very nature spawns an incredible range of physical and psychic immiseration. From Reich to Mailer, for example, cancer is recognized as the growth of a general madness blocked and denied. Before civilization disease was generally nonexistent. How could it have been otherwise? Where else do degenerative and infectious diseases, emotional maladies, and all the rest issue if not from work, toxicity, cities, estrangement, fear, unfulfilled lives—the whole canvas of damaged, alienated reality? Destroying the sources will eradicate the suffering. Minor exigencies would be treated by herbs and the like, not to mention a diet of pure, non-processed food.

It seems evident that industrialization and the factories could not be gotten rid of instantly, but equally clear that their liquidation must be pursued with all the vigor behind the rush of break-out. Such enslavement of people and nature must disappear forever, so that words like production and economy will have no meaning. A graffito from the rising in France in '68 was simply "Quick!" Those partisans apparently realized the need to move rapidly forward all the way, with no temporizing or compromise with the old world. Half a revolution would only preserve domination and cement its hold over us.

A qualitatively different life would entail abolishing exchange, in every form, in favor of the gift and the spirit of play. Instead of the coercion of work—and how much of the present could continue without precisely that coercion?—an existence without constraints is an immediate, central objective. Unfettered pleasure, creative endeavor along the lines of Fourier: according to the passions of the individual and in a context of complete equality.

What would we keep? "Labor-saving devices?" Unless they involve no division of labor (e.g. a lever or incline), this concept is a fiction; behind the "saving" is hidden the congealed drudgery of many and the despoliation of the natural world. As the Parisian group Interrogations put it: "Today's riches are not human riches; they are riches for capitalism which correspond to a need to sell and stupefy. The products we manufacture, distribute, and administer are the material expressions of our alienation."

Every kind of fear and doubt is cultivated against the prospect or possibility of transforming life, including the moment of its beginning. "Wouldn't revolt mean mayhem, hoarding, survivalist violence, etc.?" But popular uprisings seem to embody strong feelings of joy, unity, and generosity. Considering the most recent U.S. examples, the urban insurrections of the '60s, New York City '77, and Los Angeles '92—one is struck by the spontaneous sharing, the sharp drop in interracial violence and violence against women, and general sense of festival.

Our biggest obstacle lies in forgetting the primacy of the negative. Hesitation, peaceful coexistence—this deficiency of desire will prove fatal if allowed to be ascendant. The truly humanitarian and pacific impulse is that which is committed to relentlessly destroying the malignant dynamic known as civilization, including its roots. Time is a stunting, confining imposition of culture, naming is a domination—like counting, an aspect of the distancing of language. In the horrible extremity of today we can see the need to return all the way to the earth, to the multi-sensual intimacy of nature that obtained before symbolization made living a reified, separated caricature of itself.

Enchantment might be savored even more brightly this time, for knowing what our ancestors didn't realize must be avoided.

Tearing up the concrete could begin immediately, as my late friend Bob Brubaker once counseled. Literally, under the pavement, it's the beach!

1993

AGE OF GRIEF

A pervasive sense of loss and unease envelops us, a cultural sadness that can justly be compared to the individual who suffers a personal bereavement.

A hyper-technologized late capitalism is steadily effacing the living texture of existence, as the world's biggest die-off in 50 million years proceeds apace: 50,000 plant and animal species disappear each year (World Wildlife Fund, 1996).

Our grieving takes the form of postmodern exhaustion, with its wasting diet of an anxious, ever-shifting relativism, and that attachment to surface that fears connecting with the fact of staggering loss. The fatal emptiness of ironized consumerism is marked by loss of energy, difficulty in concentrating, feelings of apathy, social withdrawal: precisely those enumerated in the psychological literature of mourning.

The falsity of postmodernism consists in its denial of loss, the refusal to mourn. Devoid of hope or vision for the future, the reigning zeitgeist also cuts off, very explicitly, an understanding of what has happened and why. There is a ban on thinking about origins, which is companion to an insistence on the superficial, the fleeting, the ungrounded.

Parallels between individual grief and a desolate, grieving common sphere are often striking. Consider the following from therapist Kenneth Doka (1989): "Disenfranchised grief can be defined as the grief that persons experience when they incur a loss that is not or cannot be openly acknowledged, publicly mourned, or socially supported." Denial on an individual level provides an inescapable metaphor for denial at large; personal denial, so often thoroughly understandable, introduces the question of refusal to come to grips with the crisis occurring at every level.

Ushering in the millennium are voices whose trademark is opposition to narrative itself, escape from any kind of closure. The modernist project at least made room for the apocalyptic; now we are expected to hover forever—as if much of even survival seems likely—in a world of surfaces and simulation that ensure the "erasure" of the real world and the dispersal of both the self and the social. Baudrillard is of course emblematic of the "end of the end," based on his prefigured "extermination of meaning."

We may turn again to the psychological literature for apt descriptive points. Deutsch (1937) examined the absence of expressions of grief that occur following some bereavements and considered this a defensive attempt of the ego to preserve itself in the face of overwhelming anxiety. Fenichel (1945) observed that grief is at first experienced only in very small doses; if it were released full-strength, the subject would feel overwhelming despair. Similarly, Grimspoon (1964) noted that "people cannot risk being overwhelmed by the anxiety which might accompany a full cognitive and affective grasp of the present world situation and its implications for the future."

With these counsels and cautions in mind, it is nonetheless obvious that loss must be faced. All the more so in the realm of social existence, where in distinction to, say, the death of a loved one, a crisis of monumental proportions might be turned toward a transformative solution, if no longer denied.

Repression, most clearly and presently practiced via postmodern fragmentation and superficiality, does not extinguish the problem. "The repressed," according to Bollas (1995) "signifies the preserved: hidden away in the organized tensions of the unconscious, wishes and their memories are ceaselessly struggling to find some way into gratification in the present—desire refuses annihilation."

Grief is the thwarting and deadening of desire and very much resembles depression; in fact, many depressions are precipitated by losses (Klerman, 1981). Both grief and depression may have anger at their root; consider, for example, the cultural association of black with grief and mourning and with anger, as in "black rage."

Traditionally, grief has been seen as giving rise to cancer. A contemporary variation of this thesis is Norman Mailer's notion that cancer is the unhealthiness of a deranged society, turned inward, bridging the personal and public spheres. Again, a likely connection among grief, depression, and anger, and testimony, I think, to massive repression. Signs abound concerning weakening immune defenses; along with increasing material toxins, there seems to be an rising level of grief and its concomitants. When meaning and desire are too painful, too unpromising to admit or pursue, the accumulating results only add to the catastrophe now unfolding.

To look at narcissism, today's bellwether profile of character, is to see suffering as an ensemble of more and more closely related aspects. Lasch (1979) wrote of such characteristic traits of the narcissistic personality as an inability to feel, protective shallowness, increased repressed hostility, and a sense of unreality and emptiness. Thus narcissism, too, could be subsumed under the heading of grief, and the larger suggestion arises with perhaps greater force: there is something profoundly wrong, something at the heart of all this sorrow, however much it is commonly labeled under various separate categories.

In a 1917 exploration, "Mourning and Melancholia," a puzzled Freud asked why the memory of "each single one of the memories and hopes" that is connected to the lost loved one "should be so extraordinarily painful." But tears of grief, it is said, are at base tears for oneself. The intense sorrow at a personal loss, tragic and difficult as it most certainly is, may be in some way also a vulnerability to sorrow over a more general, almost trans-species loss.

Walter Benjamin wrote his "Theses on History" a few months before his premature death in 1940 at a sealed frontier that prevented escape from the Nazis. Breaking the constraints of Marxism and literariness, Benjamin achieved a high point of critical thinking. He saw the angel of history blown by a gale out of Paradise. He saw that civilization, from its origin, is that storm evacuating Eden, saw that progress is a single, ongoing catastrophe.

Alienation and anguish were once largely, if not entirely, unknown. Today the rate of serious depression, for example, doubles roughly every ten years in the developed nations (Wright, 1995).

As Peter Homans (1984) put it very ably, "Mourning does not destroy the past—it reopens relations with it and with the communities of the past." Authentic grieving poses the opportunity to understand what has been lost and why, also to demand the recovery of an innocent state of being, wherein needless loss is banished.

1995

In Memoriam

Memory is a basic human faculty that, despite its vagaries and problematics, we pretty much take for granted. Memory is so much always at hand, so basic to our ability to grasp reality, that it might seem impossible to accurately understand. Stephen Braude (1992), for instance, concluded that it is "plausible to regard memory as a phenomenon that is literally unanalyzable."

But what of the "anthropology" of memory? In a formulation that Adorno and Horkheimer (1947) perhaps did not take far enough, "every reification is a forgetting," and reification, the conversion of the living and autonomous into things, into objects, is the foundation of civilization. Domestication is its pronounced realization. How much, then, has memory been defined or deformed by domestication, by a world in which the very structure of experience has been essentially altered? And if reification is a forgetting, it follows that the demystification and dissolution of reification must involve a remembering. According to phenomenologist Edward Casey (1987), "We have forgotten what memory is, and can mean; and we make matters worse by repressing the fact of our own oblivion."

Memory is socially and culturally constructed. Every model of memory is thus culturally specific, and, as Melion and Küchler (1991) point out, the pursuit of memory promotes and maintains cultural formation itself. Politico-cultural practices, in dialectical interplay, influence the shape of memory. Arthur G. Miller (1991), for example, studied the ways in which "pre-Hispanic calendrics and territorial management strategies fashioned memory as a process of selective remembering and forgetting, governing patterns of labor and loyalty."

Russell provided a rather famous philosophical argument to the effect that, for all we know, the world might have sprung into existence five minutes ago complete with our "memories" of childhood, etc. We unconsciously strive to not be a part of memory that alienation has forged, knowing that Russell's questioning does nothing to lessen the force of that memory. History has been cynically referred to as the science of forgetting, perhaps because what it remembers is inadequate to an understanding of our sadness, our incompleteness. As the poet Carnevali (1967) said, "memories weep or mourn, all memories do."

The origins of our condition and its long, painful passage must be re-collected if memory is to claim its own memory. In *The Phenomenology of Mind* Hegel claimed that memory "forms the passage from representation to thought." But since representation and thought are themselves non-neutral, this formulation does little to uncover the roots of what has been so deeply obscured.

Three hundred years ago, Robert Fludd saw memory as reflected in the organization of the external world. He saw its contours represented by those of some Renaissance technologies, especially theaters. Today acquisition, storage, and retrieval of memory data is the dominant model, obviously based on memory as a computer. Now we experience an increasingly programmed and impoverished collective experience, one of whose primary effects is an imposed cultural memory that legitimates dominated life. And the very defining of memory is inseparable from the texture and organization of social existence. Its embeddedness in the prevailing state of division of labor is a key aspect of its variability and limitations.

What can we say of memory in its current condition, and its connections to other cultural dimensions? In terms of time it presents features that may seem contrary to our unexamined associations. For example, as Brain (1966) observed, our sensation of time is not furnished by memory. Having memories "is not," in this regard, "enough, for having a memory is a present state." If time is the enemy of life

lived in the here-and-now, memory cannot be seen as its ally. Like
dreams, memory takes place outside of time. Or as Friedman (1990)
understated it, "time is relatively insignificant information in the
natural functioning of memory."

But in a life-world so divided and alienated, we seem to exist in
time itself. All of our assumptions and preconceptions proceed from
that basis, with the shape and force of time a pretty exact measure of
the division and alienation of that existence. Very much to the point is
how closely our notions of memory are tied to linear conceptions of
time, as Frances Yates brought out in *The Art of Memory* (1966).

Language also has a deep impact on memory. With language
comes the turn toward mastery, as in naming. Spengler (1922) noted
that memory is "the capacity of storing for the understanding by
means of the name, the named." The trajectory of domination is
etched in memory as it is everywhere else. Arthur J. Miller (1991)
wrote of ancient sacred knowledge rendered into text: "When memory
became scripture, the past was cast as linear narrative, delimiting the
future within the scope of previous events."

Mnemosyne, or memory, was celebrated by the Greeks as the
mother of the muses, but the conversion of myth into written language
extends a debilitation begun by language itself. Kuberski (1992) goes so
far as to say, "this is the last stop of memory, when it becomes a text."

Language takes on a life of its own, ending up in our current postmodern condition in which, it is often averred, there is nothing left
but language. Words reduce and deform the experiences they symbolize; there is no language that would represent memory without such
modification. Memories are resistant to being translated into words.
Referring to the clinical setting, Donald Spence (1982) observed a
"perennial conflict facing the patient between what is true and what is
describable."

Almost three hundred years ago, Vico counted imagination as one
of memory's three aspects. Gaston Bachelard (1964) provides contemporary reflection on the relationship of memory and imagination, a
connection whose vitality should not be devalued. Meanwhile, Baudrillard repeatedly assures us that we can no longer imagine a different
world. To remember and to see a better future are related faculties,
their atrophy a mutual condition.

Memory is not a matter of objects brought to consciousness but is a part of the dynamics of consciousness (Rosenfield 1992). Wittgenstein rejected the Lockean view of memory as a storehouse; Proust virtually equated memory and perception in his notion of "involuntary" memory. Of course, it can also be a form of conditioning, depending upon the social environment and method (or lack thereof).

For Freud, memory occupied the entire psyche. But, he observed, remembrance is made difficult due to repression of dangerous childhood wishes and feelings. The Freudian thesis posits early sexuality as the seat of all such charged emotional memories, though it can be read in a wider sense. Enid Balint (1993) described a repression of memories more basic than those of a sexual nature, involving reactions against the nature of a young child's reality. Experiencing an incoherent world, the infant fails to establish an acceptable view of it. "If the baby cannot build up such a world, it may be because he cannot bear the dissimilarities he perceives (or the way he is perceived), so his perceptions are disavowed. . . .these disavowals may lead to complete loss of memory of the whole world in which unacceptable perceptions were made." The implications regarding memory and critique are obvious.

The original fragmentation and separation of humanity by the reifying force of domestication has produced the idea that the psyche consists of different parts functioning independently of each other and thus legitimately considered independently. Neurology has been unable to determine where and how memories exist in our brains; in fact, unlike computers, they seem to have "no space at all allotted solely to memory" (Herbert 1993).

The misguided effort of science to "pin down" memory—or consciousness in general—recalls Freud's rather contrary position in this area. One of his most eccentric and generally ignored beliefs (1915) was that the individual's memory reproduces an inherited recollection of the entire human species. Jim Culbertson (1963, 1976, 1982) has argued that consciousness, including memory, permeates all of nature and is present even in its smallest parts. In an eccentricity that seems to parallel Freud's, Culbertson claims that remembrance is not a representation of that which is irretrievably past, but a partial re-experiencing of the event itself. Recall involves a "clear-loop link" to the actual moment in spacetime where the event is still eternally present. Fellow physicist Nick Herbert (1993) presents a similar, if slightly more conventional, view of mind as pervasive and deeply embedded in nature. But again, the meaning of memory is best fathomed in context, as another site of struggle with domination. The ruling order seeks to enlist memory as an ally in its never-ceasing will to legitimation. It must serve as a mechanism of subjection, a means of sustaining hegemony. For our part, we have striven, since the advent of civilization, to resist this colonization, this shaping of memory's influence against us. Inherently contestatory, memory must battle, for its integrity, the deodorizing effects of nostalgia and the numbing of its vitality by routine.

Early on in the modern era Edmund Burke recognized the danger to the established order represented by a clear recollection of changes in society. Against such subversive memories he found custom to be an obscuring factor, a potent contribution to authority.

From the beginning of the nineteenth century, roughly speaking, an industrializing West decisively broke up old patterns of life and struggled for complete control. Industrial capitalism depends upon mastery of both public and private realms for its stability, and its proponents rather quickly discovered the "inadequacy of available memory mechanisms" (Terdiman 1993) for the totalizing needs of capital. The basic dynamics of modern capital, however, provided the core answer to this challenge.

Exchange is as old as division of labor. Goods move and become different as they circulate; memories are displaced and altered over time via increasingly complex exchange relationships. Proceeding inseparably, embedded in each other, technology and class society produce commodities that are more and more reified and autonomous. Borrowing from Marx and Lukacs, Richard Terdiman's attention to the "memory crisis" of the 19th century (1993) included reference to what he called "the frozen and forgotten history of the object."

Once again, origins are of central importance in understanding our present extremity. The development of the commodity mirrors the trajectory of alienation itself, its beginnings always more clouded. Bordieu (1977) called this suppression a "genesis amnesia." As with time, technology, and other basics, the memory of the production of a world of commodities is veiled from its consumers. The enigma of the commodity is thus a memory disorder, one that becomes suppressed, less troubling as the myth of progress grows by consumption.

Refusing the deflection of consciousness that progress is constantly issuing, Herbert Marcuse looked rather in the opposite direction. He was struck by the question of how past human suffering can be redeemed. "To forget," he reasoned (1955), is "the mental faculty which sustains submissiveness and renunciation. . . . Against this surrender to time, the restoration of remembrance to its rights, as a vehicle of liberation, is one of the noblest tasks of thought." It was in this vein that the Hungarian writer Gyorgy Konrad referred (1992) to Eastern European dissidents as almost alone upholding remembrance; the others must eliminate what they failed to do: "Most people have an interest in losing memory."

Heidegger stressed the point that the past is irrecoverably absent, while his student, Marcuse, saw that it is memory's ability to reverse the flow of time that makes it a utopian faculty. The repressed "remains unaltered by the passage of time" (Freud 1933) as personally painful or traumatic episodes are sealed from one's awareness. But Marcuse was alert to a similar repression of pleasurable activities enacted and enforced by the needs of a pervasively confining and immiserating society. "Forgetting past suffering and past joy alleviates life under a repressive reality principle. In contrast, remembrance spurs the drive for the conquest of suffering and the permanence of joy" (1978).

Today the utopian hopes of Marcuse are definitely out of fashion. Our postmodern era is one of cynicism and even despair, embodying, as Frederic Jameson put it (1984), the "cultural logic of late capitalism." Human yearnings are eclipsed by the cold strata of images and hypertechnology; surface sensation, gadget titillation, jaded disinterest: increasingly a landscape of cyborgs programmed by amnesia. Jameson's "Postmodernism and Consumer Society" (1982) concluded that "Our entire contemporary social system has little by little begun to lose its capacity to retain its own past."

Jean-François Lyotard is a central postmodern thinker; characteristically, there is no component of remembrance in his approach. The overall picture of defeat, in fact, finds Lyotard denouncing memory for its use-value to the system: like everything else, capital pulls memory into its orbit and appropriates its functions (1973, 1989). Memory is explicitly condemned as a moment of theory, moreover, theory being a foolish struggle against forgetfulness, as Christa Bürger aptly noted (1991).

Memory has not been plumbed deeply enough as indispensable ally to theory. Adorno warned against a theory of origins and even Marcuse failed to reach back far enough. Meanwhile, the all but enveloping postmodern zeitgeist is equally opposed to remembering as to critical social theory.

The unthinking acceptance, indeed, "virtual worship of technology" (Lash and Friedman, 1991) is an important PM trait that is closely related to its deficiencies regarding memory and theory. When technology is treated as a given (or worse, as a favorable "natural" development), we find that human, historical memory becomes supplanted by technology's memory. An inevitable, unconscious contingency that is far more trusted and relied upon than the kind it overrides, and with an undeniable ideological force.

If the hidden or unexamined—the forgotten—exerts a domination over us, the point of recollecting the past is to understand the force of its implicit truth-claim upon the present. The cumulative weight of the past "weighs like a nightmare" on the minds of the living, wrote Marx. To flee the past, so much of it—yes—but to know how and why means, in large part, memory. Marx's contemporary, Melville, expressed a dissent from the amnesia that was already gathering a century and a half ago, in the wreck of the Pequod in *Moby Dick*. Ahab's final order to the crew, to "sink all coffins and all hearses to one common pool!", stands for an evacuation of collective memory. But Ishmael, as he clings to the coffin inscribed with "hieroglyphic marks" of exterminated races, disobeys. "And I only am escaped alone to tell thee."

Until modern times the word memory extended across the vast range of the Latin *memor*, "mindful," *mens*, "the mind," and all the words that display the Indo-germanic roots *men-*, *mon-*, *mn-*, words related to thinking, intending, and being conscious or mindful in any way. The sense of memory was so broad as to encompass both death and love, for example. "How paltry the word memory has become since then!", in the judgment of Kroll (1990).

A technological context reduces memory to information retrieval, with a tendency toward enlarged colonization of what is whole, sensual, lived. Virtual Reality is offered to an impoverished spirit; memory implants may not be far off. Nostalgia, the other side of the coin and mirror image of progress, appeals to the feeling that the past offered pleasures no longer attainable. As Proust put it, the only paradises are those we have lost.

If we can see that art, and culture itself, are symptoms of human fragmentation, why is it impermissible to consider re-establishing the unity which has been lost? Referring to the ideal of living wholly in the present moment, futurologist John Holmdahl once playfully proposed an "Amnesia Foundation" toward that end. But to get there, we need not the suppression of memory, but its realization and supersession. Instrumental reason must be jettisoned along the way; perhaps even dialectical thinking, still drawing on memory, can one day be let go of, with new or unrecognizable senses and abilities coming into play in lieu of so many layers of atrophy and deformation.

1994

WHY I HATE STAR TREK

The reigning cultural mythos, including its pseudo-oppositional currents, is agreed on one thing: *Star Trek* is good for you. The vast popu-
larity of this impossibly weak, artificial, repressive series (actually there
were three series, over the past 25 years or so) is a puzzling and sad
symptom of an absence of both vitality and reflection. Of the many
stupid but popular aspects of culture, few have such a range of fans,
such a range of possibilities for extending a little the wave-lengths of
control.

One could cite the translation of the original *Star Trek* series into
no less than 49 languages, the seemingly insatiable appetite for even
the most obscure Trek trivia on the part of a large subculture, and the
burgeoning quantity of books, movies, conventions, etc. that constitute a sizeable industry. But *Star Trek* got my attention in a more personal way. A friend had a breakdown and discovered, on his locked
psychiatric ward, that *Star Trek* was prescribed viewing. At about the
same time I became aware that it is apparently also mandatory in the
home of neighbors of mine, a hippie/"alternative lifestyle" family that
is otherwise pretty anti-TV.

Even quite a few "anarchists" are, of their own volition, very big
Trek fans. Which brings to mind one of its most repulsive features, its
predication on a strict, martial hierarchy. ("Isn't that right, Number

One?") The order-giving/ order-taking military framework is always present and constitutes the model of social reality, for the crew is never seen in a different context. The evolution of the program during its three incarnations is also worth noting, for subtle shifts in this authoritarian model.

Captain Kirk, the original supreme leader, was a bit of a cowboy, even a maverick in some very slight ways. But Captain Riker, in series #2, "The Next Generation," is very much the corporate boss, totally inseparable from his role as absolute authority. And in a significant sense, even the dynamics or movement of the whole operation comes to an end over time. "Deep Space Nine," the third and final series, dispensed with the *Enterprise* (so very aptly named for a deeply entrepreneurially-spirited orientation) and takes place on a stationary space platform. No more trek; corresponding perfectly to a world where, since the collapse of bureaucratic state capitalism beginning in the late 1980s, modern capital now dominates everything, everywhere.

What *Star Trek* conveys about technology is probably its most insidious contribution to domination. Not only is a structure of hierarchical orders a constant; so is the high-tech, anti-nature foundation of the drama as a whole. Always at home in a sterile container in which they represent society, the crew could not be more cut off from the natural world. In fact, as the highest development in the mastery and manipulation of nature, *Star Trek* is really saying that nature no longer exists.

The android/computer Data, successor to Spock, is the central figure in an episode that illustrates perfectly the elevation of the machine. Data continually "experiences" disturbances that are initially thought to be a sort of electrical malfunctioning in "his" circuitry. Slowly the idea is introduced that "he" is actually having dreams. Much warm and fuzzy emotion envelopes this supposedly marvelous development, this triumph of consciousness. Never mind that the message is more hideous than uplifting. What we are seeing, by imputing human feelings to technology, is a celebration of the very framework that is debasing inner nature as it destroys outer nature. People behaving more and more like machines while machines become increasingly "human" is a horrible development not limited to *Star Trek*, but certainly applauded and thereby advanced by it.

Considered as an exercise in acting and characterization, *Star Trek* is chillingly true to the reversal that the episode just cited typifies. The glaring thing about it as drama is how lifeless and plastic the characters are. In fact, they are so machine-like and one-dimensional as to be virtually interchangeable. The Irish actor Colm Meany ("Deep Space Nine") has turned in vibrantly alive movie performances; in *Star Trek* he seemed to be in a coma, devoid of life, Irish or otherwise. Maybe it is soothing for some viewers to see so little going on on the part of non-individuals.

And this robot-like quality is, in turn, related to the decidedly anti-sensual spirit of Trek reality. Intensification of technology as a way of life is part of it, as is a sort of moral condemnation of sex. This, too, is a constant, seen in the very texture of the program. The uniforms are one example; they are never dispensed with, and provide a cadet-like image, the stuff of puerile fantasy. This parallels, on a slightly different level, the current fascination in American society with angels, sexless and benignly powerful. Overall, *Star Trek* is as sanitized and boring as Barney or Walt Disney.

An episode of "The Next Generation" featuring Captain Picard and the widow of his best friend exemplifies the anti-sexual theme. While dodging aliens, in a long "action" sequence possessed of less tension than that of a weak "B" western, they learn that they've always been attracted to each other. Neither had expressed such feelings, however, due to her married state, but now they encounter each other unencumbered. It is made perfectly clear that there is no reason whatsoever for them to hold back, yet the tale ends with them bidding a wistful, unconsummated farewell forever to the other. I cannot imagine a script giving a more unqualified no to love: even when there is not a reason in the galaxy to repress oneself, do it anyway. Breathtaking!

Gene Roddenberry (*Star Trek*'s creator, in case there's anyone on earth who doesn't know it) was a police science/pre-law major in his college days. After service in World War II, he joined the Los Angeles Police Department. He next began writing scripts for such television series as *Highway Patrol* and *Dragnet*. Roddenberry's background as a liberal cop seems perfect as guiding light for the TV phenomenon that, it could almost be said, invented Political Correctness.

Women, gays, the disabled, minorities are treated sympathetically on *Star Trek*, a not unusual corporate television gesture. This minimum requirement should not blind us to the slightly less obvious problems of content. Sadly, Ursula LeGuin, considered by many a utopian/anarchist writer, seemed to see little else besides *Star Trek*'s PC rating in her "Appointment with the *Enterprise*: an Appreciation," written for the May 14, 1994 *TV Guide*. She gushed over the late series in the classic superficiality of the liberal, managing to see a marvelous morality play, and ignoring its worship of authority and a monstrous techno-future.

Good riddance to *Star Trek*!

With help from Marty Hichens

1994

PBS, Power, And Postmodernism

The Public Broadcasting System produces "programming" toward a more manageable society. In fact, it is the network rather expressly for managers, and what it airs can best be understood by keeping in mind this service to the managing class. The exact ratio of corporate to government funding of PBS is inconsequential to its basic nature and function.

Typically, it launders the image of oil giants and other corporate uglies via their tax-deductible underwriting of high culture, such as opera. Even more basically, it provides the illusion of an "independent" source of information while enforcing the dominant constraints as to what constitutes the acceptable or reputable in ideas and information.

PBS is "innovative" in one real sense: as a consistent promoter of the latest in high-tech impoverishment. Those who understand the importance of the computerization of life—both Clinton and Gingrich, for instance—realize the vital PBS contribution in this area. Its completely neutered "environmentalism" never hints at questioning the hierarchical organization of social existence which daily generates the global eco-crisis. This "green" veneer serves, in practice, as perfect accompaniment to the real goal, namely, the highest "creative" productivity of capital.

PBS projects a superior code of diversity, tolerance and fairness, under which the essentials of modern, bereft, commodified life continue unaffected. This pretense of a calm, confident, rational social world is in stark contrast to the actual horrors and dislocations, psychic and public, of a stricken society. Stately British dramas like "Masterpiece Theater" further this soothing overall tone of ruling class control. Small wonder that PBS sponsors are so often management services, computer firms, corporate lawyers and others whose explicit function is the running of society in important capacities.

All this is fairly transparent and hardly new. More recent is what seems to be a growing connection between PBS and the prevailing culture of postmodernism. A self-promotion spot highlights this nascent marriage between the managerial hegemony PBS aspires to and the reigning cultural hegemony of postmodernism. The text of the promo encompasses virtually every important facet of the new PM creed, and it is easy to see how it serves explicit control aims. PBS celebrates itself—and the divided society it serves—in the same oath of allegiance:

America's Storyteller

Welcome to a place that is always just
beginning, that rouses itself day to day
and year to year to admire what it's
made, starting with nothing, then
rushes to invent itself all over again.

Ordinary people, doing extraordinary
things; knowing what goes on now goes
on to shape tomorrow.

Welcome to the land that is never
exactly what you think it is and will
never stay that way for long.

There are a million stories in the
streets of the cities we never finish
building. We intend to tell them all.

The postmodern "death of the subject" announces the end of the individual, dissolved in language. After the likes of Heidegger and Lacan, it is language itself that does the talking, which parallels the real: capital has swallowed up the human actor. And so our text begins; it is "the place" which is the subject, not its inhabitants.

This place is "always just beginning." A remarkably bald way of expressing the postmodern refusal of history and of origins. History, after all, is just so many arbitrary fictions; pick one—or, more characteristically, don't even bother—they are equally valid/invalid. As for origins, well, that's a bigger fool's errand yet. There are no origins; things have always been this way. Everything before this (media) moment is erased. This place is "always just beginning."

And that is so admirable! This place "rouses itself"—in order "to admire what it's made." This is the narcissism of a putrescent society in love with itself, able to focus so admiringly with the invaluable aid of know-nothing postmodernism. What it's made of is never made clear. To enumerate the specifics of this empty place, in all their terrifying emptiness, might tend to ground the flight of this paean of admiration.

"Starting with nothing"—another reason to admire the achievements of our "place." Here, too, is the embrace of an almost total ignorance. Self-chosen ignorance at that, which is so important to the fact of "postmodern culture" as oxymoron. "Starting with nothing." Never mind the unsuspecting peoples who had to be systematically sacrificed to enable the admirable wonders of today. Never mind the wondrous part of this planet that existed, naturally and freely, somehow prior to the glories erected by this "place." "Starting with nothing." No blood on anyone's hands.

Skipping over the innocuous second stanza, "Welcome to the land that is never exactly what you think it is." Here is another cardinal postmodern tenet: the pointlessness of analysis. Meaning is an illusion, or, as the PM deconstructionists say, "all interpretation is misinterpretation." In practice, the corollary is, let the experts run things; their rule and technology are inevitable and unfathomable, anyway. The Information Society, the dream of managers and their PBS, "is never exactly what you think it is." You are incapable, by definition, of understanding your subjugation to power. So sit back, tube out, and we'll perfect it.

This land also "will never stay that way [the way you mistakenly thought it was] for long." More classic postmodernism: ever-shifting signification, undecidability. Of course it is fine that the situation is both opaque and fluid: this guarantees your perpetual ignorance and slavery.

"The streets of the cities we never finish building." Capital and its high-tech embodiment dwarf you, and never rest. This "place" goes on forever. The contribution of postmodernism to PBS is inestimable, as this piece of pure PM makes utterly clear.

1995

Who Is Chomsky?

Noam Chomsky is probably the most well-known American anarchist, somewhat curious given the fact that he is a liberal-leftist politically and downright reactionary in his academic specialty of linguistic theory. Chomsky is also, by all accounts, a generous, sincere, tireless activist, which does not, unfortunately, confer his thinking with liberatory value.

Reading through his many books and interviews, one looks in vain for the anarchist or any thorough critique. When asked point-blank, "Are governments inherently bad?" his reply (28 January 1988) is no. He is critical of government policies, not government itself, motivated by his "duty as a citizen." The constant refrain in his work is a plea for democracy: "real democracy," "real participation," "active involvement," and the like.

His goal is for "a significant degree of democratization," not the replacement of political rule, albeit democratic rule, by a condition of no rule called anarchy. Hardly surprising, then, that his personal practice consists of reformist, issues-oriented efforts like symbolic tax resistance and ACLU membership. Instead of a critique of capital, its forms, dynamics, etc., Chomsky calls (1992) for "social control over investment. That's a social revolution." What a ridiculous assertion.

His focus, almost exclusively, has been on U.S. foreign policy, a narrowness that would exert a conservative influence even for a radical thinker. If urging increased involvement in politics goes against the potentially subversive tide toward less and less involvement, Chomsky's emphasis on statecraft in itself gravitates toward acceptance of states. And completely ignoring key areas (such as nature and women, to mention only two), makes him less relevant still.

In terms of inter-governmental relations, the specifics are likewise disappointing. A principal interest here is the Middle East, and we see anything but an anarchist or anti-authoritarian analysis. He has consistently argued (in books like *The Fateful Triangle*, 1983) for a two-state solution to the Palestinian question. A characteristic formulation: "Israel within its internationally recognized borders would be accorded the rights of any state in the international system, no more, no less." Such positions fit right into the electoral racket and all it legitimizes. Along these lines, he singled out (*Voices of Dissent*, 1992) the centrist Salvadoran politician Ruben Zamora when asked whom he most admired.

Chomsky has long complained that the present system and its lap-dog media have done their best, despite his many books in print, to marginalize and suppress his perspective. More than a little ironic, then, that he has done his best to contribute to the much greater marginalization of the anarchist perspective. He has figured in countless ads and testimonials for the likes of *The Nation, In These Times*, and *Z Magazine*, but has never even mentioned *Anarchy, Fifth Estate*, or other anti-authoritarian publications. Uncritically championing the liberal-left media while totally ignoring our own media can hardly be an accident or an oversight. In fact, I exchanged a couple of letters with him in 1982 over this very point (copies available from me). He gave a rather non-sequitur, pro-left response and has gone right on keeping his public back turned against any anarchy point of view.

Chomsky's newest book of interviews, *Class Warfare*, is promoted in the liberal-left media as "accessible new thinking on the Republican Revolution." It supposedly provides the answers to such questions as "Why, as a supporter of anarchist ideals, he is in favor of strengthening the federal government." The real answer, painfully obvious, is that he is not an anarchist at all.

Long a professor of linguistics at Massachusetts Institute of Technology, he achieved fame and fortune for his conceptions of the nature of language. Professor Chomsky sees language as a fixed, innate part of some "essential human nature" (Barsamian 1992). Language develops along an intrinsically determined path, very much like a physical organ. In this sense, Chomsky says language "simply arose" (1988) and that we should study it as "we study any problem in biology" (1978). In other words, language, that most fundamental part of culture, has no real relationship with culture and is a matter of instinct-driven formation through biological specialization.

Here, as everywhere else, Chomsky cannot even seem to imagine any problematics about origins of alienation or fundamental probings about what symbolic culture really is, at base. Language for Chomsky is a strictly natural phenomenon, quite unrelated to the genesis of human culture or social development. A severely backward, non-radical perspective, not unrelated to his unwillingness—this "anarchist" of ours— to put much else into question, outside of a very narrow political focus.

The summer 1991 issue of *Anarchy* magazine included "A Brief Interview with Noam Chomsky on Anarchy, Civilization, & Technology." Not surprisingly, it was a rather strange affair, given the professor's general antipathy to all three topics. The subject of anarchy he ignored altogether, consonant with his avoidance of it throughout the years. Responding to various questions about civilization and technology, he was obviously as uncomfortable as he was completely unprepared to give any informed responses. Dismissive of new lines of thought that critically re-examine the nature of civilization, Chomsky was obviously ignorant of this growing literature and its influence in the anti-authoritarian milieu.

Concerning technology, he was, reluctantly, more expansive, but just as in the dark as with the question of civilization. His responses repeated all the discredited, unexamined pro-tech clichés, now less and less credible among anarchists: technology as a mere tool, a "quite neutral" phenomenon to be seen only in terms of specific, similarly unexamined uses. Chomsky actually declares that cars are fine; it's only corporate executives that are the problem. Likewise with robotics, as if that drops from heaven and has no grounding in domination of nature, division of labor, etc., etc. In closing, he proclaimed that "the only thing that can possibly resolve environmental problems is advanced technology." Yes: more of the soul-destroying, eco-destroying malignancy that has created the current nightmare!

In the fall of 1995 Chomsky donated much of the proceeds from a well-attended speech on U.S. foreign policy to Portland's Freedom and Mutual Aid center, better known as the local anarchist info-shop. As if to honor its generous benefactor appropriately, the info-shop spent the money first of all on a computer system, and several months later financed a booklet promoting the info-shop and the ideas behind it. Among the most prominent quotes adorning the pamphlet is one that begins, "The task for a modern industrial society is to achieve what is now technically realizable." The attentive reader may not need me to name the author of these words, nor to point out this less than qualitatively radical influence. For those of us who see our task as aiding in the utter abolition of our "modern industrial society," it is repellent in the extreme to find its realization abjectly celebrated.

In issues of *The Progressive* and *Z Magazine* during 1996 and 1997, Chomsky has actually argued that no one should support a "devolution" of Big Brother authority—a movement of power from the federal government to state and local levels. This bankrupt and disgraceful "anarchist" (!) angle has been enough to create a furor among even some of the utterly reformist partisans of those tepid mags.

Most of the above mainly belongs to the well-known, dreary, superficial field of waning leftism, but more pernicious is its apparent influence on those supposedly committed to the goal of anarchy.

Black & Red's latest (1997) offering is a reprint of Chomsky's *Objectivity* and *Liberal Scholarship*, which discusses the shockingly novel and radical thesis that liberals have been known to conceal/distort historical truth. The re-publication ot this piece of memorabilia was assisted (and introduced) by individuals of *Fifth Estate*, which is itself in decline by the measure of its growing leftist component. *FE* was once a vibrant, cutting-edge project. Now its milieu in Detroit can find nothing better than a thirty-year-old, already-published relic to give expression to its meager resources.

Chomsky, like Bookchin, represents the failed inadequate critique of the past, resolutely unwilling or unable to confront the enveloping crisis on all levels. It is past time to go forward and engage the real depths of the disaster facing all of us.

1997

"Hakim Bey," Postmodern "Anarchist"

I've been getting increasingly annoyed by the word-salad posturing of Bey and find "Primitives & Extropians" one of the weaker offerings yet from this postmodern liberal. I will confine myself to some of the stand-out dopiness from what is shot through with inaccuracies, evasions, pontificating, ego-stroking, and shallowness.

On the level of content "P's & E's" is little short of absurd. He pitches his piece, most basically, as a comparison of two viewpoints, "two anarchist tendencies." But how even the most air-headed could make the extreme techno-fascist imperialism of extropy into an "anarchist" tendency is quite beyond me. In fact, it worships every hideous high-tech manifestation of the total mastery of nature and the obliteration of every trace of the sensual, autonomous individual. To quote from one of its priests, Carnegie-Mellon's Hans Moravec, "The final frontier will be urbanized, ultimately into an arena where every bit of activity is a meaningful computation: the inhabited portion of the universe will be transformed into a cyberspace . . . We might then be tempted to replace some of our innermost mental processes with more cyberspace-appropriate programs purchased from Artificial Intelligence, and so, bit by bit, transform ourselves into something much like them. Ultimately our thinking procedures could be totally liberated from any traces of our original body, indeed of any body."

(*Extropy*, #10, 1993). To term something so viciously evil "anarchist" suggests stupidity compounded by bad faith.

Bey's method is as appalling as his claims to truthfulness, and essentially conforms to textbook postmodernism. Aestheticism plus knownothingism is the PM formula; cynical as to the possibility of meaning, allergic to analysis, hooked on trendy word-play, "Primitivists & Extropians" displays these features exquisitely.

A point of view that tries to be a consistent, well-researched, tentative exploration is deemed absolutist, rigid, aggressive, the product of a "presumptive vanguard of the pure." Bey, however, is inconsistent, messy, open, impure, non-exclusive, etc. He elevates diversity, the multiplicity of situations, the refusal of the world to conform to simple formulations. What is galling is how stark and even nightmarish our situation really is, hip verbiage aside. Frederic Jameson put it ably in his *Seeds of Time* (1994): "How is it possible for the most standardized and uniform social reality in history, by the merest ideological flick of the thumbnail . . . to reemerge as the rich oil-smear sheen of absolute diversity and of the unimaginable and unclassifiable forms of human freedom?"

Bey completely buys into the PM illusion that society is too "complex" to yield to any profound indictment. A further unveiling of our trendy author reveals a liberal, whose "utopian" future might well include, he discloses, "wrangling about 'acceptable emission standards' or forest preservation." Further, "the human (animal/animate) scaling of economy and technology—this, however untidy, I would call utopia." How basically reformist! It is little wonder that Bey opens this whole mess of an article by declaring that "the anarcho-primitivists have backed themselves into a situation where they can never be satisfied without the total dissolution of the totality."

A liberal like Bey has really no quarrel with the totality, whereas I foolishly have thought that the threshold definition of a radical, of one who yearns for a qualitative break with the whole deranged setup, is precisely dissatisfaction with the totality.

More than half of this pathetic exercise is Bey peddling his patented Temporary Autonomous Zone prescription. The TAZ "seems to be the only manifestation of the possibility of radical conviviality," is bigger than "mere ideas," is able to "reconcile the wilderness and

cyberspace . . . in fact, has already done so." Reads to me like it is Bey
who advances his candidacy for Absolute Rightness, not those who
seek, in an anti-ideological and visionary spirit, to learn from our
origins and identify the basics, in reality, of our deep imprisonment.
Liberatory analysis and practice have, I would say, far better chances
for success from clear thinking and unlimited desire than from stylistic
mantras about the glories of inconsistency and hip-sounding, three-
word solutions in capital letters.

1996

CITY OF LIGHT

Pigs will be pigs. You've got to wonder about anyone who'd choose to be one. Just as you have to wonder how many people chose/choose not to know that Rodney King beatings happen every day.

But the 1992 insurrection in L.A. was not fundamentally about the latest high-profile police atrocity, nor was it mainly a matter of race relations. Of course, the media worked overtime to argue otherwise, endlessly showing a white trucker being beaten by blacks, in order to equate him with Rodney King and trivialize the whole matter. Pushing most of the story out of the way, this tactic says, one "brutal and senseless" act cancels the other and things are not really that bad, except for such behavior. As if excesses committed by a population enraged beyond measure are the same as a calculated, vicious act by those who are not. More importantly, what is truly "brutal and sense-less" is remaining passive about systematic degradation and not rising up wrathfully.

The media "coverage" was simply outrageous. Almost none of it hesitated to openly take sides against the slave revolt and array every kind of oppositional thinking against it. An outbreak that cost some 60 lives, burned and looted 5,000 businesses to the tune of $1 billion, and required 8,500 troops and countless cops from all over Southern California to contain, was attributed to a few "hoodlums and opportunists"—an incredible lie in itself. All media attention seemed to turn to politicians and church leaders—for their help in denouncing the events unfolding, those cops who speak for the very few. The media behavior only reminds one that its job is always to advertise the culture defined by the commodity and its rules (viz. work).

On May 1st a group of German anarchists in Berlin unfurled a banner declaring their solidarity with the people of Los Angeles and attacked a nearby group of neo-Nazis. In a radio interview May 6th, permitted safely after the fact, sociologist Harry Edwards pointed out that what happened "was not a black vs. white thing. Everyone was out in the streets, old and young and every color." He also made it clear that people with jobs took part, including employees who destroyed their employers' businesses. So much for the vain hope of capital that investment in new businesses will create social peace.

The rioting was not confined to the ghetto. In L.A., it spread to downtown, Westwood, mid-Wilshire and Hollywood, as desert-camouflaged armor guarded shopping malls for nearly 50 miles in every direction. The violence could not be isolated in South Central Los Angeles any more than the depth of alienation can that exists all across this rotting culture. The decline of voting to depths that challenge the very legitimacy of a phoney representation is one excellent example.

Those who wish to remain slaves as every authentic aspect of society, and nature along with it, are looted every day still summon up their defenses of slavery. Others, everywhere, who will not suppress their anger, their passion to live, find an inspiration in the explosion of those whose pride and dignity could not be suppressed. As Marc Fumaroli put it earlier this year, "the new generation is now discovering that the state of being a consumer, and above all a 'cultural' consumer, is the most humiliating and deceptive of all."

1992

WE ALL LIVE IN WACO

The quest for authenticity and community, completely denied and rendered desperate, finds its home in Jonestown and Waco. The sense of truly being alive and of belonging has almost nowhere to go in the society whose two fastest growing classes are the homeless and prisoners. Daily existence is increasingly that of despair, depression, and derangement, punctuated by news of the latest serial murder spree or global eco-disaster, consumed as horrible entertainments in the emptiness.

Debord expressed the situation accurately: "It should be known that servitude henceforth truly wants to be loved for itself, and no longer because it would bring some extrinsic advantage. Previously, it could pass for a protection; but it no longer protects anything." Even the apparatus of oppression concedes virtually the same point: Forbes, organ of finance capital, commemorated its 75th anniversary with a cover-story theme of "Why We Feel so Bad when We Have it so Good." In the Psychological Society at large, in which the only reality is the personal, its hallmark denial and delusion are challenged, almost ironically, by the definitively impoverished realm of the personal. More and more clearly, the choice is between craven servitude or a qualitative break with the entire force-field of alienation.

In a cult everything that an individual has is invested, the only guarantee against the total refusal of that cult. How else, for example, could it be endured that wives and children were offered up to David Koresh and blind submission obtained rather than revolt? Evidently autonomy and self-respect can be freely given over when the world so thoroughly devalues them.

None of us is immune from the horrors, commonplace and spectacular; the immune system itself, in fact, seems to be giving way, and this is not confined to AIDS or TB. The stress of work, according to a March report of the UN's International Labor Organization, is advancing to the point of a "worldwide epidemic." The overall situation is gravely worse than when Nietzsche observed that "most people think that nothing but this wearying reality of ours is possible."

Current reality has become impossible and continues to lose credibility. We must be outsiders, never represented, investing nothing in the death march we are expected to help reproduce. The ultimate pleasure lies in destroying that which is destroying us, in the spirit of the Situationists, who, when asked how they were going to destroy the dominant culture, replied, "In two ways: gradually at first, then suddenly."

1993

Whose Unabomber?

Technogogues and technopaths we have had with us for some time. The Artificial Intelligence pioneer Marvin Minsky, for instance, was well-known in the early 1980s for his description of the human brain as "a three-pound computer made of meat." He was featured in the December 1983 issue of *Psychology Today*, occasioning the following letter:

Marvin Minsky:

With the wholly uncritical treatment—nay, giddy embrace—of high technology, even to such excrescences as machine "emotions" which you develop and promote, *Psychology Today* has at least made it publicly plain what's intended for social life.

Your dehumanizing work is a prime contribution to high tech's accelerating motion toward an ever more artificial, de-individuated, empty landscape.

I believe I am not alone in the opinion that vermin such as you will one day be considered among the worst criminals this century has produced.

In revulsion,
John Zerzan

A dozen years later the number of those actively engaged in the desolation of the soul and the murder of nature has probably risen, but support for the entire framework of such activity has undoubtedly eroded.

Enter Unabomber (he/she/they) with a critique, in acts as well as words, of our sad, perverse, and increasingly bereft technological existence. Unabomber calls for a return to "wild nature" via the "complete and permanent destruction of modern industrial society in every part of the world," and the replacement of that impersonal, unfree, and alienated society by that of small, face-to-face social groupings. He has killed three and wounded 23 in the service of this profoundly radical vision.

There are two obvious objections to this theory and practice. For one thing, a return to undomesticated autonomous ways of living would not be achieved by the removal of industrialism alone. Such removal would still leave domination of nature, subjugation of women, war, religion, the state, and division of labor, to cite some basic social pathologies. It is civilization itself that must be undone to go where Unabomber wants to go. In other words, the wrong turn for humanity was the Agricultural Revolution, much more fundamentally than the Industrial Revolution.

In terms of practice, the mailing of explosive devices intended for the agents who are engineering the present catastrophe is too random. Children, mail carriers, and others could easily be killed. Even if one granted the legitimacy of striking at the high-tech horror show by terrorizing its indispensable architects, collateral harm is not justifiable.

Meanwhile, Unabomber operates in a context of massive psychic immiseration and loss of faith in all of the system's institutions. How many moviegoers, to be more specific, took issue with *Terminator 2* and its equating of science and technology with death and destruction? Keay Davidson's "A Rage Against Science" (*San Francisco Examiner*, April 30, 1995) observed that Unabomber's "avowed hatred of science and technological trends reflects growing popular disillusionment with science."

A noteworthy example of the resonance that his sweeping critique of the modern world enjoys is "The Evolution of Despair" by Robert Wright, cover story of *Time* for August 28, 1995. The long article discusses

Unabomber's indictment soberly and sympathetically, in an effort to plumb "the source of our pervasive sense of discontent."

At the same time, not surprisingly, other commentators have sought to minimize the possible impact of such ideas. "Unabomber Manifesto Not Particularly Unique" is the dismissive summary John Schwartz provided for the questioning of society, as if anything like that goes on in classrooms. Ellul, Juenger and others with a negative view of technology are far from old hat; they are unknown, not a part of accepted, respectable discourse. The cowardice and dishonesty typical of professors and journalists could hardly be more clearly represented.

Also easily predictable has been the antipathy to Unabomber-type ideas from the liberal-left. "Unabummer" was Alexander Cockburn's near-hysterical denunciation in *The Nation*, August 28/September 4, 1995. This pseudo-critic of U.S. capitalism rants about Unabomber's "homicidal political nuttiness," the fruit of an "irrational" American anarchist tradition. Cockburn says that Unabomber represents a "rotted-out romanticism of the individual and nature," that nature is gone forever and we'd better accept its extinction. In reply to this effort to vilify and marginalize both Unabomber and anarchism, Bob Black points out (unpublished letter to the editor) the worldwide resurgence of anarchism and finds Unabomber expressing "the best and the predominant thinking in contemporary North American anarchism, which has mostly gotten over the workerism and productivism which it too often used to share with Marxism."

In spring '95 Earth First! spokesperson Judi Bari labeled Unabomber a "sociopath," going on to declare, definitively but mistakenly, that "there is no one in the radical environmental movement who is calling for violence." This is not the place to adequately discuss the politics of radical environmentalism, but Bari's pontificating sounds like the voice of the many anarcho-liberals who wish to go no further in defense of the wild than tired, ineffective civil disobedience, and who brandish such timid and compromised slogans as "no deforestation without representation."

The summer '95 issue of *Slingshot*, tabloid of politically correct Berkeley militants, contained a brief editorial trashing Unabomber for creating "the real danger of government repression" of the radical milieu. The fear that places blame on Unabomber overlooks the simple fact that any real blows against the Megamachine will invite responses from our enemies. The specter of repression is most effectively banished by doing nothing.

For their part, the "anarchists" of *Love and Rage* (August/September 1995) have also joined the anti-Unabomber leftist chorus. Wayne Price's "Is the Unabomber an Anarchist?" concedes, with Bob Black, that "most anarchists today do not regard the current development of industrial technology as 'progressive' or even 'neutral,' as do Marxists and liberals." But after giving this guarded lip-service to the ascendancy of Unabomber-like ideas, Price virulently decries Unabomber as "a murderer dragging noble ideas through the mud" and withholds even such political and legal support that he would accord authoritarian leftists targeted by the state. *Love and Rage* is defined by a heavy-handed, manipulative organize-the-masses ideology; approaches that are more honest and more radical are either ignored or condemned by these politicians.

But this selective mini-survey of opposition to Unabomber does not by any means exhaust the range of responses. There are other perspectives, which have mainly, for obvious reasons, been expressed only privately. Some of us, for one thing, have found a glint of hope in the public appearance, at last, of a challenge to the fundamentals of a depraved landscape. In distinction to the widespread feeling that everything outside of the self is beyond our control, the monopoly of lies has been broken. It might be said that Unabomber's (media) impact is here today, only to be forgotten tomorrow. But at least a few will have been able to understand and remember. The irony, of course, is that lethal bombings were necessary for an alternative to planetary and individual destruction to be heard.

The concept of justice should not be overlooked in considering the Unabomber phenomenon. In fact, except for his targets, when have the many little Eichmanns who are preparing the Brave New World ever been called to account? Where is any elemental personal responsibility when the planners of our daily and global death march act with complete impunity?

The ruling order rewards such destroyers and tries to polish their image. The May 21, 1995 *New York Times Magazine*'s "Unabomber and David Gelerntner" humanizes the latter, injured by a Unabomber bomb at Yale, as a likable computer visionary preparing a "Renaissance of the human spirit." From no other source than the article itself, however, it is clear that Gelerntner is helping to usher in an authoritarian dystopia based on all the latest high-tech vistas, like genetic engineering.

Is it unethical to try to stop those whose contributions are bringing an unprecedented assault on life? Or is it unethical to just accept our passive roles in the current zeitgeist of postmodern cynicism and know-nothingism? As a friend in California put it recently, when justice is against the law, only outlaws can effect justice.

The lengthy Unabomber manuscript will go undiscussed here; its strengths and weaknesses deserve separate scrutiny. These remarks mainly shed light on some of the various, mostly negative commentary rather than directly on their object. It is often the case that one can most readily learn about society by watching its reactions, across the spectrum, to those who would challenge it.

"Well, I believe in FC/Unabomber—it's all over the country . . . his ideas are, as the situationists said, 'in everyone's heads'; it's just a matter of listening to your own rage," from a Midwesterner in the know. Or as Anne Eisenberg, from Polytechnic University in Brooklyn, admitted, "Scratch most people and you'll get a Luddite."

And from the *Boulder Weekly*, Robert Perkinson's July 6, 1995 column sagely concluded: "Amidst the overwhelming madness of unbridled economic growth and postmodern disintegration, is such nostalgia, or even such rage, really crazy? For many, especially those who scrape by in unfulfilling jobs and peer longingly toward stars obscured by beaming street lights, the answer is probably no. And for them, the Unabomber may not be a psychopathic demon. They may wish FC the best of luck."

1995

Domestication News

Worth noting is a concise article in the March 4, 1993 issue of the British journal Nature. Almost 4,000 years of agriculture in central Mexico yield a dramatic picture to the research efforts of archaeologists O'Hara, Street-Perrot, and Burt. Conclusively debunked is the notion that traditional farming methods were more benign that more modern methods.

Severe soil erosion and other forms of environmental degradation commenced, in fact, with agriculture itself. By the time of the Spanish conquest (1521 A.D.), contrary to widespread belief, Mesoamerica presented anything but a pristine landscape. "Erosion caused by the Spanish introduction of plough agriculture," the authors observe from exhaustive soil samples, "was apparently no more severe than that associated with traditional agricultural methods." As they explain later in the article, "it is hard to distinguish any specific impact of the introduction of plough agriculture and draught animals by the Spanish after A.D. 1521."

The point is plain: domestication is domestication, and embodies a qualitatively negative logic for the natural world. Agriculture per se brings a ruinous, unidirectional impact, despite the wishful thinking of those who envision a coexistence with domestication, consisting of benign, "green" methods that would reverse the global destruction of the land.

The devastation exists on a much more basic level, whose reality must be faced. As the article concludes, "There is a move by many environmental agencies both in Mexico and elsewhere for a return to traditional forms of agriculture, as they are considered to be better for the environment. As our findings indicate that traditional farming techniques cause significant erosion, it is unlikely that a return to prehistoric farming methods would solve the problem of environmental degradation."

1993

WE HAVE TO DISMANTLE ALL THIS

The unprecedented reality of the present is one of enormous sorrow and cynicism, "a great tear in the human heart," as Richard Rodriguez put it. A time of ever-mounting everyday horrors, of which any newspaper is full, accompanies a spreading environmental apocalypse. Alienation and the more literal contaminants compete for the leading role in the deadly dialectic of life in divided, technology-ridden society. Cancer, unknown before civilization, now seems epidemic in a society increasingly barren and literally malignant.

Soon, apparently, everyone will be using drugs; prescription and illegal becoming a relatively unimportant distinction. Attention Deficit Disorder is one example of an oppressive effort to medicalize the rampant restlessness and anxiety caused by a life-world ever more shriveled and unfulfilling. The ruling order will evidently go to any lengths to deny social reality; its techno-psychiatry views human suffering as chiefly biological in nature and genetic in origin.

New strains of disease, impervious to industrial medicine, begin to spread globally while fundamentalism (Christian, Judaic, Islamic) is also on the rise, a sign of deeply-felt misery and frustration. And here at home New Age spirituality (Adorno's "philosophy for dunces") and the countless varieties of "healing" therapies wear thin in their delusional pointlessness. To assert that we can be whole/enlightened/healed within the present madness amounts to endorsing the madness.

The gap between rich and poor is widening markedly in this land of the homeless and the imprisoned. Anger rises and massive denial, cornerstone of the system's survival, is now at least having a troubled sleep. A false world is beginning to get the amount of support it deserves: distrust of public institutions is almost total. But the social landscape seems frozen and the pain of youth is perhaps the greatest of all. It was recently announced (10/94) that the homicide rate among young men ages 15 to 19 more than doubled between 1985 and 1991. Teen suicide is the response of a growing number who evidently cannot imagine maturity in such a place as this.

The overwhelmingly pervasive culture is a fast-food one, bereft of substance or promise. As Dick Hebdige aptly judged, "the postmodern is the modern without the hopes and dreams that made modernity bearable." Postmodernism advertises itself as pluralistic, tolerant, and non-dogmatic. In practice it is a superficial, fast-forward, deliberately confused, fragmented, media-obsessed, illiterate, fatalistic, uncritical excrescence, indifferent to questions of origins, agency, history or causation. It questions nothing of importance and is the perfect expression of a setup that is stupid and dying and wants to take us with it.

Our postmodern epoch finds its bottom-line expression in consumerism and technology, which combine in the stupefying force of mass media. Attention-getting, easily-digested images and phrases distract one from the fact that this horror-show of domination is precisely held together by such entertaining, easily digestible images and phrases. Even the grossest failures of society can be used to try to narcotize its subjects, as with the case of violence, a source of endless diversion. We are titillated by the representation of what at the same time is threatening, suggesting that boredom is an even worse torment than fear.

Nature, what is left of it, that is, serves as a bitter reminder of how deformed, non-sensual, and fraudulent is contemporary existence. The death of the natural world and the technological penetration of every sphere of life, what is left of it, proceed with an accelerating impetus. *Wired*, *Mondo 2000*, zippies, cyber-everything, virtual reality, Artificial Intelligence, on and on, up to and including Artificial Life, the ultimate postmodern science.

Meanwhile, however, our "post-industrial" computer age has resulted in the fact that we are more than ever "appendages to the machine," as the 19th century phrase had it. Bureau of Justice statistics (7/94), by the way, report that the increasingly computer-surveilled workplace is now the setting for nearly one million violent crimes per year, and that the number of murdered bosses has doubled in the past decade.

This hideous arrangement expects, in its arrogance, that its victims will somehow remain content to vote, recycle, and pretend it will all be fine. To employ a line from Debord, "The spectator is simply supposed to know nothing and deserve nothing."

Civilization, technology, and a divided social order are the components of an indissoluble whole, a death-trip that is fundamentally hostile to qualitative difference. Our answer must be qualitative, not the quantitative, more-of-the-same palliatives that actually reinforce what we must end.

1995

He Means It—Do You?

Today opposition is anarchist or it is non-existent. This is the barest minimum coherence in the struggle against an engulfing totality.

And while ten years ago the milieu generally called anti-authoritarian was largely syndicalist, those leftist residues are fading out altogether. Very few now find a vista of work and production at all liberatory.

As the smell of this false and rotting order rises to the heavens, registering an unprecedented toll on all living beings, faith in the whole modern world evaporates. Industrialism and its ensemble looks like it has been a very bad idea, sort of a wrong turn begun still earlier. Civilization itself, with its logic of domestication and destruction, seems untenable.

After all, is there anyone who is happy in this desolation?

Lovely new indicators of how it is panning out include increasing self-mutilation among the young and murder of children by their own parents. Somehow a society that is steadily more impersonal, cynical, de-skilled, boring, artificial, depressing, suicide-prompting, used up, drug-ridden, ugly, anxiety-causing and futureless brings a questioning as to why it has come to this/what's it all about.

Leftism with its superficial program is nearly extinct. Its adherents have folded their tents of manipulation and, in some cases, moved on to far more interesting adventures.

Anarchism, if not yet anarchy, is the only scene going, even if the blackout on the subject is still in effect. As if to match the accelerating decomposition of society and displacement of life at large, determined resistance is also metamorphosing with some rapidity. The rout of the left, following the swiftly declining prestige of History, Progress, and techno-salvation, is only one development. The old militants, with their ethic of sacrifice and order, their commitment to economy and exchange, are already fixed on the museum shelves of partial revolt.

Enter the Unabomber and a new line is being drawn. This time the bohemian schiz-fluxers, Green yuppies, hobbyist anarcho-journalists, condescending organizers of the poor, hip nihilo-aesthetes and all the other "anarchists" who thought their pretentious pastimes would go on unchallenged indefinitely—well, it's time to pick which side you're on. It may be that here also is a Rubicon from which there will be no turning back.

Some, no doubt, would prefer to wait for a perfect victim. Many would like to unlearn what they know of the invasive and unchallenged violence generated everywhere by the prevailing order—in order to condemn the Unabomber's counter-terror.

But here is the person and the challenge before us.

Anarchists! One more effort if you would be enemies of this long nightmare!

1997

HOW RUINOUS DOES
IT HAVE TO GET?

Recent developments make an all-encompassing crisis plain to see. Society could scarcely be more bizarrely unhealthy, but is getting even more so all the time.

With two million people behind bars, kids as young as two are on behavior control drugs like Ritalin. *Sunset* magazine carries pages of ads for "boot camps." "Got an angry child?" "Defiant teen?"

A recent national study disclosed that emotional disorders among children have more than doubled in the past 20 years. Homicidal outbursts at school, as deeply shocking as they are, correspond to murderous rampages at work or at Burger King. Meanwhile, the trend toward year-round schooling feeds into the current prospect of a lifetime of more and more hours at work.

Last November a *U.S. News & World Report* survey announced that over 90 percent of students cheat. No surprise, where a similarly high percentage of citizens feel cynicism/no confidence concerning most of the ruling institutions.

Youthful smoking is on the rise; so are binge drinking, and health-threatening obesity. And as with adults, kids' levels of anxiety, stress, isolation, and boredom are going up. TV fare is shock- and peep-show tabloid-oriented for the increasingly jaded. *USA Today* for

July 18 pondered "Why America is so short-tempered," as road rage erupts and parents get violent—to the point of murder—at Little League games.

It was recently reported that drug abuse and addiction in Oregon went up 232 percent from 1995 to 1999. On the national level, one out of every three people say they have felt close to a nervous breakdown at some point, according to a study released in early July. The assortment of "healing" and alternative therapy approaches multiplies, perhaps in proportion to a massive and pervasive denial of the root causes of all the suffering and estrangement.

Meanwhile, afflictions such as chronic fatigue syndrome and fibromyalgia debilitate many; no specific causes can be found. It is as if a growing number of people are simply becoming allergic to society itself.

So many are now taking pharmaceutical drugs (e.g. antidepressants) that they now constitute a significant pollutant. An April issue of *Science News* reported this new form of contamination of water and soil.

Thus we now see immiseration in the personal and social spheres meeting up with the impoverishment of our physical environment. A graphic suggestion that the pain and emptiness felt by human subjects of capital and technology is connected to the ongoing destruction of nature (global warming, accelerating species extinction, oceans dying, etc.).

If the salaried thinkers of the dominant emptiness largely continue to ignore the glaring fact of engulfing alienation, the word is definitely beginning to spread nonetheless. There is an alternative consciousness: for example, in the anti-culture of hundreds of underground, do-it-yourself zines and pirate radio projects. And it is even showing up above ground, in films like *Matrix* and *Fight Club*, in novels like Alan Lightman's *The Diagnosis*, and in the work of Bret Easton Ellis. Critique is making itself felt in many areas.

A culture this bereft cannot long sustain itself. Especially if we are equal to the task of demolishing it in favor or life, health, freedom, authenticity.

2000

How Postmodernism Greases The Rails For The Cyborg Future

The reigning, pervasive cultural ethos is postmodern, with its sharply narrowed ambitions concerning thought, its tendency to shade into the cynical.

It began in large part as French reaction against the grand and total claims of Marxism. Emerging and spreading about 20 years ago, in a period of reaction with almost no social movements, postmodernism bears the imprint of a period of conservatism and lowered expectations. It is also already a result of the "cyborg" society in which a technical imperative tends to subsume or co-opt alternatives.

Postmodernism tells us that we can't grasp the whole, indeed that the desire for an overview of what's going on out there is unhealthy and suspect, even totalitarian. I don't argue specifically with postmodernism's rejection of Marxism. We have seen, after all, how grand systems—"metanarratives," as they are fashionably referred to—have proven oppressive rather than liberatory.

Skeptical about the claims and results of previous systems of thought, postmodernism has in fact jettisoned pretty nearly all desire or hope of making sense of reality as we experience it. PM abandons the "arrogance" of trying to figure out the origins, logic, causality, or structure of the world we live in.

Instead, postmodernists focus on surfaces, fragments, margins. Reality is too shifting, complex, indeterminate to decipher or judge. Too "messy," too "interesting" to allow for fixed conclusions, as Donna Haraway puts it in her well-known "Cyborg Manifesto."

Meaning and value are old-fashioned illusions, and so is the practice of writing with clarity. The postmodern style is notorious for its word play, dense language games, and fondness for contradiction. To cite Haraway's "Cyborg Manifesto" again, she concedes that "the main trouble with cyborgs, of course, is that they are the illegitimate offspring of militarism and patriarchal capitalism"—but that in no way dims her enthusiasm for a cyborg (part human, part machine), high tech future!

Shared experience and direct experience are two major casualties of an increasingly technified society. But Haraway and the postmodern crowd in general are uncritical of the techno imperative that is so rampantly gaining ground and leaching away what little quality and texture is left in our everyday lives. Of course, once one renounces any attempt to comprehend the overall situation, the door is wide open for technology and capital to fill the vacuum. Things grow stark and menacing in every sphere, but conclusions are to be avoided.

Postmodernism celebrates evanescent flows, a state of no boundaries, the transgressive. In the actual world, however, this translates as an embrace of the unimpeded movement of capital, the experience of consumer novelty. As the dimensions of personal robusticity and social interaction steadily erode, along with meaning and value, a consumer society in cyberspace becomes the uncontested next stage of human existence.

Postmodernism gives up on understanding how and why the cyborg future is overtaking us. Division of labor, domestication, the nature of technology—not to mention less abstract factors like drudgery, toxicity, the steady destruction of nature—are integral to the high-tech trajectory. Of no concern, evidently, to postmodernists, who continue to cling to the subtle, the tentative, the narrowly focused.

Virtual reality is an example that mirrors the postmodern fascination with surfaces, explicitly rejoicing in its own depthlessness—one obvious way in which it is the accomplice of the Brave New World development. No challenge there, no challenge even plausible in the collapse and refusal of the possibility of understanding the totality. The political counterpart of postmodernism is pragmatism, the tired liberalism that accommodates itself to the debased norm.

The decay of meaning, passion, inner vibrancy has been going on for a while. Max Weber spoke of disenchantment, for instance. But postmodernism is the culture of no resistance to this juggernaut. The good news is that there are signs of life, signs that folks in various places are refusing a cyborg future.

2001

So . . . How Did You
Become An Anarchist?

I was one of the Baby Boom generation's first arrivals, born in Salem, Oregon two years before the end of World War II. My parents and my older sister Jackie had moved to Oregon from Nebraska in 1940, looking for a break from tough times in the Midwest of the Great Depression. Before they came west, Dad worked at a gas station six, and every other week, seven days a week. Getting by was not easy. Dreadful winters and not always enough food for three.

The times were less precarious when John and Lorene—both of Bohemian forbears as far back as anyone knew—and their nine-year-old daughter started over on the West Coast. The prospect of war was spurring the economy. Hard times were ending in most places. I showed up in 1943; my brother Jim a month after World War II ended, two years later.

Married in 1929 and having endured a decade of Depression, my folks were among many who feared that war's end would mean another economic downturn. But Cold War military spending precluded the return of lean years, and instead helped kick off the consumer-spending economic expansion of the '50s. I grew up in those years, in a fairly typical small-town, Catholic, nuclear family world, within the larger world of new things like TV, the H-bomb, freeways, and a mainly unexamined, triumphalist U.S. world view. I can remember—it must have been 1952—bicycling around the neighborhood with a pack of friends shouting "We Like Ike!" And around that age, maybe ten, fearing and hating "communists." We had by this time moved from Salem to nearby Woodburn, an even smaller town, quite an unlikely place to have found any Reds.

My first baby step away from the conformist know-nothingism of the rabidly all-American '50s was to become a strong Adlai Stevenson-for-President supporter in 1956. In what way, if any, he was different from Eisenhower (who drubbed him in 1952 and 1956) I couldn't have said. But I think this enthusiasm was a slight stirring, clueless as it was.

By the mid-'50s both the U.S. and the U.S.S.R. possessed nuclear weapons, so strategic competition became focused on missile development—the Space Race. The enforced political orthodoxy was buttressed by a major emphasis on science and technology. Boys were encouraged to devote themselves to these pursuits, in the national interest. In 1957 the Soviets launched the first artificial satellite, Sputnik. Their achievement intensified the American focus on math, sciences, engineering, and the like.

Ron, Steve, and I were in the 7th and 8th grades at this time. Caught up in the prevailing atmosphere, we were young science nerds with our own version of competitive experimentation. We'd gone from chemistry sets to the construction of small bombs, thanks to materials ordered from chemical supply companies. A pound of sulphur cost $1.00, easily affordable even with our meager allowances. Magnesium wire was more expensive, and was paid for by our summer work as harvesters in the fields near Woodburn. One of our pastimes was coming up with gunpowder-like compounds. We competed to see whose compound would oxidize fastest while leaving the smallest noncombustible traces. Whoever was least efficient was dubbed that week's "Residue King." I recall that Steve was usually the mocked monarch. When we entered high school, we left our interest in explosives behind. Plus the fact that my dad came across the container for our biggest effort yet, and confronted me about it. He wasn't angry, but rather shaken, grasping how much destruction we could have unleashed.

After eight years at St. Luke's School I got a further four years at the hands of Benedictines in Mount Angel, just about ten miles from Woodburn. Hands were literally involved at Mt. Angel Prep, where priests frequently resorted to physical punishment. High school at this small, boys-only place next to a monastery was essentially medieval. Along with Latin and Church History, the teachers had the divine right to clock you whenever they lost their tempers, and promoted brutality among the fairly rowdy student body. Juniors and seniors were encouraged to shave the heads of any freshman or sophomores caught smoking on the school grounds, and for greater or repeated infractions there was the "belt line." This meant that the malcontent had to run a school assembly gauntlet, whipped by the belts of all students. Those who didn't participate were forced to run the gauntlet in turn.

To gain acceptance, I played football until my senior year. The Friday night games really weren't bad. I was far from being an accomplished player, but the games were a picnic compared to practices. By my senior year I'd become "one of the guys" and decided to forego a last season of afternoon torture. At that point it wasn't worth the daily afternoon ordeal of brutal drills.

I mainly stayed out of trouble until just before graduating, when a couple of the holy Fathers discovered that their A- student had been less the model character than they'd thought. I got whacked in the face a few times for my minor troublemaking.

Apparently somewhat like another bright little bomb-maker at the time—Ted Kaczynski in Illinois—fitting in was not always easy. I did have some close friends, but generally felt out of place and confused by many prevailing norms. I have a vivid recollection even now of watching the popular late '50s sitcom, "The Adventures of Ozzie and Harriet." Certainly there wasn't anything even slightly adventurous (or funny) about this family of zombies, and the tinny, canned laughter made me feel uneasy and left out. Ricky Nelson, Ozzie and Harriet's younger son, was the program's teen heartthrob, while I had no idea at all what to say to girls. Very slow in this area for some time.

Maybe I wasn't much more confused or estranged than the average adolescent in my vague, uninformed appetite for something different. The Beat Generation, as interpreted in cartoon-like fashion by *Life*

magazine, represented exotic rebellion to me. Dirty beatniks! Not
everyone, it seemed, was a smiling, patriotic consumer. Portland,
Oregon's Reed College seemed a pretty beat place when I visited in my
senior year, including people sitting on the floor and dogs in the book-
store. The campus exuded a non-conformist, intellectual atmosphere
that really grabbed me. But the priests at my school were decidedly
appalled at my desire to apply to such a hotbed of godless, bohemian
communism. I needed three letters of recommendation from teachers
and couldn't get even one.

I was thrilled, however, to get a scholarship to Stanford, and
enrolled Fall, 1961. The Farm, as it has been called since railroad
baron Leland Stanford founded it in the 1890s, was beginning its
ascendancy, paralleling the rise of adjacent Silicon Valley and the
gradual, overall shift of power in the U.S. from the East coast to the
Pacific Rim. I was rather awed by its palm-, eucalyptus-, and sports-
car-studded 10,000 acres, complete with lake, fire department, stables,
golf course, etc. And frankly wondered if I would make the grade,
especially against the many incoming freshmen from real prep schools:
eighteen-year-olds incomparably more sophisticated than me, familiar
with such things as foreign films, folk music, the blues, and Camus
(whose name I didn't even know how to pronounce).

One rich kid I knew very slightly dropped out after only a few
weeks, declaring in a letter to the campus daily that he'd already done
his "penance" academically and was bored by required, introductory
courses. I recall standing with my mouth open as he packed his bags to
go off to Switzerland for the skiing.

But I learned fairly quickly that flunking out was unlikely, and
from that point on an inchoate disillusionment began to set in. As a
would-be beatnik who remained a Catholic, I wasn't really turned on
by college classes. It was exciting to select interesting-sounding courses
at the beginning of every term, only to feel later that they were just
successive pre-packaged elements in a competitive grind for grades.
Stanford was and is a lot of very intelligent people, minus original
thinking: a pretty conservative place.

So I went about in my army fatigue jacket with no real friends,
the bloom fading from the rose. It was hard to maintain real interest,
and my grades began to slip. A sojourn in Europe, at Stanford-in-Italy

in Florence, at the end of my sophomore year, helped some. Especially because I made a few very close friends in the Florentine villa that was home for six months. And it was in Italy that I first began to take a critical look at social and political life. To improve my Italian I subscribed to *Umanità*, the Communist Party daily. I was struck by the stark poverty in Naples when I hitchhiked there. Another watershed during that overseas sojourn in 1963 was the bombing of a Birmingham church, a racist attack that killed four black children. I don't remember discussing it or thinking about it at length, but it had an impact on me.

Hitchhiking to Naples that summer, I was struck by a tableau in a very poor district. An old man and a teenage boy were studying together in an old building; the former was apparently teaching the lad something, in the neighborhood hall of the Italian Communist Party. I remember coming across them and feeling moved by their connection with each other. This was perhaps the very beginning of my political life, the start of a replacement (or grounding) of values that had before this time been religious.

In the summer of '63 I also hitchhiked to Assisi. My Christian faith had all but evaporated; I went there to give it a last shot. St. Francis, with his love for animals and his innocence, appealed to me. But I found no rescusitation of interest in Catholicism. In fact, the church at that historic place was curiously modern, and the priest in charge was actually from Ohio. Not inspiring.

Back on the Farm, my focus on school resumed a tendency to blur. I was Class of '65, but by early that year I literally couldn't concentrate. Upon taking an exam I would find that virtually none of the material I'd read came to mind. Some kind of minor breakdown was happening, so I got a medical leave of absence, returning to Oregon and enrolling at a tiny Willamette Valley college in order to avoid the mounting Vietnam war draft.

Mt. Angel College, another Benedictine place of learning, was metamorphosing in an interesting "sign of the times" direction in 1965. The liberal arts college had been a safe, Catholic alternative to more worldly schools and was often a place where parents sent wayward kids for moral improvement. Like Sarah, nabbed for selling pot at her California high school.

Well, the '60s were already under way in some unlikely places, like totally out-of-the-way Mt. Angel College, in 1965. And of course sending young people there who were already weirdos and discontents only hastened the process by which the inmates overran the asylum. Early hippie students and offbeat teachers (especially in the art department) lured straighter types into this obscure locus of the just-emerging "counter-culture." By 1968, the institution's president would be defrocked for siding with students against Benedictine authority. Already, in temporary exile in Oregon, it began to seem to me that a new day was arriving. In any case, it was a generally fun, healing place to be, just when I really needed it.

Meanwhile, starting just before I dropped out in early '65, something new was under way in the Bay Area environs near Stanford. It was at this time, in Berkeley, that the first large-scale anti-Vietnam War protest took place. A very dramatic evening march with a sadly anti-climactic ending.

Thousands of us streamed along down Telegraph Avenue, heading for the Oakland Army depot on San Francisco Bay. The aim was to proceed south through Berkeley, west through Oakland, all the way to the base, and then interfere with its operations. Most of the supplies fueling the war were being shipped from that particular arms depot.

We drew up to Ashby Avenue, next to the Berkeley-Oakland boundary, and stopped. Across the intersection of Telegraph and Ashby were hundreds of Oakland cops, a large phalanx of pigs in riot gear, barring our way.

Various speakers discussed this impasse, stressing the need to move forward anyway. The mood of the crowd grew stronger in response to the challenge we faced. Grew equal to the fear we felt, and then some.

But at this crucial point, Ken Kesey got to the makeshift podium and began playing "Home on the Range" on a harmonica. Slow and plaintive, the tune served to deflate the resolve of the thousands of protestors. And the march was simply called off. There was some announcement about meeting the next day, as I recall, but the evening's showdown was over. The main thrust of the ensuing commentary was that cooler and wiser heads had prevailed. No one was hurt; common sense and nonviolence had overcome temporary passion.

And within a very few months, the U.S. government had decided on all-out war in Vietnam. An escalating campaign killed upwards of four million Asians over the ensuing ten years.

It didn't dawn on me until much later that there was very likely a connection between what happened on that night in Berkeley early in 1965 and the course of genocidal war in Southeast Asia. Foreign policy may have hinged on the protest that didn't happen. Public response to war is generally a key factor to be reckoned with, and what occurred in Berkeley was token resistance, at best. Since no real opposition was expected, the authorities had no political reason to hold back.

If we had gone forward, people would have been hurt, almost certainly. Some might even have been killed. But the government might well have decided that serious resistance could be expected if it moved forward with a greatly intensified war.

In other words, we failed that night, and millions died. All the ritual peacenik demos of the '60s and early '70s failed. The war ended in 1975 because Vietnamese kept fighting and because American troops began refusing to fight. The route of serious resistance at home was ruled out very early on.

After my time off in Oregon, at Mt. Angel College (it felt mainly like time off, in that relaxed, small-town bohemia), I returned to Stanford in the fall of '65 to do my last two terms. "The Farm" was the same stodgy, isolated place it had always been, but by this time something was definitely in the air. Stanford was catching up with Mt. Angel, and the Haight-Ashbury and Berkeley were now in high gear, if you'll pardon the pun.

The one outrageous scene wasn't on campus—big surprise—but in adjacent Palo Alto and East Palo Alto. Ken Kesey and fellow partyers including Neal Cassidy (soon to be called the Merry Pranksters), the Grateful Dead (a local band that had been known until recently as the Warlocks), and LSD, a new, defenses-melting drug, combined in all-night phenomena advertised as Acid Tests. ("Can You Pass the Acid Test?")

With a couple of friends who were more in the know, I attended an Acid Test in a vintage ex-roller rink. We opened some swinging doors and the first thing I saw was Neal Cassidy, standing nearby with a microphone in his mouth, having several simultaneous conversations with people who weren't there. I backed out of the doors in a hurry, having stumbled onto full-out insanity. After a few short look-ins, coming inside briefly but staying near the front entrance, I got used to the prevailing madness. I wasn't ready yet to sample the acid Kool-Aid, but enjoyed the daring zone of anti-normality, including a slide show by Kesey, "America Needs Indians."

A few months later I went to L.A. for an Acid Test in a large pornography film studio on Pico Boulevard. In the morning we drove out to the beach, and I saw snowmen on all the lawns and an aircraft carrier up ahead of us on the freeway. We collapsed on the sand and woke up many hours later, badly sunburned.

I even had a course or two that I actually enjoyed, with the finish line coming into view. A degree in political science is surely a monument to wasted time, but I remember a substantial seminar on Marxism, and I began to delve more into history, which should have been my major all along—a better chance to learn some content.

In my final term I lucked into a colloquium on the Russian Revolution, taught by none other than the head of the provisional government in 1917, Alexander Kerensky. Premier between the fall of the Czar in March and the Bolshevik takeover in October, he was now an elderly gentleman, his white hair crew-cut. He was also, not too surprisingly, quite passionate about his fall from power and the "unprincipled" tactics of his successful rival Lenin. Sitting next to him at a screening of Eisenstein's classic silent film, "Ten Days That Shook the World," I watched him in profile as much as I watched the film. In a pivotal scene, the crowd breaks into the palace; the actor playing Kerensky appears on a grand staircase, first running up and then running down, a symbol of his political vacillation in the face of contending social forces. Sitting in the dark in early 1966, almost 40 years after that momentous day, Kerensky watched, agitated and upset, reliving his own history.

I graduated at the end of winter term and the April 1 date on my A.B. degree was not completely lost on me. By then, the '50s were finally at an end and things were beginning to get crazy, especially in the Bay Area. I recall an episode one evening in nearby Menlo Park before I left Stanford. In a car with Neal Cassady and a classmate who was a friend of his, we pulled into a gas station, where Neal jumped out to deal with the high-school-age attendant. He popped the hood, went around checking the tires, climbed in and out of the car, while feverishly bombarding the kid with comments and questions, including a complicated query about green stamps (a promotional giveaway of the day). The attendant's mouth was agape and he was probably as freaked as I had been upon my first encounter with Cassady. He moved slowly backward, broke into a run, and fled into the night down a side street. Our mad driver concluded that green stamps would not be forthcoming and drove off, gasoline on the house.

I returned to Oregon and got a job washing dishes in a big retirement complex near Portland. With the troop buildup in Vietnam heading toward half a million, the draft was nailing everyone in sight. Without my student deferment, it was clear that official greetings would be in the mail within a month or two.

No thanks to Stanford, I'd become increasingly aware of the repressive and destructive nature of the reigning system, and was by now totally opposed to the Vietnam war. Two friends and I pledged that we'd go to Mexico together should we pass the draft board physical.

At the Selective Service center in Portland that spring of 1966, the three of us were more than a little worked up. In fact, I'd gotten drunk and overturned my VW into a ditch a few nights before. Luckily, the passengers and myself were not injured.

John and I played the physical as a kind of psychodrama, with emphasis on the psycho. John as a crazed, manic weirdo, me as a virtually catatonic weirdo. (In less than a year the induction centers would be a lot more wised up to such fakery.) Ken, who'd had a tree fall on his foot, breaking most of its bones, was fairly quickly sent home. "You can't march on that. Just have your doctor send us the x-rays," the Army examiner said. Guess who, some months later and unbeknownst to John and me, ended up in Vietnam.

With a permanent deferment, I promptly returned to California and got a job at the Shell Oil refinery in Martinez, just north of Berkeley. But the work ranged from generally boring to occasionally dangerous, and in a few months I headed for the Haight-Ashbury.

At this point I need to explicitly restrict the scope of this mini-memoir, because I can't see another way forward with it. In the interest of protecting the privacy of others, this account will avoid most personal relationships. I'll skirt the pitfalls of saying too little or too much about others—and, I must admit, the pitfall of how to honestly acquit myself in an area of great importance. Certain people have meant a lot to me personally, and still do.

1966 was the banner year for the fabled Haight-Ashbury neighborhood of San Francisco. On block after square block, suddenly there were hippies everywhere. LSD, free rock music, instant camaraderie. . . . A new scene was booming, change was definitely in the air. People were partying and laughing at the old world. Kesey and the Pranksters had moved up the Peninsula from the Stanford environs; Kesey had been busted twice for pot and failed to appear in court. Conforming to the spirit of the Haight, he would appear in adjacent Golden Gate Park in outrageous disguises to thumb his nose at the many cops— including FBI—who were after him. So many knew it was him, but the heat was in the dark; quite hilarious, even though he was caught fairly soon, driving in a car on a Bay Area freeway.

Dropouts were arriving from all over and the place was becoming quite the exotic tourist attraction. A showdown of sorts came on Easter weekend, 1967. City Hall decided that bus service was to be diverted from Haight Street to the streets on either side of it, apparently to better accommodate the almost bumper-to-bumper traffic of "straights" driving through to gawk at the colorful inhabitants. It was pretty clear that the choice was to acquiesce to this policy or to defend the Haight as a liberated zone.

Only a handful of us showed up to block traffic and oppose the increased-traffic plan. Hippies, then as now, proved passive rather than resistant, and the fate of the 'hood was sealed. The heyday of Haight-Ashbury was over, and in rather short order a joyful, expansive spirit was replaced by a large-scale "back to the land" retreat and a sharp rise in the use of non-psychedelic hard drugs among those remaining. Berkeley, on the other hand, was still coming on, as a very politicized center of anti-war organizing and other increasingly militant directions. In late summer '66 I got arrested at a big, stupid "civil disobedience" anti-war demo and spent 15 days in the Contra Costa County jail. This was the first and last time I was lame enough to present myself to be arrested.

But I'm getting ahead of myself. Before the end of the year, I'd run out of money and taken a job as a public welfare caseworker for the City and County of San Francisco. At age 23, I was still just beginning to think about how the world ran and what I could do about it. The four years I spent at the Department of Social Services were to prove, as they say, a learning experience.

In fact, an experience of some consequence happened soon after I took the job. I happened to work in the vicinity of a guy who was about to retire—a quiet old lifer named Donnelly who'd never uttered a peep against the workings of the welfare system. At ten minutes to 5:00 p.m. on his very last day, he was given the boot. Incredible as it sounds, the downtown brass fired him at the last moment, so as to avoid paying his retirement pension.

Not too surprisingly, there was an enormous uproar. It was an unbelievable outrage, especially now that "the Sixties"—that part of the decade that tried to count for something—was now showing up. The union, a local of the Services Employees International (SEIU), always beloved by liberals, said that nothing could be done, and refused to make any effort on Donnelly's behalf. This was a classic instance of the collusion and corruption of unions in general.

Virtually overnight, an independent union was formed. A militant, do-it-yourself outfit, hated by Organized Labor as much as by City Hall. It was exciting and instructive to be a part of this wide-open experiment in radical democracy. We decided against having any paid organizers or officers, and rejected signing any contract with the City and County. Membership would be strictly voluntary, ruling out the possibility of a "closed shop" arrangement in which union dues become an automatic paycheck deduction. I served as vice-president in 1967 and president in 1968. Our union—sedately named the Social Services Employees Union—came to encourage members to invent positions according to their agitational interests and then "run" for election to the new positions as a kind of ratifying process. Dues were whatever amount an individual chose to contribute. SSEU militants drew up an organizers' manual intended to encourage a prairie fire of constant challenges to the authority of the welfare bureaucracy. Workers—caseworkers, clerks, public hospital employees—were invited, for example, to file endless grievances, through a process designed to spread participation with unlimited assistance and open testimony. All negotiations were designed to be transparent, with every concession merely an opening to further demands. We constantly exposed the logic of public policy as repressive control of poor people, and the police role of Organized Labor in its parallel control of employees.

Early on, we held a public meeting with Emmett Grogan and the Diggers, to explore possible common round in the area of radically-based social services. But we found very little commonality. Our organizing-on-the-job approach didn't appeal to the Diggers, who were free-wheeling drop-outs.

The ultimate goal was to destabilize the system from the inside and to achieve an alliance between welfare workers and welfare recipients. We failed, misreading our possibilities for spontaneous action in general and our role as paid agents of government in particular. A rare example of connection occurred when the bureaucracy tried to fire a very active union militant. Scores of public assistance clients showed up at City Hall and turned the tide, saving Charley's job. But without an explicit critique of the overall setup, SSEU was fated to play a reformist, if noisy part; similarly, there was no convincing reason why our welfare clients should find themselves working with us.

But for a time, we felt we'd discovered a liberating "third way," steering between an inherently complicit unionism and the various groupings of authoritarian Marxism, so prevalent in the '60s. Journalists would get the word and excitedly write feature stories about our experimental effort. Not a single story was published, however, demonstrating what we saw as a kind of contemporary fascism. Government, unions, and business united against this kind of independent activity. We tried to spread our little contagion to other, mainly white-collar workplaces, and did get asked for organizing advice. A couple of times, the Black Panthers sought our help in terms of members who drove buses and cable cars. For all the Panthers' militant courage in the streets, they were at a loss in terms of protecting themselves on the job. All these experiences tended to encourage our workerist illusions.

SSEU was what I mainly did from late 1966 to early 1971, with occasional weekend rioting across the Bay in Berkeley during '68 and '69. As time went on in the Department of Social Services, my (unpaid, of course) union role more and more outstripped my case-worker role, and organizing began to feel problematic in itself. I was increasingly bothered by what seemed like a fatal flaw inherent in the organizing mode. I still feel that organizing entails trying to get people to do things without fully revealing the program, vision, or agenda that's behind the organizing. Of course, if there's no transcendent radical orientation and goal behind the effort, then it's just reform, pure and simple. But if there is a radical goal, more or less hidden, then how can the organizing activity not be seen as inherently manipulative?

During most of this period, it had seemed to me that unless one had a job there could be no leverage on society. Action in the streets, however militant and dangerous, was misplaced, could not have much effect. But this outlook was losing its appeal for me. Transparency was becoming a more important factor, as I thought about ways to try to overturn the dominant order. In this sense, some of the ideas of the Situationists had a big effect on my thinking, from the time I first learned about them, around 1970. Their no-holds-barred critiques of the many varieties of leftism appealed to me in a big way. I was never in full accord with all their theses, but the non-manipulative, up-front quality of the Sits was instantly refreshing.

The radical, often visionary outlook of the Situationist International did not, alas, reach the U.S. (and the West coast in particular) in time to influence "The Movement" much at all. Similarly, the radical women's movement didn't arrive until 1969, too late to have a chance to deepen and enlighten the '60s. As for the anarchists, I'm not aware that they played more than a very slight role. Anarchists seemed pretty invisible, their activities usually confined to the archaic, mini-bureaucratic realm of the IWW. These anarcho-syndicalists were characteristically uncritical of unionism, the prevailing leftism, and other impediments to revolution. They seemed virtually unaware of the global wave of opposition during the '60s.

In the early 1970s I took notice of how much organizing I'd been doing and also, how much writing. The writing was mostly about the deeply collaborationist nature of unions, their key role in a state/business/organized labor system that is designed to freeze out independent, potentially radical modes of activity. Mainly via their legally binding labor-management contracts and strictly bureaucratic structures, unions enforce and legitimate the conditions and the very existence of wage labor. Coinciding with the height of my interest in this subject arose a much-publicized "revolt against work" phenomenon. Suddenly a spate of articles appeared that acknowledged widespread absenteeism, employee turnover, sabotage, drug use on the job, wildcat strikes, etc. A kind of non-political or underground resistance seemed to have replaced the public radicalism of the '60s. A more explicit kind of underground opposition was also present at this time, exemplified by groups like the Black Liberation Army and Weather Underground.

In early 1971 I began graduate studies in U.S. history at San Francisco State, earning an M.A. degree the following year. This was chiefly a way to pursue my research/writing interests and to indulge my own aversion to work. "Organized Labor and the Revolt Against Work" was published in a 1973 issue of the radical theory journal *Telos*.

After a month or so in Europe, I enrolled at the University of Southern California in the fall of '72. This mediocre place was adequate for my purposes, and it was primarily my own labor studies/social control topics that I pursued there until 1975. Approaching the completion of a Ph.D. program and having never intended to become a professor, it was time to move on. During the last two years at USC I had been a teaching assistant, a job whose light duties offered free tuition and office space. In fact, my failure to be properly obsequious in the feudal game of prostrating oneself before an all-powerful doctoral committee of "superiors" had placed me increasingly on their shit list, as I discovered. Just before I took the two weeks of written qualifying exams required for Ph.D. candidacy, I was told that my assistantship would not be renewed for the following year. Every professor I'd worked for had allegedly had problems with me. Since none of them had every expressed dissatisfaction to me personally, I concluded that this move was simply intended to mess me up during the exams that were to commence the next day. I passed the exams and resigned, expressing my contempt in a flippant postcard to the chairman of my committee.

There was a little problem of about $13,000 (mainly in student loans), but at that time debt could be disposed of easily. With the help of some kind of "people's law services" in Echo Park, I filed for bankruptcy on the entire amount. Redfaced with anger, the judge demanded to know what would happen if everyone were to do the same, what of the deserving poor, etc. We both knew he had no choice but to sign away what I owed. In the elevator going downstairs from the courtroom, my people's lawyer expressed some agreement with the judge's attitude. If there had been any doubt, that remark made it a certainty that he wasn't going to be paid either.

So ended three years in L.A. Returning to San Francisco in 1975, it was clear that the days of contestation were not only gone, but were unlikely to return anytime soon. I continued to publish in Telos off an on during the '70s, and thanks to Fredy Perlman I discovered and began a relationship with *Fifth Estate* of Detroit before the end of '75. Writing, drinking a lot, getting by on short-term jobs, unemployment benefits, a few small-time scams.

I was also thinking about what the '60s meant—how far the movement did and didn't go, why it ended—questions along those lines. My work had become more history- and theory-oriented, as can happen when contemporary reality becomes less promising. Exploring the roots of unionism, I discovered the Luddite revolts and delved into early industrial capitalism. The idea that the factory system arose in large part to corral and subdue a dispersed and autonomous population was a big revelation, and led to further questions about technology. If a mode of production initiated in the late 18th century had, built-in, a social control intentionality, where else was this kind of dimension also present? I began to consider that perhaps technology is never neutral, that it expresses or embodies the values desired by a dominant group.

1977 was the year of the original punk rock explosion in San Francisco, imported from its birth in the U.K. about a year earlier. No one thought its vehemence was the rebirth of the '60s, but it occasioned an exciting outburst of nihilist energy. Punk might be thought of as a kind of aftershock of the '60s quake, although many punkers were explicitly contemptuous of that earlier scene (especially of hippies). The first blast of raw, angry punk was bracing as hell, and some went further than music performance. For instance, a small bunch went up to Pacific Heights more than once to bash new Mercedes, BMWs, and the like with chains and metal bars. More characteristic, of course, were the drug O.D.s that occurred all along, even during the 1977 heyday, as well as later.

By early '78 the initial rush was over, particularly for the more political types like myself who secretly hoped that punk might actually re-ignite significant resistance. '60s illusions and groundless idealism were effectively dead and the new defiance of punk went deeper, even with its cynical overlay. Or so it seemed for a season.

By this time alcohol had become a serious problem for me, adversely affecting my relationships (that's putting it euphemistically) and bringing the writing pretty much to a stop. At the end of the decade I'd been kicked out of a group household for stupid, drunken behavior and was living with some illegals in a Mission district flat furnished with broken castoffs. I suppose the latter was appropriate, given that I'd helped burn the furniture where I lived before, for no known reason. During the next couple of years I routinely drank myself into blackout states, with killer hangovers and zero memory of the nights before. My only steady income came from selling my plasma twice a week.

Meanwhile, San Francisco was becoming less and less tolerable. Both the rents and the number of insane people wandering the streets were on the rise. So many people in the Bay Area, but no one, apparently, fighting the ugly, lying system. My friend Joe was doing a life term at Folsom, and I was never far from feelings of impotent rage over that. In an evasive effort to curb my drinking I ended up completely hooked on tranquilizers, needing more and more of them and still not drinking less. In short, I was a mess.

In March 1981, I moved back to Oregon. In the Portland Greyhound station I saw a crowd gathering around a black man who was holding a very small portable TV and chuckling. The news was coming in that Reagan had been shot. Nearby, a contingent of Oregon State University students were preparing to board their bus to Corvallis. I could hear outright laughter and joking about the shooting among members this group. They were bound for a campus known as fairly conservative, at a moment when it wasn't clear whether Reagan was dead or alive.

That spring and summer I worked in Newport, on Oregon's central coast, first at a shrimp cannery and then as a waiter. One weekend some friends from Seattle visited me and a stray comment, not pursued at the time, registered and got under my skin. As we drove to a lake to go swimming, someone said, "I don't think the term revolution has meaning anymore." My unspoken reaction was twofold: I didn't like hearing that, and I knew for some reason that it was true.

As noted above, I'd already been doing some historical exploring of the role of technology in society. My friend's comment deepened the questioning and also brought contemporary radical practice into my research. His remark implied that the efforts of the '60s just weren't deeply oriented enough to have qualified as liberatory. "Revolution" now seemed inadequate, and I was challenged by the question of what would go far enough.

Back in Los Angeles, in the mid-'70s, I had put out flyers that sported the name "Upshot" and an Echo Park P.O. box address. This was influenced by our SSEU habit of daily agitational leaflets, and by critiques that the Situationists embodied in their pamphlets. Sometimes one or two other people helped with the Upshot flyers, and the practice had persisted in San Francisco during the second half of the decade. I resumed creating flyers on my own after moving to Eugene in the fall of 1981.

Library facilities at the University of Oregon constituted the main reason for the move, the better to pursue answers to various questions about the depth of alienated society and what a dis-alienated world might consist of. On a more prosaic level, my main source of income continued to be twice-weekly visits to the local plasma center. My own alienation was underlined as I stood in line early one morning waiting for the center to open. A woman in an expensive car, stopped at a traffic light, looked at our disreputable ranks with evident disgust. I remember feeling pleased to be standing where I was, not part of the terrorized-by-consumer-goods class.

The early '80s were a take-off point for high-tech developments, especially computerization in general, and the appearance of personal computers in particular. New and grandiose predictions from the Artificial Intelligence people seemed emblematic of a new stage of estrangement and dehumanization, succinctly expressed by AI pioneer Marvin Minsky's pronouncement that "the brain is a three-pound computer made of meat." It was hard not to notice that social existence was being rapidly technified as a key part of growing estrangement. We were becoming more and more separated from the natural world, each other, and even our own experience.

It began to occur to me that the sense of time, and time as a cultural dimension, were fundamental to the development of this massive alienation. I spent most of 1982 exploring time as a fairly exact measure of alienation, appearing and developing in tandem with it. According to anthropologists, humans once lived in the present, with little or no consciousness of that very elusive thing we call time. How is it that we are now so ruled by time, as some kind of external, almost palpable presence over our consciousness? Time seems to be the first form of estrangement. The separation from the now that has grown so markedly that our lives are much more past and future than present to us.

When I didn't have to work, the U of O library was my haunt, seven days a week at times. At this time I began to see what a paradigm shift had occurred, during the past couple of decades, in how anthropologists and archaeologists viewed the state of humankind before agriculture. Though Homo species had been around for more than two million years, the "breakthrough" had happened only 10,000 years ago, with the domestication of animals and plants. And the overall picture of humans before agriculture had long portrayed a precarious, violent, benighted existence. Outside of civilization (which quickly followed once we had achieved domestication), life had been, in Hobbes' famous dictum, "nasty, brutish, and short."

The new view is a virtual reversal of that general outlook. The literature and its supporting evidence have established gatherer-hunter human life—99 percent of our span as Homo—as one of ample leisure time, no organized violence, a strong degree of gender autonomy and equality, and healthy, varied, robust lives. In broadest overview, this is what is taught now in Anthropology 101. Scholars who used to ask, "Why did it take our ancestors so long to adopt agriculture?" now wonder, "Why did they ever do it?"

We've always known what followed the trading in of a foraging lifeway for that of farming: war, private property, subjugation of women, ecological destruction, and the state, to name a few results. Now we see what preceded it and what a horrible bargain it was, and continues to be. The logic of domestication is ever clearer, as civilization demonstrates its destructive impacts on every level from the personal to the biospheric.

Five years of the 1980s were taken up with essays on time, language, number, art, and agriculture, published in *Fifth Estate*. They all deal with origins of our present imprisonment, whose foundation may be traced to the intertwined advance of division of labor and symbolic culture, leading to and extending domestication. These explorations were published in *Elements of Refusal* (Seattle: Left Bank Books, 1988) and are much of the basis for *Future Primitive* (Brooklyn: Autonomedia, 1994).

In the mid-'80s "Upshot" became "Anti-Authoritarians Anonymous," flyers and posters by Dan and myself. In that era of retrenchment and reaction, almost no radical activity could be found. We had to content ourselves with cultural critique, often employing the detourning of ads and other public images, and ridiculing the pious nonsense of the local pacifists. We didn't exactly rouse the populace to insurrection, but it was nice to find out that our broadsides came to adorn a few folks' walls.

Quiet times, but in addition to writing projects and the AAA flyers I enjoyed a growing and far-flung correspondence. Thanks to wonderful Alice, I was able to stop the alcohol abuse. It was also good to come to have a closer tie with my family, beginning about this time. Not only just the moving back to Oregon in 1981, but especially a rapprochement with my conservative father. He'd been burned by Nixon's Watergate debacle and more or less concluded that the political system—including Social Security—didn't have much of a future. He was now less inclined to condemn my shirker, non-commercially-viable ways. Some do "mellow with age," and it was apparent that he enjoyed my visits. In the '90s it would also be evident, to dust off another cliché, that the child becomes parent to the parents. My sister, living next door to them, a hundred miles closer, shouldered far more of the responsibility for them in their last years. But a basically close family drew closer, and after our parents' deaths my sister and I have drawn still nearer each other.

If the first half of the 1960s are more properly thought of as part of the dreaded '50s, the first half of the '90s belonged to the dead zone of the preceding decade. These were the years of Milli Vanilli, the Waco inferno, Kurt Cobain's suicide, the O.J. Simpson trial, and the high-water mark of postmodern cynicism and collaboration. There was also the L.A. rising in 1992, and the end of Apartheid in South Africa the year before, but overall American life seemed to embody the continuing stasis of a too-slowly rotting culture. The fall of the state capitalist Soviet Union in 1990 gave market capitalism a boost toward a more global, closed system. The penetration of capital into new spheres of daily life paralleled a colonization that was being speeded up all over the world with technology, as ever, its close partner. Not only do Cyberspace and Virtual Reality express avoidance and denial in terms of what was and is being obliterated of nature and direct experience. They also represent new realms for domination itself. A growing misogyny is perhaps the ugliest, worsening aspect of a society that is becoming increasingly separated from the authenticity of direct accountability.

In the mid-'90s the wind began to turn and instances of resistance cropped up, including the dramatic appearance of the Zapatista movement in southern Mexico and the seemingly unstoppable "Unabomber" attacks on various people bringing on the Brave New World.

I'd moved across town in '83 from the University area to the Whiteaker, Eugene's oldest and only diverse neighborhood. In fact, I've lived on or within a half block of 4th and Adams, and have been part of a 22-household housing co-op there since late 1987. The fact that it is essentially run by women is such a big plus in terms of meetings and other interactions—the main reason, it occurs to me, why I've stayed involved for so long.

Nearby, Icky's Tea House (1993–97) was the site of the first stirrings of resistance in the 'hood. Aside from some of the frequent punk music shows there, virtually everything was free, including a bike repair corral, lending library, and weekly film evenings. Copwatch was born there, and a benefit for Ted Kaczynski was held in May, 1996. Icky's was an anti-commercial haven for various folks who didn't feel at home in the prevailing work-pay-die ethos. The cops increasingly harassed the place, aided decisively by a local liberal columnist and the liberal owner of a neighborhood natural food grocery. The latter campaigned furtively to pressure the building's owner to sever Icky's lease and to cause the last-minute veto of a grant from a church. Good ol'

Icky's went under after four years, victim of the surrounding pig culture and some of its enforcers.

The Unabomber became very big news in 1995, following his last fatal parcel. It had been sent to Gilbert Murray of Sacramento, head of public relations for the clear-cutting of the remaining forests in the Western states. *The New York Times* determined that my writings were quite similar to the critique of technology ideas being expressed in Unabomber public statements. I agreed to talk with a reporter about the nature of technology, its deeply negative logic, etc. The result was a longish, early May piece in the *Times* that ended the obscurity in which I'd operated.

The authorities' futile efforts to end the by-then seventeen-year stretch of bombings by the Unabomber (a name jointly conferred by the FBI and the media) made headlines in the summer of '95. I got the impression that I was among the suspects that season when my mail was interfered with for some weeks, and my house was burglarized. Several letters that I knew were sent to me never arrived, and the break-in resulted in the removal of only two items: my address book and a pair of fairly old sneakers.

In the fall the *Washington Post* published "Industrial Society and its Future," the so-called "Unabomber Manifesto." In essence, the essay demonstrates that the progress of technological society means less and less freedom and fulfillment for the individual. Federal authorities recommended the release of this extremely cogent 30,000-word treatise, following its author's promise to suspend his bombing campaign if it was made widely available. Ted Kaczynski's brother David snitched on him to the FBI after noting strong similarities between Ted's writings and "Industrial Society"; he was arrested in April '96 at his tiny Montana cabin.

Our correspondence soon commenced and I first visited him, at the Sacramento County Jail, one year later. There were no fewer than three members of his legal team present at our visit, and enroute I was asked to try to persuade him to accept their version of an insanity defense. Amazed at such a request, I ignored it. Between April '97 and Ted's sentencing in May 1998, we had four encounters. I would take the overnight Amtrak and go to his Federal Defenders' offices for a legal escort to the jail. Ted's lawyers, headed by Quinn Denvir and

Judy Clarke, told me that a lawyer's presence was necessary to secure the privacy of visits. Only later it became clear that the primary consideration wasn't so much to make sure that we couldn't be overheard by the authorities as it was for the lawyers to monitor and police our interactions.

I found Kaczynski very sharp and unassuming, with a sense of humor. His comments and questions always seemed appropriate and spontaneous, though at times he could be a bit formal. Facing the death penalty and always with legal accompaniment, the situation in terms of visits wasn't ideal for free and relaxed communication. But it wasn't only our similar ideas about technology that made for some pre-established rapport. Although we discussed very little about our family histories, we shared some personal background that probably contributed to our speaking a common language. Of Slavic heritage, we'd both grown up in the pro-math and science Sputnik era and as kids made bombs with our chemistry sets. We were bright achievers who later turned our backs on academe, pursuing "independent study." In fact, we each had younger brothers who were social workers, and fathers who succumbed to cancer.

During the summer of '97, with Ted's trial set to begin in the fall, I began to feel some of the mounting pressure. More than obviously, the real heat was on him; but quite willingly, I'd gotten pulled into the pre-trial drama—without benefit of being really included. With a stroke, it seemed, the Unabomber critique had opened a new era of possibility, and this was and is of enormous importance to me. More to the point, there was a specific life on the line, a person I was getting to know, involving a heavy emotional identification. My problem was that I was in the dark as to what role I really had in his defense. At times it seemed that he was relying on me for something, but weeks of silence might follow an intense letter, with occasional, but sometimes cryptic phone calls from his lawyers, which never clarified things.

A related frustration had to do with the desire a few of us had to try to campaign on his behalf, mainly by drawing attention to the cogent ideas of "Industrial Society and its Future." Lydia in Boston had used a semi-serious "Unabomber for President" effort in '96 to draw attention to critical Unabomber theses, and a scattered handful of us were in touch, wanting to expand pro-Ted efforts. The defense attorneys had made it clear that they were opposed to politicizing the case, as if that dimension of it wasn't already entirely obvious. So I saw Ted in August and made the pitch for his permission to go ahead in that direction. His response, not what we'd hoped to hear, echoed the larger dilemma of the case. He said something like, "Wow, that sounds good. I hope you can persuade my lawyers!"

Jury selection began in November, and when Ted entered the courtroom for the first time he nodded to me, precipitating a minor stampede of reporters my way during morning recess. "Who are you?" "Do you know Kaczynski?" etc. I said nothing and was shielded by a junior member of the legal team, my anonymity remaining intact. Through the second floor window of the Sacramento federal courthouse, I looked out on a block-long row of press tents and satellite dishes of the national and international press corps.

A flurry of expected motions and counter-motions next brought the trial itself into view as the end of 1997 loomed. December revealed the essence of what had been going on behind the scenes for some time, ably told, by the way, in Bill Finnegan's March 16, 1998 *New Yorker* article, "Defending the Unabomber." Ted's federal defender lawyers were anti-death penalty liberals, whose entire focus was saving his life. It seems that the feds had promptly reneged on the FBI promise of a year and a half earlier to David Kaczynski (dubbed "the Unasquealer" by David Letterman), to not seek the death penalty if he would betray his brother. In pursuit of their objective the lawyers finessed Kaczynski along, keeping him in the dark by controlling all access to outside reality and denying that they were really fashioning an insanity defense. That they were lying to him began to become quite apparent when their almost daily comments to the press belied this entirely, while he was doing everything he could to prove his sanity and thus the meaning or necessity of the Unabomber actions. Ted's lawyers, by this point, were constantly portraying their client to the reporters as delusional and paranoid schizophrenic.

Into January the defense strategy was rather openly a race to the wire, the lawyers' effort to hold onto an insanity orientation up to the decisive point in the trial before Kaczynski figured out what they were really doing in his name. By this time, various media types could see what was happening. Before each day's proceedings some of them would even call out cynical taunts to Denvir and Clarke: "Got control of him?" One could see their anger, as illusions faded away. Judge Burrell made it clear that he saw Ted as quite sane, offering his judgment on one occasion, in camera, that the attorney's client had a better grasp of the case than they did.

Finally it began to dawn on Kaczynski that the lawyers had not been truthful, and he started to rethink his trusting reliance on them. I had been loath to volunteer my impressions and doubts, which admittedly had been slow in forming. And mail to Ted was always routed through his lawyers' office; by this time I suspected that they were keeping some letters from him. As with visits, the mail needed the legal transit for "security reasons"; this guaranteed the lawyers' control over what Ted could discuss or read.

He now phoned me on occasion, mainly to ask me to help him connect with radical San Francisco lawyer Tony Serra, though he was hesitant about firing the lawyers he'd depended upon for so long. Serra told me to let Ted know that it was urgent for him to fire the lawyers; the time to make such a move was running out. Serra's office set up a 24-hour phone line to receive word from me about what Ted decided, in case he couldn't communicate directly.

In mid-January 1998, the clock did indeed run out for Ted. He tried to sack his lawyers in favor of Serra, and when that was denied asked to be permitted to represent himself. The judge ruled that it was too late for either course, and further decreed that the trial would go forth not only with his present representation, but also with their insanity argument as his defense.

What Ted most feared had come to pass: he and his thinking would be portrayed to the world as crazy. After a failed suicide attempt, he accepted a plea agreement of life in prison for an admission of guilt. Further humiliation was avoided and his life was spared, at the cost of not being allowed to establish that he was not a madman.

In terms of my own minor role in all this, something happened about a month earlier that "outed" me a good deal more than the May '95 New York Times article had done. At the beginning of December, Ted asked me to arrange for Christine Craft to visit him. She was a writer for the *Sacramento Weekly* who had been in court every day and whose accounts, often critical of the way the defendant was being treated, impressed him.

I called and got her excited assent to the prospect of a visit. I told her to contact the Federal Defenders office if her name wasn't on his visitors' list at the jail, and that they would assist her. She got a runaround for days going into weeks and finally received the word that the lawyers weren't going to permit her to see Ted. Of course, this was transpiring as the attorneys focused on holding in place their deception concerning the insanity plea, at a critical juncture in the proceedings. They weren't about to let her possibly blow their control over him via his direct access to media.

Christine was phoning me several nights a week to recount her frustration, while at the same time the lawyers were working hard to poison Ted's opinion of her. They portrayed her as a scheming, publicity-seeking snoop with no legitimate interest in him.

Late in the month when it had been made clear that no visit was going to happen, Ms. Craft decided to do a story anyway and tell, among other things, her tale of being denied the chance to speak with Ted Kaczynski. I felt, as Ted had initially, that she was a very fair-minded, responsible individual and that she was obviously entitled to do a piece on what had been going on. But she needed to be able to include the part about being invited to see him, how that came about. This included me, and meant that her end-of-December *Sacramento Weekly* article brought a deluge of media attention my way. Having really very few other connections to Kaczynski, journalists flocked to my house and phoned at all hours for a while. I didn't talk to any of them until the plea agreement was reached a month later.

Several months previously I had arranged, through the Cultural Forum of the Associated Students of the University of Oregon, to give a talk on campus in late January 1998. It turned out that the event took place just a few days after the front page news of the plea agreement. During those few days I'd talked with media folks locally, which brought major free publicity to the talk and necessitated two successive changes to larger-capacity campus venues.

More than 500 people showed up for my comments on the nature and direction of technology. It's possible that some were disappointed by my avoidance of any "What's the Unabomber really like?"-type material. However, I ended the speech with the suggestion that there might be a parallel between Kaczynski and John Brown. Brown made an anti-slavery attack on the federal arsenal at Harpers Ferry, West Virginia in 1859. Like Kaczynski, Brown was considered deranged, but he was tried and hung. Not long afterward he became a kind of American saint of the abolitionist movement. I offered the hope, if not the prediction, that T.K. might at some point also be considered in a more positive light for his resistance to industrial civilization. During the question-and-answer period, a Native American woman and a teenage boy each expressed their respect and admiration for Kaczynski.

The best thing about this campus presentation was that it prompted two young anarchists to visit me some time later. Icky's was no more, but a new, militant presence was soon at work. Overall, 1998 would see an awakening that continues to grow, and has seemed especially pronounced in Eugene and the Whiteaker neighborhood in particular.

Various repressive responses were soon felt. In fact, they had begun in the neighborhood the preceding fall, when the City closed Scobert Park, ignoring a rough consensus that the community had arrived at through a series of open meetings. The little park was entirely fenced off, but opposition swiftly appeared. Along with signs and banners and folks doing a sleep-in, the fence disappeared during its first night on duty around the park. In the morning it was replaced, and the next night it was once again removed. This went on for a few days until the City gave up. Victory for the neighborhood!

Summer of '98 saw local government attempt to cut down about thirty old maple trees along three blocks in the heart of the Whiteaker. This decimation of the area's loveliest feature would have been a demoralizing blow. At the same time, in a series of secret meetings, a move was underway to bring the federal "Weed and Seed" program to our hotbed of emerging resistance and alternative ways. "Weed and Seed" offers federal money to poor locales in return for permission to crack down on any and all "law-breakers": weed out the bad elements and get seed funds for, say, a community center. Both of these challenges to the integrity of the neighborhood were loudly rebuffed in no uncertain terms by the solidarity of the residents who would have been affected.

In other words, the resurfacing of opposition to business as usual was met early on by various efforts at counter-attack. But a renewed social movement was quickly developing, and in its militancy was adopting radically new tactics.

In October '98 an anti-Nike demonstration crossed the line from respectful symbolic protest to a real, non-legal act. To draw attention to Nike's already notorious use of sweatshop labor, a standard march and picket at the local outlet proceeded as usual, but the event soon took on a different character. Several people, masked up and wearing black, entered the store and trashed it by breaking a few items and throwing apparel out the door into a fountain below. A bold departure from the old gestures that never seem to show contempt for basics of the work/consume/destroy nature treadmill.

In fact, night-time property damage was fast asserting itself and raising the ante of discussion in Eugene. Targets of political vandalism in the Whiteaker included a natural foods store whose owner worked overtime to close Icky's Teahouse, the van owned by a cop residing in the neighborhood, and a yuppie restaurant, which to many represented an opening wedge to gentrification (higher rent for poor people). The last place closed after a steady pattern of graphic, hostile acts.

Property destruction, mainly broken windows and spray-painted graffiti, was hotly debated at first but has become more widely accepted and even espoused as a necessary tactic. The same shift has occurred in terms of increasingly militant tactics, seen as a needed escalation against an all-destructive global system of capital and technology. Those of us who know that the reigning setup must be stopped and dismantled have for some time pushed for substantive resistance, and it has certainly grown. From Seattle '99 to Prague 2000, Quebec City 2001 and beyond, a strong resolve is in evidence, with "black bloc" and like-minded militancy.

The new level or stage of contestation began to be noticed outside of Eugene. The winter of '98–99 was marked by continued radical efforts, including the birth of the *Black-Clad Messenger*, an enduring publication dedicated to indicting the whole trajectory of domination, including its technological and civilization-based logic, and pushing for even stronger responses. A June '99 *Wall Street Journal* article called "Disaffected Youth Dust off a Combustible Philosophy" was a lengthy and scurrilous smear-job, full of inaccuracies, that sought to put the heat on us.

But before the month was out, the spirit of anarchy in Eugene delivered a counter-blow that significantly exceeded what had already gone on. "Reclaim the Streets" on June 18 was a day of worldwide anti-capitalist demonstrations, whose high point occurred in London as thousands occupied part of the city center and disrupted the stock exchange for a few hours. The Eugene edition of RTS began (like the smaller Nike affair eight months earlier) as a rather standard-issue protest gathering, and took a surprising turn. To sum up, about 200 people conducted a roaming riot that went on for almost five hours, with banks and other businesses damaged and the cops repeatedly in retreat. It was a glorious outburst of energy against the Megamachine, although anarchist Rob Thaxton (AKA Rob los Ricos), among eighteen arrested, was later sentenced to seven years in prison for hitting a heavily armored cop with a rock in defense of himself and a comrade. The anti-World Trade Organization "Battle of Seattle" that got the world's attention five months later had been prefigured in the streets of little old Eugene, Oregon.

Meanwhile, of course, a movement that is more and more anarchist in orientation goes forward all over the world. And the anarchy scene has itself changed rather fundamentally in recent years, away from the traditional, production/progress-embracing outlook, toward the primitivist critique or vision and its Luddite/feminist/decentralization/anti-civilization aspects.

Certainly no one knows if the side of life, health, and freedom can prevail against a system that has already produced an unprecedented assault on all living beings. The global war on outer nature is matched only by the assault, day after day, upon inner nature; but resistance is waxing in strength and I am extremely hopeful. Increasingly, people see what is at stake and how basic and far-reaching our alternatives need to be. How wonderful it is that after several decades, people are rising to the challenge. Nothing is more excellent than to have the opportunity to be alive in these days and be a part of a marvelous and necessary effort.

These remarks, by the way, are in no way comprehensive. They only skim the surface, mentioning some highlights and leaving out so much, perhaps especially in terms of the richness, diversity, and the conflicts, too, here in the Eugene anarchist community. I will leave it to others to fill in the rest, and correct my judgment or emphasis. Our very future depends, similarly, upon everyone playing their part and making the difference. In closing, I want to express my love to my two daughters. The one I gave so little to but who has never cut me off, and the one who adopted me, as undeserving as I am. The healed world awaits us all.

2001

No Way Out?

Agriculture ended a vast period of human existence largely characterized by freedom from work, non-exploitation of nature, considerable
gender autonomy and equality, and the absence of organized violence.
It takes more from the earth than it puts back and is the foundation of
private property. Agriculture encloses, controls, exploits, establishes
hierarchy and resentment. Chellis Glendinning (1994) described agriculture as the "original trauma" that has devastated the human psyche,
social life, and the biosphere.

But agriculture/domestication didn't suddenly appear out of
nowhere, 10,000 years ago. Quite possibly, it was the culmination of a
very slow acceptance of division of labor or specialization that began in
earnest in Upper Paleolithic times, about 40,000 years ago. This process
is behind what Horkheimer and Adorno termed "instrumental reason"
in their *Dialectic of Enlightment*. Although still touted as the precondi-
tion for "objectivity," human reason is no longer neutral. It has
somehow become deformed, with devastating impact: our reason impris-
ons our true humanity, while destroying the natural world. How else to
account for the fact that human activity has become so inimical to
humans, as well as to all other earthly species? Something had already
started to take us in a negative direction before agriculture, class stratification, the State, and industrialism institutionalized its wrongness.

This disease of reason, which interprets reality as an amalgamation of instruments, resources, and means, adds an unprecedented and uncontrolled measure of domination. As with technology, which is reason's incarnation or materiality at any given time, reason's "neutrality" was missing from the start. Meanwhile, we are taught to accept our condition. It's "human nature" to be "creative," goes part of the refrain.

Division of labor gives effective power to some, while narrowing or reducing the scope of all. This can be seen in the production of art as well as in technological innovation. The distinctive work of individual masters is apparent in the earliest cave art, and craft specialization is an essential aspect of the later development of "complex" (AKA stratified) societies. Specified roles facilitated a qualitative rupture with long-standing human social patterns, in a remarkably short period of time. After two or three million years of an egalitarian foraging (AKA hunter-gatherer) mode of existence, in only 10,000 years, the rapid descent into a civilized lifeway. Since then, an ever-accelerating course of social and ecological destructiveness in every sphere of life.

It's also remarkable how complete the experience of civilization was from its very first stages. K. Aslihan Yener's *Domestication of Metal* (2000) discusses complex industry in civilization's opening act, the Early Bronze Age. She charts the organization and management of tin mining and smelting in Anatolia beginning in 8,000 BC. The archaeological evidence shows irrefutably that erosion, pollution, and deforestation were very significant consequences, as the earliest civilizations laid waste to much of the Middle East.

With civilization, how it is is how it's always been. Russell Hoban's 1980 novel, *Riddley Walker*, provides keen insight into the logic of civilization. What some call Progress, the narrator identifies as Power:

> "It come to me then I know it Power dint go away. It ben and it wer and it wud be. It wer there and drawing. Power want it you to come to it with Power. Power wantit what ever cud happen to happen. Power wantit every thing moving frontways."

The nature of the civilization project was clear from the beginning. As the swiftly arriving product of agriculture, the intensification of domination has been steady and sure. It's telling that humans' first monuments coincide with the first signs of domestication (R. Bradley in Mither, 1998). The sad linearity of civilization's destruction of the natural world has been interrupted only by symptoms of self-destruction in the social sphere, in the form of wars. And when we recall with B.D. Smith (1995) that domestication is "the creation of a new form of plant and animal," it becomes obvious that genetic engineering and cloning are anything but strange aberrations from the norm.

The contrast with thousands of generations of forager (hunter-gatherer) life is staggering. There is no dispute that these ancestors put sharing at the center of their existence. Throughout the anthropological literature, sharing and equality are synonymous with the forager social organization, characterized as bands of 50 or fewer people. In the absence of mediation or political authority, people enjoyed strong expressive bonds face-to-face with one another and in intimacy with nature.

Hewlett and Lamb (2000) explored the levels of trust and compassion in an Aka band of foragers in central Africa. The physical and emotional closeness between Aka children and adults, they concluded, is closely related to their benign orientation to the world. Conversely, Aka people see their environment as generous and supportive, at least in part, because of the unrestricted bonds among themselves. Colin Turnbull observed a very similar reality among the Mbuti in Africa, who addressed greetings to "Mother Forest, Father Forest."

Agriculture is the founding model for all the systematic authoritarianism that followed, certainly including capitalism, and initiating the subjugation of women. Very early farming settlements contained "as many as 400 people" (Mithen et al, 2000). We know that expanding population was not a cause of agriculture but its result; this suggests a basic dynamic of the population problem. It appears that societies organized on a truly human scale fell victim to the exigencies of domestication. It may be that we can only solve the planet's overpopulation problem by removing the root cause of basic estrangement from one another. With the advent of domestication, reproduction was not only rewarded economically; it also offered a compensation or consolation for so much that had been eradicated by civilization.

Amid the standardizing, disciplinary effects of today's systems of technology and capital, we are subjected to an unprecedented barrage of images and other representations. Symbols have largely crowded out everything real and direct, both in the daily round of interpersonal interactions and in the accelerating extinction of nature. This state of affairs is generally accepted as inevitable, especially since received wisdom dictates that symbol-making is the cardinal, defining quality of a human being. We learn as children that all behavior, and culture itself, depend on symbol manipulation; this characteristic is what separates us from mere animals.

But a close look at Homo over our many, many millennia challenges the inexorability or "naturalness" of the dominance of symbols in our lives today. New discoveries are making newspaper headlines with increasing frequency. Archaeologists are finding that more than a million years ago, humans were as intelligent as ourselves—despite the fact that the earliest evidence to date of symbolic activity (figurines, cave art, ritual artifacts, time recordings, etc.) date to only 40,000 years ago or so. People used fire for cooking 1.9 million years ago; and built and sailed seagoing vessels at least 800,000 years ago!

These people must have been very intelligent; yet they left no tangible trace of symbolic thought until relatively recently. Likewise, although our ancestors of a million years ago had the I.Q. to enslave each other and destroy the planet, they refrained from doing so, until symbolic culture got going. Civilization advocates are making a concerted effort to find evidence of symbol use at a much earlier time, paralleling the unsuccessful effort in recent decades to locate evidence that would overturn the new anthropological paradigm of pre-agricultural harmony and well being. So far, their searches have not borne fruit.

There is an enormous time gap between clear signs of mental capacity and clear signs of any symbolizing at all. This discrepancy casts serious doubt on the adequacy of a definition of humans as essentially symbol makers. The apparent congruence between the beginnings of representation and the beginnings of what is unhealthy about our species seems even more important. Basic questions pretty much formulate themselves.

One such question concerns the nature of representation. Foucault argued that representation always involves a power relation. There may be a connection between representation and the power imbalance that is created when division of labor takes over human activity. In a similar vein, it is difficult to see how large social systems could have come about in the absence of symbolic culture. At a minimum, they appear to be inseparable.

Jack Goody (1997) referred to "the continuing pressure to represent." Along with an easily identified impulse to communicate, is there not also something much less positive going on? For all those generations before civilization, folks did many things with their minds—including communicating—but they didn't get symbolic about it. To re-present reality involves a move to a complete, closed system, of which language is the most obvious example and perhaps the original instance. Whence this will to create systems, to name and to count? Why this dimension that looks suspiciously like instrumental reason, with its essentially dominating core?

Language is routinely portrayed as a natural and inevitable part of our evolution. Like division of labor, ritual, domestication, religion? Complete the progression and we see that the end of the biosphere and total alienation are likewise "natural" and "inevitable." Whether or not there can be a way out of the symbolic order is the pressing question.

"In the beginning was the Word"—the convening of the symbolic domain. After Eden's freedom was revoked, Adam named the animals and the names were the animals. In the same way, Plato held that the word creates the thing. There is a moment of linguistic agreement, and from then on a categorized frame is imposed on all phenomena. This pact attempts to override the "original sin" of language, which is the separation of speech and world, words and things.

Many languages start out rich in verbs, but are gradually undone by the more common imperialism of the noun. This parallels the movement to a steadily more reified world, focusing on objects and goals at the expense of process. In similar fashion, the vivid naturalism of cave art gives way to an impoverished, stylized aesthetic. In both cases, the symbolic deal is sweetened by the promise of an enticing richness, but in each case the long-term results are deadly. Symbolic modes may begin with some freshness and vitality, but eventually reveal their actual poverty, their inner logic.

The innate sensual acuity of human infants steadily atrophies as they grow and develop in interaction with a symbolic culture that continues to infiltrate and monopolize most aspects of our lives. A few remnants of the unmediated, the direct still survive. Lovemaking, close relationships, immersion in wild nature, and the experience of birth and death awaken our senses and our intelligence, stimulating an unaccustomed hunger. We long for something other than the meager, artificial world of re-presentation, with its second-hand pallor.

Communication remains open to those invigorating flashes that pass, nonverbally, between people. All the crabbed, crimped, conditioned channels might be chucked, because we can't live on what's available. As levels of pain, loss, and emptiness rise, the reigning apparatus pumps out ever more unsatisfying, unsustaining lies.

Referring to telepathy, Sigmund Freud wrote in *his New Introductory Lectures on Psychoanalysis*, "One is led to a suspicion that this is the original, archaic method of communication." Enculturated down to his toes, Freud didn't celebrate this suspicion, and seemed to fear the life force that accompanied such non-cultural dynamics. Laurens van der Post (e.g. *The Lost World of the Kalahari*, 1958) related several first-hand observations of telepathic communication, over considerable distances, among the people who used to be called "Bushmen." M. Pobers and Richard St. Barbe Baker, also writing in the 1950s, witnessed telepathy by indigenous people before they were colonized by civilization. I mention this in passing as one glimpse of the reality of the non-symbolic, a direct connection that actually existed not long ago, and that could be revived amid the ruins of representation.

Language and art may have originally appeared and united in ritual, a cultural innovation intended to bridge a new separation between people and their world. The term "animism" is often used, dismissively or even pejoratively, to describe the belief that non-human beings and even objects are inhabited by "spirits." Just as the term "anarchism" is a summary description of anarchy, a pervasive viewpoint or state of being that rejects hierarchy, "animism" fails to capture the transformative quality of a shared awareness. In the case of anarchy, there is an awareness that living in equality with with other humans necessitates the rejection of all forms of domination, including leadership and political representation. "Animism" refers to the extension of that awareness to other life forms and even to "inanimate" dwellers on the planet such as rocks, clouds, and rivers. The fact that there is no word related to animism, analogous to anarchy, is an index of how distanced we are from this awareness, in our present state. Green anarchy explicitly states that anarchy must embrace the community of living beings, and in this sense takes a step toward reawakening this awareness.

Did humans lose the awareness of belonging to an earthly community of living beings with the advent of domestication, division of labor, and agriculture? The construction of monuments and the beginnings of animal and human sacrifice would tend to support this hypothesis. Characteristically, the scapegoated victim is held responsible for communal misfortune and suffering, while the fundamental reasons for the community's loss go unrecognized and unmitigated. Ritual involves "enormous amounts of energy" (Knight in Dunbar, Knight and Power, 1999); it is usually loud, multimediated, emotional, and redundant, testifying to the felt depth of the underlying crisis.

The movement from animism to ritual parallels the transformation of small, face-to-face groups into large, complex societies. Culture takes over, with specialized professionals in charge of the realm of the sacred. The longing for that original feeling of communion with other beings and egalitarian intimacy with one's fellow humans can never be appeased by ritual activities developed within a hierarchical social system. This tendency culminates in the teachings of transcendant religions, that since the meaning of our lives has nothing to do with life on earth, we should pin our hopes on a heavenly reward. Conversely, as with the Aka and Mbuti described above, feelings of oneness with the earth and all its inhabitants, and a sense of the joy and meaningfulness of existence, seem to flourish when we humans live in egalitarian, face-to-face groups.

Returning to language, an agreed-upon banality is that reality is always inherently disclosed through language— that in fact reality is decisively mediated by language. Postmodernism ups this ante in two ways. Because language is basically a self-referential system, PM avers, language cannot really involve meaning. Further, there is only language (as there is only civilization); there is no escape from a world defined by language games (and domestication). But archaeological and ethno-

graphic evidence shows clearly that human life has existed outside representation, and nothing definitively precludes humans from living
that way again—however devoutly the postmodernists, in their accommodation to the system, may pray that this just cannot be.

The ultimate in representation is the current "society of the spectacle" described so vividly by Guy Debord. We now consume the image
of living; life has passed into the stage of its representation, as spectacle. At the same time that technology offers virtual reality to the individual, the ensemble of electronic media creates a virtual community,
an advanced symbolic state of passive consumption and learned helplessness.

But the balance sheet for the ruling order shows a mixed forecast.
For one thing, representation in the political sector is met with skepti-
cism and apathy similar to that evinced by representation in general.
Has there ever been so much incessant yammer about democracy, and
less real interest in it? To represent or be represented is a degradation, a
reduction, both in the sense of symbolic culture and in terms of power.

Democracy, of course, is a form of rule. Partisans of anarchy
should know this, though leftists have no problem with governance.
Anarcho-syndicalists and other classical anarchists fail to question any
of the more fundamental institutions, such as division of labor, domestication, domination of nature, Progress, technological society, etc.

To quote Riddley Walker again, as an antidote: "I cud feal some
thing growing in me it wer like a grean sea surging in me it wer saying,
LOSE IT. Saying, LET GO. Saying, THE ONLYES POWER IS NO
POWER." The heart of anarchy.

Heidegger, in *Discourse on Thinking*, counseled that an attitude of
"openness to the mystery" promises "a new ground and foundation
upon which we can stand and endure in the world of technology
without being imperiled by it." An anti-authoritarian orientation does
not consist of this passive attitude, of changing only our consciousness.
Instead, technology and its accomplice, culture, must be met by a res-
olute autonomy and refusal that looks at the whole span of human
presence and rejects all dimensions of captivity and destruction.

2001

BIBLIOGRAPHY

Aaronson, Bernard, "Time, Time Stance, and Existence," *The Study of Time*, vol. 1, ed. Fraser, Haber and Müller (New York, 1972)

Adorno, Theodor, *Aesthetic Theory* (Minneapolis, 1997); *Prisms* (Cambridge, 1981); *Dialectic of Enlightenment* (New York, 1972)

Alford, C. Fred, *Narcissism* (New Haven, 1988)

Anfam, David, *Abstract Expressionism* (New York, 1990)

Arlow, Jacob, Psycholanalysis and Time," *Journal of the American Psychoanalytical Association*, vol. 34, 1986

Ashton, Dore, *About Rothko* (New York, 1983)

Bachelard, Gaston, *The Poetics of Space* (New York, 1964)

Balint, Enid, *Before I Was* (New York, 1993)

Barrow, John D., *The Physical Universe* (Berlin, 1991); *Pi in the Sky* (Oxford, 1992)

Bergler, E. and G. Roheim, "Psychology of Time Perception," *Psychoanalytic Quarterly*, vol. 15, 1946

Binford, Lewis, "Butchering, Sharing and the Archaeological Record," *Journal of Anthropological Archaeology*, vol. 3 (1984); "Human Ancestors: Changing Views of Their Behavior," *Journal of Anthropological Archaeology*, vol. 4 (1987)

Bloch, Marc, *Feudal Society* (Paris, 1940)

Blumenberg, Hans, *The Legitimacy of the Modern Age* (Cambridge, MA, 1983)

Bollas, Christopher, *Cracking Up: The World of Unconscious Experience* (New York, 1995)

Bonaparte, Marie, "Time and the Unconscious," *International Journal of Psychoanalysis*, 1940

Bourdieu, Pierre, *Outline of a Theory of Practice* (Cambridge, 1977)

Bower, Bruce, "Raising Trust," *Science News*, July 1, 2000.

Bradley, F.H., *Appearance and Reality* (Oxford, 1930)

Breslin, James, *Mark Rothko* (Chicago, 1993)

Breton, André, *Surrealist Manifesto* (Paris, 1924)

Brown, Norman O., *Life Against Death* (Middletown, CT, 1959)

Burkitt, Denis P., "Some Diseases Characteristic of Modern Western Civilization," *Health and the Human Condition, ed. Logan and Hunt* (North Scituate, MA, 1978)

Cambel, Ali, *Applied Class Theory* (Boston, 1993)

Capek, Milic, *The Philosophical Impact of Contemporary Physics* (Princeton, 1961)

Carnevali, Emanuel, *The Autobiography of Emanuel Carnevali* (New York, 1967)

Carpenter, Edmund, "If Wittgenstein Had Been an Eskimo," *Natural History*, February 1980

Carr, David, Time, *Narrative and History* (Bloomington, 1986)

Cassirer, Ernst, *The Philosophy of Symbolic Forms* (New Haven, 1955)

Casey, Edward, *Remembering: A Phenomenological Study* (Bloomington, 1987)

Castoriadis, Cornelius, *Philosophy, Politics, Autonomy* (New York, 1991)

Chacalos, Elias Harry, *Time and Change* (Rockville, MD, 1989)

Chomsky, Noam, *Chronicles of Dissent* (Monroe, ME, 1992); *Cartesian Linguistics* (New York, 1966)

Cioran, E.M., *On the Heights of Despair* (Chicago, 1990)

Coan, Richard, *Human Consciousness and Its Evolution* (New York, 1987)

Cohen, Abner, *Masquerade Politics* (Berkeley, 1993); *Politics of Elite Cultures* (Berkeley, 1981)

Cohen, Mark Nathan, *Health and the Rise of Civilization* (New Haven, 1989)

Condominas, George, *We Have Eaten the Forest* (New York, 1977)

Conkey, Margaret, "To Find Ourselves: Art and Social Geeography of Prehistoric Hunter-gatherers," *Past and Present in Hunter-Gatherer Societies, ed. C. Shrire* (Orlando, 1984)

Coveney, Peter and J.R.L. Highfield, *The Arrow of Time* (New York, 1991)

Craven, David, "Abstract Expressionism, Automatism and the Age of Automation," *Art History*, March 1990.

Culbertson, James, *The Minds of Robots* (Urbana, 1963); *Sensations, Memory and the Flow of Time* (Santa Margarita, CA, 1976); *Consciousness: Natural and Artificial* (Roslyn Heights, NY, 1982)

Darby, W. Thomas, *The Feast: Meditations on Politics and Time* (Toronto, 1982)

Davies, P.C.W., *The Physics of Time Asymmetry* (Berkeley, 1977); *Space and Time in the Modern Universe* (Cambridge, 1977); *Edge of Infinity* (London, 1981); *God and the New Physics* (New York, 1983)

Desmond, William, *Perplexity and Ultimacy* (Albany, 1995)

Doka, Kenneth, *Disenfranchised Grief* (Washington DC, 1989)

Derrida, Jacques, *Margins of Philosophy* (Chicago, 1982); *Positions* (Chicago, 1981)

d'Espagnat, Bernard, *Reality and the Physicist* (Cambridge, 1989)

Deutsch, H., "Absence of Grief," *Psychoanalytic Quarterly*, vol. 6 (1937)

Donald, M., *Origins of the Modern Mind* (Cambridge, MA, 1991)

Dooley, L. "The Concept of Time in Defense of Ego Integrity," *Psychiatry*, vol. 4, 1941

Douglas, Mary, *Natural Symbols* (London, 1973)

Dummett, Michael, *Truth and Other Enigmas* (Cambridge, MA, 1978)

Dunbar, Robin, Chris Knight, and Camilla Power, eds., *The Evolution of Culture* (New Brunswick, NJ, 1999)

Eissler, K.R., *The Psychiatrist and the Dying Patient* (New York, 1955)

Eliade, Mircea, *Myth of the Eternal Return* (Princeton, 1954); *The History of Religions* (Chicago, 1985)

Engels, Friedrich, *Dialectic of Nature* (Moscow, 1934)

Farb, Peter, *Humankind* (Boston, 1978)

Fenichel, Otto, *The Psychoanalytic Theory of Neurosis* (New York, 1945)

Feuerbach, Ludwig, *Lectures on the Essence of Religion* (New York, 1967)

Feynman, Richard, *What Do You Care What Other People Think?* (New York, 1988)

Fine, Reuben, *Narcissism, the Self, and Society* (New York, 1980)

Foster, Mary LeCron, *Symbol as Sense* (New York, 1980)

Foucault, Michel, *Madness and Civilization* (New York, 1973)

Fraser, J.T., *Of Time, Passion, and Knowledge* (Princeton, 1990); *Time and Mind* (Madison, CT, 1989)

Frazier, J.G., *The Golden Bough: A Study in Magic and Religion*, XLIX (New York, 1932-36)

Freud, Sigmund, "Mourning and Melancholia," *The Complete Works of Sigmund Freud*, vol. 14 (1914-1916) (London, 1957); *Totem and Taboo* (London, 1940)

Freund, Peter, *The Civilized Body* (Philadelphia, 1982)

Fried, Michael, "Jackson Pollock," *Artforum*, September 1965.

Friedman, William J., *About Time* (Cambridge, MA, 1990)

Gabel, Joseph, *False Consciousness* (Oxford, 1975)

Gamble, Clive, *Timewalkers* (Cambridge, MA, 1994)

Gans, Eric, *The End of Culture* (Berkeley, 1985)

Geertz, Clifford, "The Impact of the Concept of Culture on the Concept of Man," *New Views of the Nature of Man*, ed. J.R. Platt (Chicago, 1965)

Germain, Gilbert B., *A Discourse on Disenchantment* (Albany, 1992)

Getty, Adele, *Goddess* (London, 1996)

Giddons, Anthony, *A Contemporary Critique of Historical Materialism* (Berkeley, 1981)

Girard, R., *Violence and the Sacred* (Baltimore, 1977)

Gleick, James, *Genius: the Life and Science of Richard Feynman* (New York, 1992)

Gooddy, William, *Time and the Nervous System* (New York, 1988)

Goodman, Felicitas, *Ecstasy, Ritual and Alternative Reality* (Blooming-ton, 1988)

Goody, Jack, *The Logic of Writing and the Organization of Society* (Paris, 1986)

Grinspoon, Lester, "Fallout Shelters and the Unacceptability of Disquieting Facts," *The Threat of Impending Disaster*, ed. Grosser, Wechsler, Greenblatt (Cambridge, 1964)

Grunberger, Bela, *Narcissism* (New York, 1979)

Guyau, J.-M., *Genesis of the Idea of Time* (Paris, 1890)

Haken, H., *Dynamic Patterns in Complex Systems* (Singapore, 1988)

Hartcollis, Peter, *Time and Timelessness* (New York, 1983)

Hauser, Arnold, "The Conception of Time in Modern Art and Science," *Partisan Review*, 1956

Hawking, Stephen, *A Brief History of Time* (New York, 1988)

Heidegger, Martin, *Basic Writings* (New York, 1969)

Hermelint, Beate and N. O'Connor, *Psychological Experiments with Autistic Children* (New York, 1970)

Herrman, Paul, *Conquest by Man* (New York, 1954)

Gribben, John, *Timewarps* (New York, 1979)

Hirn, Yrgö, *The Origins of Art* (London, 1900)

Horkheimer, Max, *Dawn and Decline* (New York, 1978)

Hoban, Russell, *Riddley Walker* (New York, 1980)

Howes, David, *The Varieties of Sensory Experience* (Toronto, 1991)

Humphrey, Nicholas, *A History of the Mind* (New York, 1992)

Husserl, Edmund, *The Crisis of European Sciences and Transcendental Phenomenology* (Evanston, 1970); *Le Discours et le Symbole* (Paris, 1962)

Ingold, Tim, "Tools, Techniques and Technology," Tools, *Language and Cognition in Human Evolution*, ed. Gibson and Ingold (Cambridge, 1993)

Isaac, Glynn, "Early Stone Tools," *Problems in Economic and Social Archaeology*, ed. Sieveking et al (London, 1976)

Jameson, Frederic, *Postmodernism: The Cultural Logic of Late Capitalism* (Durham, 1991)

Jansons, K.M., "A Personal View of Dyslexia and of Thought Without Language," *Thought Without Language*, ed. Welskrantz (Oxford, 1988)

Jenkins, Paul, quoted in *To a Violent Grave: An Oral Biography of Jackson Pollock*, Jeffrey Potter (New York, 1985)

Kaprow, Allen, *Selections* (New York, 1967)

Kertesz, A., "What Do We Learn from Recovery from Aphasia?," *Advances in Neurology*, ed. S.G. Waxman (New York, 1988)

Kingsley, April, *The Turning Point: the Abstract Expressionists and the Transformation of American Art* (New York, 1992)

Konrad, Gyorgy, *A Feast in the Garden* (New York, 1992)

Korzybski, Alfred, *Science and Sanity* (Lakeville, CT, 1948)

Kramer, Hilton, *The Age of the Avant-Garde*, 1956–1972 (New York, 1973)

Kristeva, Julia, *Language, the Unknown* (New York, 1989)

Kuberski, Philip, *The Persistence of Memory* (Berkeley, 1992)

Kuspit, Donald, *Clement Greenberg, Art Critic* (Madison, 1979)

Landau, Iddo, "Why Has the Question of the Meaning of Life Arisen in the Last Two and a Half Centuries?" *Philosophy Today*, Summer 1967

Landsberg, Peter Theodore, *The Enigma of Time* (Bristol, 1982)

Lasch, Christopher, *The Culture of Narcissism* (New York, 1979)

Leach, Edmund, *Political Systems of Highland Burma* (Boston, 1954)

Lecours, A.R. and Joanette, Y., "Linguistic and other aspects of parox-ysmal aphasia," in *Brain and Language*, #10 (1980)

Leggett, A.J., *The Problems of Physics* (Oxford, 1987)

Leroi-Gourhan, A., *Religions of Prehistory* (Paris, 1964)

Le Roy, Eduoard, *The New Philosophy of Henri Bergson* (New York, 1913)

Lévi-Strauss, *Claude, Myth and Meaning* (London, 1978); *Tristes Tropiques* (New York, 1972)

Levinas, Emmanuel, *Otherwise Than Being* (The Hague, 1981)

Lieberman, Philip, *On the Origins of Language* (New York, 1975)

Lindley, David, *The End of Physics* (New York, 1993)

Loewald, H., "Superego and Time," *International Journal of Psycho-analysis*, vol. 43, 1962

Lomas, Peter, review of Adam Phillips: *Terrors and Experts, Times Literary Supplement*, May 3, 1996

Lommel, Andreas, *Shamanism; the Beginnings of Art* (New York, 1967)

Lumsden, C.J. and E.O. Wilson, *Promethean Fire: Reflections on the Origins of Mind* (Cambridge, MA, 1983

Lyotard, Jean-François, *Pacific Wall* (Venice, 1989); *The Postmodern Condition* (Minneapolis, 1984); *The Differend* (Minneapolis, 1988)

Malinowski, Bronislaw, *Sex, Culture and Myth* (New York, 1962)

Mallove, Eugene, *The Quickening Universe* (New York, 1987)

Marcuse, Herbert, *The Aesthetic Dimension* (Boston, 1978); *Eros and Civilization* (Boston, 1955); *One Dimensional Man* (Boston, 1964)

Mattison, Robert, *Robert Motherwell: the Formative Years* (Ann Arbor, 1987)

McFarland, Thomas, *Shapes of Culture* (Iowa City, 1987)

McTaggart, John, *Philosophical Studies* (London, 1934)

Mead, George Herbert, *Self and Society* (Chicago, 1934)

Meerloo, Joost, *Mental First Aid* (New York, 1966); *Along the Fourth Dimension* (New York, 1970)

Melion, Walter and Suzanne Küchler, *Images of Memory* (Washington DC, 1991)

Merleau-Ponty, Maurice, *Phenomenology of Perception* (New York, 1962)

Mithen, Steven, ed., *Creativity in Human Evolution and Prehistory* (London, 1998)

Montagu, Ashley, *Touching* (New York, 1971)

Morgan, George W., *The Human Predicament* (Providence, 1968)

Morris, Richard, *Dismantling the Universe* (New York, 1983)

Motherwell, Robert, *Possibilities* (New York, 1947); *Selections: the Collected Writings* (New York, 1992)

Nancy, Jean-Luc, *The Birth to Presence* (Stanford, 1993)

Novalis, *Schriften*, vol. II (Stuttgart, 1965–77)

O'Hara, Frank, *Jackson Pollock* (New York, 1959)

Pagels, Heinz, *The Cosmic Code* (New York, 1983)

Park, David, "The Myth of the Passage of Time," *The Study of Time,* vol. 1, ed. Fraser, Haber, and Müller (New York, 1972)

Parkin, David, "Ritual as Spatial Directon and Bodily Division," *Understanding Rituals*, ed. de Coppett (London, 1992)

Pater, Walter, *Appreciations* (New York, 1901)

Paz, Octavio, *Alternating Current* (New York, 1973)

Peirce, C.S., *Collected Papers*, vol. 5 (Cambridge, 1931-58)

Penrose, Roger, *The Emperor's New Mind* (Oxford, 1989)

Penta, Leo J., "Resistance to the Rule of Time," *Philosophy Today*, Summer 1993

Perry, William S., *Children of the Sun* (London, 1927)

Peterson, Dale and Jane Goodall, *Visions of Caliban* (Boston, 1993)

Piaget, Jean, *The Child's Conception of Number* (New York, 1952); *The Psychology of Intelligence* (New York, 1950)

Ponting, Clive, *A Green History of the World: the Environment and the Collapse of Great Civilizations* (New York, 1992)

Postone, Moishe, *Time, Labor and Social Domination* (New York, 1993)

Prigogine, Ilya and Isabella Stengers, *Order Out of Chaos* (Toronto, 1984)

Quine, W.V., *From Stimulus to Science* (Cambridge, 1995)

Radin, Paul, *Primitive Religion* (New York, 1927)

Reichenbach, Hans, *The Direction of Time* (Berkeley, 1956)

Rexroth, Kenneth, *Classics Revisited* (Chicago, 1968)

Ricoeur, Paul, *Time and Narrative*, vol. 1 (Chicago, 1984)

Rilke, Rainer Maria, *Letters of Rilke*, vol. 2 (New York, 1969)

Rorty, Richard, *Philosophy and the Mirror of Nature* (Princeton, 1979)

Rosenberg, Harold, "The American Action Painters," *Art News*, December 1952; *The De-Definition of Art* (New York, 1972); *The Tradition of the New* (New York, 1959)

Rosenfield, Israel, *The Strange Familiar and Forgotten* (New York, 1992)

Rosler, Martha, *3 Works* (Halifax, 1981)

Russell, Bertrand, *Skeptical Essays* (London, 1929)

Ryle, Gilbert, *The Concept of Mind* (London, 1949)

Sagan, Eli, *At the Dawn of Tyranny* (New York, 1985)

Sandler, Irving, *The New York School* (New York, 1978)

Schlegel, Richard, *Time and the Physical World* (East Lansing, 1961)

Sebba, Gregor, *Collected Essays: Truth, History, and the Imagination* (Baton Rouge, 1991)

Shallis, Michael, *On Time* (New York, 1982)

Shapiro, David and Cecile, *Abstract Expressionism: A Critical Record* (Cambridge, 1990)

Sheets-Johnstone, Maxine, *The Roots of Thinking* (Philadelphia, 1990)

Shore, Bradd B., *Culture in Mind* (New York, 1996)

Shreeve, James, *The Neandertal Enigma* (New York, 1995)

Simic, Charles, *Dismantling the Silence* (New York, 1971)

Sklar, Lawrence, *Philosophy and Spacetime Physics* (Berkeley, 1985); *Philosophy of Physics* (Boulder, 1992); *Space, Time, and Spacetime* (Berkeley, 1974)

Sloan, Ted, *Damaged Life: the Crisis of the Modern Psyche* (London, 1996)

Smith, J. Maynard, "Time in the Evolutionary Process," *The Study of Time*, vol. 1, ed. Fraser, Haber, Müller (New York, 1972)

Spanos, William, *Repetitions: the Postmodern Occasion in Literature and Culture* (Baton Rouge, 1987)

Spence, Donald, *Narrative Truth and Historical Truth* (New York, 1982)

Spengler, Oswald, *The Decline of the West* (London, 1922)

Squires, Euan, *The Mystery of the Quantum World* (Boston, 1986)

Staal, Frits, *The Science of Ritual* (Poona, 1982); *Agni, The Vedic Ritual of the Fire Altar* (Delhi, 1986); *Universals* (Chicago, 1988)

Stevenson, Mark, "Mayan Stone's Discovery May Confirm Ancient Text" (Associated Press, November 17, 1997)

Still, Clyfford, *Clyfford Still: Thirty-three Paintings* (Buffalo, 1966)

Synge, J.L., *Principles of Mechanics* (New York, 1959)

Syzamos, Geza, *The Twin Dimensions: Inventing Time and Space* (New York, 1986)

Taylor, J.G., "Time in Particle Physics," *The Study of Time*, ed. Fraser, Haber, Müller (New York, 1972)

Terdiman, Richard, *Present Past: Modernity and the Memory Crisis* (Ithaca, 1993)

Thomas, Lewis, *Late Night Thoughts on Listening to Mahler's Ninth Symphony* (New York, 1983)

Thompson, E.P., "Time, Work Discipline and Industrial Capitalism," *Past and Present* #38, 1967

Toda, M., "The Boundaries of the Notion of Time," *The Study of Time*, vol. 3, ed. Fraser, Lawrence, Park (New York, 1973)

Tortelli, Giovanni, *De Orthographia*, 1471

Tudge, Colin, *The Time Before History* (New York, 1996)

Turnbull, Colin, *The Forest People* (New York, 1961); *The Mbuti Pygmies* (New York, 1965)

Valéry, Paul, *The Outlook for Intelligence* (New York, 1962)

Van der Post, Laurens, *The Lost World of the Kalahari* (New York, 1958); *A Mantis Carol* (New York, 1976)

Vendler, Zeno, *Linguistics in Philosophy* (Ithaca, 1967)

Virilio, Paul, *Aesthetics of Disappearance* (New York, 1991); *Speed and Politics* (New York, 1986)

von Glasersfeld, Ernst, "Purposive Behavior," *Annals of the New York Academy of Sciences*, vol. 280, 1976

Voyat, Gilbert, *Cognitive Development among Sioux Children* (New York, 1983)

Waters, Frank, *Book of the Hopi* (New York, 1963)

Weber, Max, "Religious Rejections of the World and their Directions," in *Essays on Sociology*, Hans Gerth and C. Wright Mills, eds. (New York, 1958)

Weizenbaum, Joseph, *Computer Power and Human Reason* (San Francisco, 1976)

Werner, Heinz, *Comparative Psychology of Mental Development* (New York, 1940); *Symbol Formation* (with Bernard Kaplan) (New York: 1963)

White, Leslie, *The Science of Culture* (New York, 1949)

Whorf, Benjamin Lee, *Language, Thought, and Reality* (Cambridge, MA, 1956)

Wittgenstein, Ludwig, "Wittgenstein's Lecture on Ethics," *Philosophical Review* 74 (1965)

Wynn, Thomas, *The Evolution of Spatial Competence* (Urbana, 1989)

Yener, K. Aslihan, *The Domestication of Metals* (Boston, 2000)

Zohar, Danah, *Through the Time Barrier* (London, 1982)

Zweig, Paul, *The Heresy of Self-Love* (Princeton, 1980)

also available from feral house

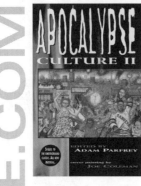

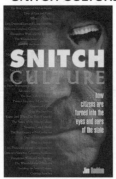